The Communicative Approach to Language Teaching

The Communicative Approach to Language Teaching

C. J. Brumfit and K. Johnson

Oxford University Press

1979

Oxford University Press
Walton Street, Oxford OX2 6DP

Oxford London Glasgow
New York Toronto Melbourne
Wellington Cape Town
Nairobi Dar es Salaam
Kuala Lumpur Singapore
Hong Kong Tokyo Delhi Bombay
Calcutta Madras Karachi

ISBN 0 19 437078 X

Set in Monotype Imprint

Printed and bound in Great Britain
by Morrison & Gibb Ltd
London and Edinburgh

Acknowledgements

Acknowledgements are made to the following publishers from whose texts earlier versions of the extracts and papers have been taken:

Research Planning Conference on Language Development Among Disadvantaged Children, Yeshiva University June 1966 for 'On Communicative Competence' which is reprinted from *Sociolinguistics* published by Penguin.

Edward Arnold (Publishers) Ltd., for 'Towards a sociological semantics', published in *Explorations of the functions of language* (see also *Language as Social Semiotic* by the same author);

AIMAV, for 'Directions in the Teaching of Discourse', and the 'Status of pedagogical grammars', both published in *Theoretical Linguistic Models in Applied Linguistics*, 1973; and for 'The deep structure of discourse and the use of translation', and 'Notional syllabuses and the concept of a minimum adequate grammar', from *Linguistic Insights in Applied Linguistics*, 1974;

Julius Groos Verlag, for 'Grammatical, situational and notional syllabuses' from Proceedings of the Third International Congress of Applied Linguistics, Copenhagen 1972, Vol. II (applied sociolinguistics), pp 254–265, Heidelberg 1974; and for 'Teaching the communicative use of English' from International Review of Applied Linguistics in Language Teaching (IRAL) Vo. XII/1, 1974, pp 1–21;

Council of Europe, for 'Draft outline of a European unit/credit system for modern language learning by adults in and Systems development in adult language learning' in *Systems development in adult language learning* 1973; and for *The Threshold Level* 1975. These texts were commissioned by the Council of Europe as part of a research and development programme concerning the implementation of a European unit/credit system for modern language learning by adults;

Oxford University Press for 'The teaching of English as communication' from the ELT Journal, Vol. 27, No. 1;

British Council for 'Language Learning through Communication Practice' from ELT Documents 77/1;

University of Chicago Press for 'How not to interfere with Language Learning' published in International Journal of American Linguistics 32, I, II, 77–83.

Acknowledgements are made to the following publishers from whose texts the extracts in Section 5 have been taken:

Macmillan, London and Basingstoke for extracts as follows: Pupil's Book page 41, Teacher's Guide pages 214–6, and Teacher's Tapescript pages 36–7 from *Kaleidoscope English for Juniors: Stage 1* (University of York/Macmillan Education);

English Language Teaching for the Arab World/Oxford University Press for pages 76–8 of Pupil's Book 1 of the *Crescent English Course* by T. O'Neill and P. Snow;

Thomas Nelson & Sons Ltd. for pages 88–9 of the Teacher's Book of *Say what you mean in English* by J. Andrews;

Longman Group Ltd. for Unit 10, pages 91–3 of Student's Book of *Strategies* by B. Abbs, A. Ayton, and I. Freebairn;

Cambridge University Press for 'Asking for Help, Section A, oral practice' from Student's Book, Unit 8 of *Approaches* by K. Johnson and K. Morrow; and for pages 41–3 of the Student's Book of *Functions of English* by L. Jones;

Oxford University Press for pages 30–1 of Student's Book of *English in Physical Science* by J. P. B. Allen and H. G. Widdowson.

Contents

Preface

'Communicative Language Teaching' has in recent years become a fashionable term to cover a variety of developments in syllabus design and, to a lesser extent, in the methodology of teaching foreign languages. Teachers and applied linguists wishing to examine the fundamental arguments underlying these developments have had to rely on the publications of the Council of Europe, many of which are difficult to obtain, and on access to journals and conference proceedings which few libraries stock. This book attempts to collect many of the important papers in this field, and especially those with relevance to the teaching of English as a second or foreign language. It is hoped that through these papers it will be possible to trace the major linguistic influences on language teaching from theory through to practical application in syllabus design and teaching materials. At the same time, the few papers which have been specially written for this volume relate the linguistic theory to the broader educational context.

Language teaching, as a practical rather than a theoretical activity, draws on insights from many disciplines, and the emphasis here on broadly linguistic and sociolinguistic discussion is not intended to suggest that language teaching has been responsive only to these. The problem has been where to draw a convenient boundary. We felt that the general positions held by Hymes and Halliday—described in detail in the introduction—are central to any contemporary discussion of language teaching. There would certainly be room for another book of this length taking the argument further back historically, and further away from linguistics into the areas of anthropology, semantics, philosophy, social psychology and others which have been neglected here. However, to have attempted to cover such an enormous field in one book would have been foolhardy. The papers in this volume show various attempts to interpret language for classroom use in the light of recent theoretical developments which the authors see as significant. Any contemporary student of language teaching needs to evaluate such discussion, and it is hoped that this book will enable many more people to do so.

KJ   CJB
November 1978

The Linguistic Background

On communicative competence
D. H. Hymes
Towards a sociological semantics
M. A. K. Halliday

[It is often said that language teaching in the past few decades has shifted the emphasis away from (in Newmark & Reibel's terms) 'mastery of language use to mastery of language structure' (1968: 232). This emphasis on the teaching of structure has manifested itself in many ways. We have come to see the task of syllabus design, for example, as very much one of selecting structural items and grading them in suitable order for teaching. Our syllabuses have often been little more than ordered lists of structures, which we have then proceeded to teach by means of a strategy that has become all but universal. The strategy works like this: we present a structure, drill it, practise it in context . . . then move to the next structure (see Brumfit, this volume, p. 183). In this way we gradually, and in Wilkins' term (1976: 3) 'synthetically' build up the inventory of structural items our students can handle. And since we specify and execute our language teaching in such terms, it is natural that we should assess it in a similar way. We reward structural correctness and chastise structural inaccuracy. Success or failure in language learning, as interpreted both through examination results and through student or teacher judgement, has generally come to be assessed in terms of ability to manipulate the structures of the language.

'Mastery of language use'—teaching the student how 'to mean' as well as how 'to form' has not of course been entirely neglected. If (to employ a distinction made by Wilkins and others) we speak of meaning as having 'conceptual' ('semantico-grammatical', 'notional') and 'functional' levels, then both levels have received some attention in past language teaching, though in important respects their treatment has been inadequate. But no teacher introduces 'shall' and 'will' (for example) without relating the structure implicitly or explicitly to a conceptual meaning, usually that of futurity; nor would we teach (or be able to teach) the English article system without recourse to the concepts of countableness and uncountableness. Similarly, questions of conceptual meaning have always had a place in course design. Many courses, for example, contain a teaching unit contrasting simple past and present perfect tenses, often on the assumption not that the formal contrast will cause difficulty, but that the conceptual distinctions (like 'finished action irrelevant to the present' versus 'finished action relevant to the present') are hard for many to grasp. Similarly a course may (as in Broughton 1968: 243) treat formally different structures like 'the boy's leg' and 'the leg of the chair' in the same teaching unit because they share a conceptual feature (attribution) yet at the same time distinguish themselves conceptually (animate versus inanimate).

Nor has meaning as 'function' been entirely neglected. Language *has* been used to some communicative purpose in classroom practice (for *greeting, requesting and giving information, giving commands*, and the like) even if the purposes have been restricted and such practice over-sparse. Certainly to represent past language teaching as having taken place in a kind of communicative vacuum in which structures are learned like mathematical formulae, would be an oversimplification.

With these reservations it still remains true that 'form' rather than 'meaning' has dominated our teaching. Why should this have been so? How indeed is the direction that language teaching will follow determined at any point in history? The answer to this second question (which subsumes the first) will be provided partly by the linguist. For his view of language will influence, though not entirely determine, the language teacher's formulation of what the task of language learning involves. The linguist's answer to the question 'what is language?' will usually find reflection in the language teacher's answer to the question 'what knowledge and what skills are involved in language proficiency?'.

So it is that the language teacher's emphasis over the past few decades runs parallel to a similar emphasis within linguistics (or, more precisely, American linguistics) during the same period. The parallel is not hard to demonstrate. The proclaimed characteristic feature of Bloomfieldian and neo-Bloomfieldian American structuralism was its careful concern to restrict itself to the study of form, and the classification of the forms of a language, without reference to the categories of meaning. Linguistics was, almost exclusively, the study of language structure. Then, in the late fifties, Chomsky published his *Syntactic Structures*, and this event heralded the arrival of transformational generative grammar. The transformational theory of grammar does indeed represent a revolution in the aims of linguistic study. Taxonomic classification of structures is no longer considered adequate, and from thenceforth linguists became concerned with developing systems of rules which account for, rather than merely describe by means of lists, the structural possibilities of a language. Yet transformational grammar shares one fundamental characteristic with structural linguistics: it is the importance given to the study of language structure. In Chomsky's model syntax remains central, and however much this model has changed the aims and techniques of linguistic study, the concern with syntactic structure remains. Linguistics—in Chomsky as in Bloomfield —is by and large the study of language structure. Perhaps this is why transformational grammar, so revolutionary in linguistics, has had such little effect on language teaching. After all, the most it can offer is alternative strategies for teaching grammar—new ways of teaching the same thing.

The language teacher's emphasis on mastery of structure is, then, paralleled by a similar emphasis within linguistics. And in both fields a parallel reaction has taken place. It is a reaction against the view of language as a set of structures; it is a reaction towards a view of language as communication, a view in which meaning and the uses to which language is put play a central part. In language teaching this reaction is crystallizing itself into the 'communicative approach' which is the subject of this volume, and our exploration of the background to this approach will take us into an investigation of the ways in which general linguistic studies have manifested a parallel reaction.

A particularly powerful and lucid expression of discontent with the transformational view of linguistic study is found in Hymes' paper 'On Communicative Competence', quoted at length below. A large part of this paper is taken up with a discussion of two concepts central to Chomsky's theory: the concepts of 'competence' and 'performance'. Hymes is critical of the way Chomsky uses these terms, and in the latter part of his paper he formulates his own redefinition.

For Chomsky it is 'competence' defined as 'the speaker-hearer's knowledge of his language' (1965: 4) which is the prime concern of linguistic theory. Competence is an idealization: it is the knowledge of the 'ideal speaker-listener' operating within 'a completely homogeneous speech community'. It distinguishes itself from 'performance' which is seen as 'the actual use of language in concrete situations'. As Chomsky says (and Hymes quotes), 'a record of natural speech will show numerous false starts, deviations from rules, changes of plan in mid-course, and so on'. In these senses performance represents both an incomplete and a degenerate reflection of the ideal speaker-listener's competence, and as such is considered to be of little relevance to the theoretical and descriptive linguist.

In its original form Hymes' paper was delivered at a conference on language development among disadvantaged children, and in its first section Hymes points to the irrelevance of the Chomskian notion of competence—dealing as it does with the ideal speaker-listener in a homogeneous speech community—to the study of disadvantaged children. Indeed, says Hymes, what one is inevitably concerned with in such a study is 'performance'—the actual use of language in a concrete situation; its use moreover by speaker-listeners who are far from 'ideal' and whose language behaviour cannot be characterized as that of any 'homogeneous speech community'. Sociocultural factors, which for Chomsky are again associated with the realm of performance, will prove of prime importance in studies of this kind. For Hymes, Chomskian linguistics with its narrow concept of competence represents a 'Garden of Eden view' which dismisses central questions of use by relegating them to the area of performance. Indeed, it is a major characteristic of modern linguistics that (as Hymes says in a quotation directly relevant to the theme of this volume)

> 'it takes structure as a primary end in itself, and tends to depreciate use. . . .' (this volume, p. 8).

In the second section of his paper, Hymes exemplifies situations in which non-ideal speaker-listeners operate within a non-homogeneous speech community, situations in which one finds 'differential competence within a heterogeneous speech community'. He argues that linguistics in general (concerned with issues going far beyond the study of disadvantaged children) requires a theory which will take account of such phenomena. A theory of this sort would give central importance (a 'constitutive role') to sociocultural factors.]

On communicative competence[1]
D. H. Hymes

I

This paper is theoretical. One connotation of 'theoretical' is 'pro-gramatic'; a related connotation is that one knows too little about the subject to say something practical. Both connotations apply to this attempt to contribute to the study of the 'language problems of disadvantaged children'. Practical work however, must have an eye on the current state of theory, for it can be guided or misguided, encouraged or discouraged, by what it takes that state to be. Moreover, the language development of children has particular pertinence just now for theory. The fundamental theme of this paper is that the theoretical and the practical problems converge.

It is not that there exists a body of linguistic theory that practical research can turn to and has only to apply. It is rather that work motivated by practical needs may help build the theory that we need. To a great extent programs to change the language situation of children are an attempt to apply a basic science that does not yet exist. Let me review the present stage of linguistic theory to show why this is so.

Consider a recent statement, one that makes explicit and precise an assumption that has underlain much of modern linguistics (Chomsky, 1965, p. 3):

> Linguistic theory is concerned primarily with an ideal speaker-listener, in a completely homogeneous speech community, who knows its language perfectly and is unaffected by such grammatically irrelevant conditions as memory limitations, distractions, shifts of attention and interest, and errors (random or characteristic) in applying his knowledge of the language in actual performance.

From the standpoint of the children we seek to understand and help such a statement may seem almost a declaration of irrelevance. All the difficulties that confront the children and ourselves seem swept from view.

One's response to such an indication of the state of linguistic theory might be to ignore fundamental theory and to pick and choose among its products. Models of language structure, after all, can be useful in ways not envisioned in the statements of their authors. Some linguists (e.g., Labov, Rosenbaum, Gleitman) use transformational generative grammar to study some of the ways in which a speech community is not homogeneous and in which speaker-listeners clearly have differential knowledge of a language. Perhaps, then, one ought simply to disregard how linguists define the scope of 'linguistic' theory. One could point to several available models of language—Trager-Smith-Joos, tagmemic, stratificational, transformational-generative (in its MIT, Pennsylvania, Harvard and other variants), and, in England, 'system-structure' (Halliday and others); remark that there are distinguished scholars using each to analyse English; regret that linguists are unable to agree on the analysis of English; and pick and choose, according to one's problem and local situation, leaving grammarians otherwise to their own devices.

To do so would be a mistake for two reasons: on the one hand, the sort of theoretical perspective quoted above *is* relevant in ways that it is important always to have in mind; on the other hand, there is a body of linguistic data and problems that would be left without theoretical insight, if such a limited conception of linguistic theory were to remain unchallenged.

The special relevance of the theoretical perspective is expressed in its representative anecdote (to use Kenneth Burke's term), the image it puts before our eyes. The image is that of a child, born with the ability to master any language with almost miraculous ease and speed; a child who is not merely molded by conditioning and reinforcement, but who actively proceeds with the unconscious theoretical interpretation of the speech that comes its way, so that in a few years and with a finite experience, it is master of an infinite ability, that of producing and understanding in principle any and all grammatical sentences of language. The image (or theoretical perspective) expresses the essential equality in children just as human beings. It is noble in that it can inspire one with the belief that even the most dispiriting conditions can be transformed; it is an indispensable weapon against views that would explain the communicative differences among groups of children as inherent, perhaps racial.

The limitations of the perspective appear when the image of the unfolding, mastering, fluent child is set beside the real children in our schools. The theory must seem, if not irrelevant, then at best a doctrine of poignancy: poignant, because of the difference between what one imagines and what one sees; poignant too, because the theory, so powerful in its own realm, cannot on its terms cope with the difference. To cope with the realities of children as communicating beings requires a theory within which sociocultural factors have an explicit and constitutive role; and neither is the case.

For the perspective associated with transformational generative grammar, the world of linguistic theory has two parts: linguistic *competence* and linguistic *performance*. Linguistic competence is understood as concerned with the tacit knowledge of language structure, that is, knowledge that is commonly not conscious or available for spontaneous report, but necessarily implicit in what the (ideal) speaker-listener can say. The primary task of theory is to provide for an explicit account of such knowledge, especially in relation to the innate structure on which it must depend. It is in terms of such knowledge that one can produce and understand an infinite set of sentences, and that language can be spoken of as 'creative', as *energeia*. Linguistic performance is most explicitly understood as concerned with the processes often termed encoding and decoding.

Such a theory of competence posits ideal objects in abstraction from sociocultural features that might enter into their description. Acquisition of competence is also seen as essentially independent of sociocultural features, requiring only suitable speech in the environment of the child to develop. The theory of performance is the one sector that might have a specific sociocultural content; but while equated with a theory of language use, it is essentially concerned with psychological by-products of the analysis of grammar, not, say, with social interaction. As to a constitutive role for sociocultural features in the acquisition or conduct of performance, the attitude would seem quite negative. Little or nothing is said, and if something were said, one would expect it to be depreciatory. Some aspects of performance are, it is true, seen as having a constructive role (e.g., the cycling rules that help assign stress properly to sentences), but if the passage quoted at the outset is recalled, however, and if the illustrations of performance phenomena in the chapter from which the passage comes are reviewed, it will be seen that the note struck is persistently one of limitation, if not disability. When the notion of performance is introduced as 'the actual use of language in concrete situations', it is immediately stated that only under the idealization quoted could performance directly reflect competence, and that in actual fact it obviously could not. 'A record of natural speech will show numerous false starts, deviations from rules, changes of plan in mid-course, and so on.' One speaks of primary linguistic data as 'fairly degenerate in quality' (Chomsky, 1965, p. 31), or even of linguistic performance as 'adulteration' of ideal competence (Katz, 1967, p. 144). While 'performance' is something of a residual category for the theory, clearly its most salient connotation is that of imperfect manifestation of underlying system.

I do not think the failure to provide an explicit place for sociocultural features to be accidental. The restriction of competence to the notions of a homogeneous community, perfect knowledge, and independence of sociocultural factors does not seem just a simplifying assumption, the sort that any scientific theory must make. If that were so, then some remark to that effect might be made; the need to include a sociocultural dimension might be mentioned; the nature of such inclusion might even be suggested. Nor does the predominant association of performance with imperfection seem accidental. Certainly any stretch of speech is an imperfect indication of the knowledge that underlies it. For users that share the knowledge, the arrangement might be thought of as efficient. And if one uses one's intuitions as to speech, as well as to grammar, one can see that what to grammar is imperfect, or unaccounted for, may be the artful accomplishment of a social act (Garfinkel, 1970), or the patterned, spontaneous evidence of problem solving and conceptual thought (John, 1967, p. 5). These things might be acknowledged, even if not taken up.

It takes the absence of a place for sociocultural factors, and the linking of performance to imperfection, to disclose an ideological aspect to the theoretical standpoint. It is, if I may say so, rather a Garden of Eden view. Human life seems divided between grammatical competence, an ideal innately-derived sort of power, and performance, an exigency rather like the eating of the apple, thrusting the perfect speaker-hearer out into a fallen world. Of this world, where meanings may be won by the sweat of the brow, and communication achieved in labor (cf. Bonhoffer, 1965, p. 365), little is said. The controlling image is of an abstract, isolated individual, almost an unmotivated cognitive mechanism, not, except incidentally, a person in a social world.

Any theoretical stance of course has an ideological aspect, and that aspect of present linguistic theory is not its invention. A major characteristic of modern linguistics has been that it takes structure as a primary end in itself, and tends to depreciate use, while not relinquishing any of its claim to the great significance that is attached to language. (Contrast classical antiquity, where structure was a means to use, and the grammarian subordinate to the rhetor.) The result can sometimes seem a very happy one. On the one hand, by narrowing concern to independently and readily structurable data, one can enjoy the prestige of an advanced science; on the other hand, despite ignoring the social dimensions of use, one retains the prestige of dealing with something fundamental to human life.

In this light, Chomsky is quite correct when he writes that his conception of the concern of linguistic theory seems to have been also the position of the founders of modern general linguistics. Certainly if modern structural linguistics is meant, then a major thrust of it has been to define the subject matter of linguistic theory in terms of what it is not. In de Saussure's linguistics, as generally interpreted, *la langue* was the privileged ground of structure, and *la parole* the residual realm of variation (among other things). Chomsky associates his views of competence and performance with the Saussurian conceptions of langue and parole, but sees his own conceptions as superior, going beyond the conception of language as a systematic inventory of items to renewal of the Humboldtian conception of underlying processes. The Chomsky conception is superior, not only in this respect, but also in the very terminology it introduces to mark the difference. 'Competence' and 'performance' much more readily suggest concrete persons, situations, and actions. Indeed, from the standpoint of the classical tradition in structural linguistics, Chomsky's theoretical standpoint is at once its revitalization and its culmination. It carries to its perfection the desire to deal in practice only with what is internal to language, yet to find in that internality that in theory is of the widest or deepest human significance. No modern linguistic theory has spoken more profoundly of either the internal structure or the intrinsic human significance.

This revitalization flowers while around it emerge the sprouts of a conception that before the end of the century may succeed it. If such a succession occurs, it will be because, just as the transformational theory could absorb its predecessors and handle structural relationships beyond their grasp, so new relationships, relationships with an ineradicable social component, will become salient that will require a broader theory to absorb and handle them. I shall return to this historical conjecture at the end of this paper. Let me now sketch considerations that motivate a broader theory. And let me do this by first putting forward an additional representative anecdote.

II

As against the ideal speaker-listener, here is Bloomfield's account of one young Menomini he knew (1927, p. 395):

> White Thunder, a man around forty, speaks less English than Menomini, and that is a strong indictment, for his Menomini is atrocious. His vocabulary is small; his inflections are often barbarous; he constructs sentences of a few threadbare models. He may be said to speak no language tolerably. His case is not uncommon among younger men, even when they speak but little English.

Bloomfield goes on to suggest that the commonness of the case is due, in some indirect way, to the impact of the conquering language. In short, there is here *differential competence* within a *heterogeneous speech community*, both undoubtedly shaped by acculturation. (The alternative to a constitutive role for the novel sociocultural factor is to assume that atrocious Menomini was common also before contact. If taken seriously, the assumption would still implicate sociocultural factors.) Social life has affected not merely outward performance, but inner competence itself.

Let me now review some other indications of the need to transcend the notions of perfect competence, homogeneous speech community, and independence of sociocultural features.

In her excellent article reviewing recent studies of subcultural differences in language development in the United States, Cazden (1966, p. 190) writes that one thing is clear:

> The findings can be quickly summarized: on all the measures, in all the studies, the upper socio-economic status children, however defined, are more advanced than the lower socio-economic status children.

The differences reviewed by Cazden involve enabling effects for the upper status children just as much as disabling effects for the lower status children. Moreover, given subcultural differences in the patterns and purposes of language use, children of the lower status may actually excel in aspects of communicative competence not observed or measured in the tests summarized. And among the Menomini there were not only young men like White Thunder, but also those like Red Cloud Woman, who

> speaks a beautiful and highly idiomatic Menomini . . . (and) speaks Ojibwa and Potawatomi fluently. . . . Linguistically, she would correspond to a highly educated American woman who spoke, say, French and Italian in addition to the very best type of cultivated, idiomatic English (Bloomfield, 1927, p. 394).

There are tribes of the northeast Amazon among whom the normal scope of linguistic competence is a control of at least four languages, a spurt in active command coming during adolescence, with repertoire and perfection of competence continuing to be augmented throughout life. Here, as in much of our world, the ideally fluent speaker-listener is multilingual. (Even an ideally fluent monolingual of course is master of functional varieties within the one language.)

In this connection it should be noted that fluent members of communities often regard their languages, or functional varieties, as not identical in communicative adequacy. It is not only that one variety is obligatory or preferred for some uses, another for others (as is often the case, say, as between public occasions and personal relationships). Such intuitions reflect experience and self-evaluation as to what one can in fact do with a given variety. This sort of differential competence has nothing to do with 'disadvantage' or deficiency relative to other normal members of the community. All of them may find Kurdish, say, the medium in which most things can best be expressed, but Arabic the better medium for religious truth; users of Berber may find Arabic superior to Berber for all purposes except intimate domestic conversation (Ferguson, 1966).

The combination of community diversity and differential competence makes it necessary not to take the presence in a community of a widespread language, say, Spanish or English, at face value. Just as one puts the gloss of a native word in quotation marks, so as not to imply that the meaning of the word is thereby accurately identified, so one should put the name of a language in quotation marks, until its true status in terms of competence has been determined. (Clearly there is need for a theoretically motivated and empirically tested set of terms by which to characterize the different kinds of competence that may be found.) In an extreme case what counts as 'English' in the code repertoire of a community may be but a few phonologically marked forms (the Iwam of New Guinea). The cases in general constitute a continuum, perhaps a scale, from more restricted to less restricted varieties, somewhat crosscut by adaptation of the same inherited 'English' materials to different purposes and needs. A linguist analysing data from a community on the assumption 'once English, always English' might miss and sadly misrepresent the actual competence supposedly expressed by his grammar.

There is no way within the present view of linguistic competence to distinguish between the abilities of one of the pure speakers of Menomini noted by Bloomfield and those of whom White Thunder was typical. Menomini sentences from either would be referred to a common grammar. Perhaps it can be said that the competence is shared with regard to the recognition and comprehension of speech. While that would be an important (and probably true) fact, it has not been the intention of the theory to distinguish between models of competence for reception and the models of competence for production. And insofar as the theory intends to deal with the 'creative' aspect of language, that is, with the ability of a user to devise novel sentences appropriate to situations, it would seem to be a retrenchment, if not more, to claim only to account for a shared ability to *understand* novel sentences produced by others. In some fundamental sense, the competence of the two groups of speakers, in terms of ability to make 'creative' use of Menomini, is clearly distinct. Difference in judgement of acceptability is not in question. There is simply a basic sense in which users of Menomini of the more versatile type have a knowledge (syntactic as well as lexical) that users of White Thunder's type do not. [. . .]

Labov has documented cases of dual competence in reception, but single competence in production, with regard to the ability of lower-class Negro children to interpret sentences in either standard or sub-standard phonology, while consistently using only substandard phonology in speaking themselves. An interesting converse kind of case is that in which there is a dual competence for production, a sort of 'competence for incompetence' as it were. Thus among the Burundi of East Africa (Albert, 1964) a peasant may command the verbal abilities stressed and valued in the culture but cannot display it in the presence of a herder or other superior. In such cases appropriate behavior is that in which 'their words are haltingly delivered, or run on uncontrolled, their voices are loud, their gestures wild, their figures of speech ungainly, their emotions freely displayed, their words and sentences clumsy'. Clearly the behavior is general to all codes of communication, but it attaches to the grammatical among them.

Such work as Labov's in New York City, and examples such as the Burundi, in which evidence for linguistic competence co-varies with interlocutor, point to the necessity of a social approach even if the goal of description is a single homogeneous code. Indeed, much of the difficulty in determining what is acceptable and intuitively correct in grammatical description arises because social and contextual determin-ants are not controlled. By making explicit the reference of a description to a single use in a single context, and by testing discrepancies and variations against differences of use and context, the very goal of not dealing with diversity can be achieved—in the limited, and only possible, sense in which it can be achieved. The linguist's own intuitions of underlying knowledge prove difficult to catch and to stabilize for use (and of course are not available for languages or varieties he does not himself know). If analysis is not to be reduced to explication of a corpus, or debauch into subjectivity, then the responses and judgements of members of the community whose language is analysed must be utilized—and not merely informally or ad hoc, but in some explicit, systematic way. In particular, since every response is made in some context, control of the dependence of judge-ments and abilities on context must be gained. It may well be that the two dimensions found by Labov to clarify phonological diversity—social hierarchy of varieties of usage, and range (formal to informal) of 'contextual styles', together with markings for special functions (ex-pressivity, clarity, etc.) will serve for syntactic diversity as well. Certainly some understanding of local criteria of fluency, and con-ditions affecting it, is needed just insofar as the goal is to approximate an account of ideal fluency in the language in question. In sum, if one analyses the language of a community as if it should be homogeneous, its diversity trips one up around the edges. If one starts with analysis of the diversity, one can isolate the homogeneity that is truly there.

Clearly work with children, and with the place of language in education, requires a theory that can deal with a heterogeneous speech community, differential competence, the constitutive role of socio-cultural features—that can take into account such phenomena as White Thunder, socio-economic differences, multilingual mastery, relativity of competence in 'Arabic', 'English', etc., expressive values, socially determined perception, contextual styles and shared norms for the evaluation of variables. Those whose work requires such a theory know best how little of its content can now be specified. Two things can be said. First, linguistics needs such a theory too. Concepts that are unquestionably postulated as basic to linguistics (speaker-listener, speech community, speech act, acceptability, etc.) are, as we see, in fact sociocultural variables, and only when one has moved from their postulation to their analysis can one secure the foundations of linguistic theory itself. Second, the notion of competence may itself provide the key. Such comparative study of the role of language as has been under-taken shows the nature and evaluation of linguistic ability to vary cross-culturally; even what is to count as the same language, or variety, to which competence might be related, depends in part upon social factors (cf. Gumperz, 1964; Hymes, 1968a; Labov, 1966). Given, then, the assumption that the competency of users of language entails abilities and judgements relative to, and interdependent with, sociocultural features, one can see how to extend the notion to allow for this. I shall undertake this, by recasting first the representative anecdote of the child, and then the notions of competence and performance themselves. [...]

* * *

[In the following two sections of his paper, Hymes outlines the way in which he feels a linguistic theory should develop to provide a more constitutive role for sociocultural factors. If this is to happen, he argues, the notions of competence and performance need redefinition. In his redefinition, the salient contrast is between 'the actual' and 'the underlying'. The term 'performance' is to be used to refer strictly to the 'actual use of language', the sense in which Chomsky at least claims to be using it—though see Hymes' discussion at the end of Section III (p. 17) on an important ambiguity in the use of the word performance within transformational literature.

The result of insisting on the contrast being between 'the actual' and 'the underlying' is a far more general concept of competence than is found in Chomsky. For Chomsky competence simply means 'knowledge of the language system': grammatical knowledge in other words. But once we view competence as the overall underlying know-ledge and ability for language use which the speaker-listener possesses, then we have to accept that this involves far more than knowledge of (and ability for) grammaticality. There are, in Hymes' words, 'rules of use without which the rules of grammar would be useless' (p. 15). Indeed, if a speaker were to produce grammatical sentences without regard to the situations in which they were being used, he would certainly be considered deranged. Competence seen as overall underlying linguistic knowledge and ability thus includes concepts of appropriateness and acceptability—notions which in Chomsky are associated with performance—and the study of competence will inevitably entail consideration of such variables as attitude, motivation, and a number of sociocultural factors.

There are, then, 'several sectors of communicative competence, of which the grammatical is one'. Hymes lists four sectors. The first, 'whether or not something is formally *possible*' is roughly equivalent to Chomsky's restricted notion of competence as grammaticality. It is concerned with whether a language permits a structure as grammatical (possible) or rejects it as ungrammatical (impossible). The second sector deals with *feasibility*. A sentence like 'the mouse the cat the dog the man the woman married beat chased ate had a white tail' is grammatically possible, but is hardly feasible. Because of our restricted powers of processing, such a sentence cannot in any real sense be said to form part of our competence. The third sector covers *appropriateness to context*. The speaker-listener's underlying competence includes 'rules of appropriateness', and a sentence can be grammatically possible, feasible, but inappropriate (see Widdowson 1978, Chapter 1 for development of this point in relation to language teaching). Hymes' final sector relates to the area which we commonly refer to as 'accepted usage'. It concerns *whether or not something is in fact done*. A sentence may be possible, feasible, appropriate and not occur.

Once we consider linguistic competence in these terms, we find (Hymes claims) that it is similar to competences which underlie communicative systems other than language. In the final part of Section IV Hymes discusses his four sectors in relation to other such systems. This general applicability of the term gives Hymes particular justification for referring to 'communicative competence', in contrast to Chomsky's more narrow notion of 'grammatical competence'.]

* * *

III

Recall that one is concerned to explain how a child comes rapidly to be able to produce and understand (in principle) any and all of the grammatical sentences of a language. Consider now a child with just that ability. A child who might produce any sentence whatever—such a child would be likely to be institutionalized: even more so if not only sentences, but also speech or silence was random, unpredictable. For that matter, a person who chooses occasions and sentences suitably, but is master only of fully grammatical sentences, is at best a bit odd. Some occasions call for being appropriately ungrammatical.

We have then to account for the fact that a normal child acquires knowledge of sentences, not only as grammatical, but also as appropriate. He or she acquires competence as to when to speak, when not, and as to what to talk about with whom, when, where, in what manner. In short, a child becomes able to accomplish a repertoire of speech acts, to take part in speech events, and to evaluate their accomplishment by others. This competence, moreover, is integral with attitudes, values, and motivations concerning language, its features and uses, and integral with competence for, and attitudes toward, the interrelation of language with the other code of communicative conduct (cf. Goffman, 1956, p. 477; 1963, p. 335; 1964). The internalization of attitudes towards a language and its uses is particularly important (cf. Labov, 1965, pp. 84–5, on priority of subjective evaluation in social dialect and processes of change), as is internalization of attitudes toward use of language itself (e.g. attentiveness to it) and the relative place that language comes to play in a pattern of mental abilities (cf. Cazden, 1966), and in strategies —what language is considered available, reliable, suitable for, *vis-à-vis* other kinds of code.

The acquisition of such competency is of course fed by social experience, needs, and motives, and issues in action that is itself a renewed source of motives, needs, experience. We break irrevocably with the model that restricts the design of language to one face toward referential meaning, one toward sound, and that defines organization of language as solely consisting of rules for linking the two. Such a model implies naming to be the sole use of speech, as if languages were never organized to lament, rejoice, beseech, admonish, aphorize, inveigh (Burke, 1966, p. 13), for the many varied forms of persuasion, direction, expression and symbolic play. A model of language must design it with a face toward communicative conduct and social life.

Attention to the social dimension is thus not restricted to occasions on which social factors seem to interfere with or restrict the grammatical. The engagement of language in social life has a positive, productive aspect. There are rules of use without which the rules of grammar would be useless. Just as rules of syntax can control aspects of phonology, and just as semantic rules perhaps control aspects of syntax, so rules of speech acts enter as a controlling factor for linguistic form as a whole. Linguists generally have developed a theory of levels by showing that what is the same on one level of representation has in fact two different statuses, for which a further level must be posited. The seminal example is in Sapir (1925) on phonology, while the major recent examples are in the work of Chomsky and Lamb. A second aspect is that what is different at one level may have in fact the same status at the further level. (Thus the two interpretations of 'He decided on the floor'—the floor as what he decided on/as where he decided—point to a further level at which the sameness of structure is shown.) Just this reasoning requires a level of speech acts. What is grammatically the same sentence may be a statement, a command, or a request; what are grammatically two different sentences may as acts both be requests. One can study the level of speech acts in terms of the conditions under which sentences can be taken as alternative types of act, and in terms of the conditions under which types of act can be realized as alternative types of sentence. And only from the further level of acts can some of the relations among communicative means be seen, e.g. the mutual substitutability of a word and a nod to realize an act of assent, the necessary co-occurrence of words and the raising of a hand to realize an oath.

The parallel interpretations of 'he decided on the floor' and 'she gave up on the floor' point to a further at which the sameness in structure is shown.

Rules of use are not a late grafting. Data from the first years of acquisition of English grammar show children to develop rules for the use of different forms in different situations and an awareness of different acts of speech (Ervin-Tripp, personal communication). Allocation of whole languages to different uses is common for children in multilingual households from the beginning of their acquisition. Competency for use is part of the same developmental matrix as competence for grammar.

The acquisition of competence for use, indeed, can be stated in the same terms as acquisition of competence for grammar. Within the developmental matrix in which knowledge of the sentences of a language is acquired, children also acquire knowledge of a set of ways in which sentences are used. From a finite experience of speech acts and their interdependence with sociocultural features, they develop a general theory of the speaking appropriate in their community, which they employ, like other forms of tacit cultural knowledge (competence) in conducting and interpreting social life (cf. Goodenough, 1957; Searle, 1967). They come to be able to recognize, for example, appropriate and inappropriate interrogative behavior (e.g. among the Araucanians of Chile, that to repeat a question is to insult; among the Tzeltal of Chiapas, Mexico, that a direct question is not properly asked (and to be answered 'nothing'); among the Cahinahua of Brazil, that a direct answer to a first question implies that the answerer has no time to talk, a vague answer that the question will be answered directly the second time, and that talk can continue).

The existence of competency for use may seem obvious, but if its study is to be established, and conducted in relation to current linguistics, then the notions of competence and performance must themselves be critically analysed, and a revised formulation provided.

The chief difficulty of present linguistic theory is that it would seem to require one to identify the study of the phenomena of concern to us here with its category of performance. The theory's category of competence, identified with the criterion of grammaticality, provides no place. Only performance is left, and its associated criterion of acceptability. Indeed, language use is equated with performance: 'the theory of language use—the theory of performance' (Chomsky, 1965, p. 9).

The difficulty with this equation, and the reasons for the making of it, can be explained as follows. First, the clarification of the concept of performance offered by Chomsky (1965, pp. 10–15), as we have seen, omits almost everything of sociocultural significance. The focus of attention is upon questions such as which among grammatical sentences are most likely to be produced, easily understood, less clumsy, in some sense more natural; and such questions are studied initially in relation to formal tree-structures, and properties of these such as nesting, self-embedding, multiple-branching, left-branching, and right-branching. The study of such questions is of interest, but the results are results of the psychology of perception, memory, and the like, not of the domain of cultural patterning and social action. Thus, when one considers what the sociocultural analogues of performance in this sense might be, one sees that these analogues would not include major kinds of judgement and ability with which one must deal in studying the use of language (see below under appropriateness).

Second, the notion of performance, as used in discussion, seems confused between different meanings. In one sense, performance is observable behavior, as when one speaks of determining from the data of performance the underlying system of rules (Chomsky, 1965, p. 4), and of mentalistic linguistics as that linguistics that uses performance as data, along with other data, e.g. those of introspection, for determination of competence (p. 193). The recurrent use of 'actual' implies as much, as when the term is first introduced in the book in question, 'actual performance', and first characterized: 'performance (the actual use of language in concrete situations)' (pp. 3–4). In this sense performance is 'actual', competence underlying. In another sense, performance itself also underlies data, as when one constructs a performance model, or infers a performative device (e.g. a perceptual one) that is to explain data and be tested against them (p. 15); or as when, in a related sense, one even envisages the possibility of stylistic 'rules of performance' to account for occurring word orders not accounted for by grammatical theory (p. 127).

When one speaks of performance, then, does one mean the behavioral data of speech? or all that underlies speech beyond the grammatical? or both? If the ambiguity is intentional, it is not fruitful; it smacks more of the residual category and marginal interest.

The difficulty can be put in terms of the two contrasts that usage manifests:

1. (underlying) competence v. (actual) performance;
2. (underlying) grammatical competence v. (underlying) models/ rules of performance.

The first contrast is so salient that the status of the second is left obscure. In point of fact, I find it impossible to understand what stylistic 'rules of performance' could be, except a further kind of under-lying competence, but the term is withheld. [. . .]

It remains that the present vision of generative grammar extends only a little way into the realm of the use of language. To grasp the intuitions and data pertinent to underlying competence for use requires a sociocultural standpoint. To develop that standpoint adequately, one must transcend the present formulation of the dichotomy of com-petence: performance, as we have seen, and the associated formulation of the judgements and abilities of the users of a language as well. To this I now turn.

IV

There are several sectors of communicative competence, of which the grammatical is one. Put otherwise, there is behavior, and, underlying it, there are several systems of rules reflected in the judgements and abilities of those whose messages the behavior manifests. (The question of how the interrelationships among sectors might be con-ceived is touched upon below.) In the linguistic theory under discussion, judgements are said to be of two kinds: of *grammaticality*, with respect to competence, and of *acceptability*, with respect to performance. Each pair of terms is strictly matched; the critical analysis just given requires analysis of the other. In particular, the analysis just given requires that explicit distinctions be made within the notion of 'acceptability' to match the distinctions of kinds of 'peformance', and at the same time, the entire set of terms must be examined and recast with respect to the communicative as a whole.

If an adequate theory of language users and language use is to be developed, it seems that judgements must be recognized to be in fact not of two kinds but of four. And if linguistic theory is to be integrated with theory of communication and culture, this fourfold distinction must be stated in a sufficiently generalized way. I would suggest, then, that for language and for other forms of communication (culture), four questions arise:

1. Whether (and to what degree) something is formally *possible*;
2. Whether (and to what degree) something is *feasible* in virtue of the means of implementation available;
3. Whether (and to what degree) something is *appropriate* (adequate, happy, successful) in relation to a context in which it is used and evaluated;
4. Whether (and to what degree) something is in fact done, actually *performed*, and what its doing entails.

A linguistic illustration: a sentence may be grammatical, awkward, tactful and rare. (One might think of the four as successive subsets; more likely they should be pictured as overlapping circles.)

These questions may be asked from the standpoint of a system *per se*, or from the standpoint of persons. An interest in competence dictates the latter standpoint here. Several observations can be made. There is an important sense in which a normal member of a community has knowledge with respect to all these aspects of the communicative systems available to him. He will interpret or assess the conduct of others and himself in ways that reflect a knowledge of each (possible, feasible, appropriate), done (if so, how often). There is an important sense in which he would be said to have a capability with regard to each. This latter sense, indeed, is one many would understand as included in what would be meant by his competence. Finally, it cannot be assumed that the formal possibilities of a system and individual knowledge are identical; a system may contain possibilities not part of the present knowledge of a user (cf. Wallace, 1961b). Nor can it be assumed that the knowledge acquired by different individuals is identical, despite identity of manifestation and apparent system.

Given these considerations, I think there is not sufficient reason to maintain a terminology at variance with more general usage of 'competence' and 'performance' in the sciences of man, as is the case with the present equations of competence, knowledge, systemic possibility, on the one hand, and of performance, behavior, implementational constraints, appropriateness, on the other. It seems necessary to distinguish these things and to reconsider their relationship, if their investigation is to be insightful and adequate.

I should take *competence* as the most general term for the capabilities of a person. (This choice is in the spirit, if at present against the letter, of the concern in linguistic theory for underlying capability.) Competence is dependent upon both (tacit) *knowledge* and (ability for) *use*. *Knowledge* is distinct, then, both from competence (as its part) and from systemic possibility (to which its relation is an empirical matter). [...]

Knowledge also is to be understood as subtending all four parameters of communication just noted. There is knowledge of each. *Ability for use* also may relate to all four parameters. Certainly it may be the case that individuals differ with regard to ability to use knowledge of each: to interpret, differentiate, etc. The specification of *ability for use* as part of competence allows for the role of noncognitive factors, such as motivation, as partly determining competence. In speaking of competence, it is especially important not to separate cognitive from affective and volitive factors, so far as the impact of theory on educational practice is concerned; but also with regard to research design and explanation (as the work of Labov indicates). Within a comprehensive view of competence, considerations of the sort identified by Goffman (1967, pp. 218–26) must be reckoned with—capacities in interaction such as courage, gameness, gallantry, composure, presence of mind, dignity, stage confidence, capacities which are discussed in some detail by him and, explicitly in at least one case, as kinds of competency (p. 224).

Turning to judgements and intuitions of persons, the most general term for the criterion of such judgements would be acceptable. Quirk (1966) so uses it, and Chomsky himself at one point remarks that 'grammaticalness is only one of the many factors that interact to determine acceptability' (1965, p. 11). (The term is thus freed from its strict pairing with 'performance'.) The sources of acceptability are to be found in the four parameters just noted, and in interrelations among them that are not well understood.

Turning to actual use and actual events, the term *performance* is now free for this meaning, but with several important reminders and provisos. The 'performance models' studied in psycholinguistics are to be taken as models of aspects of ability for use, relative to means of implementation in the brain, although they could now be seen as a distinct, contributory factor in general competence. There seems, indeed, to have been some unconscious shifting between the sense in which one would speak of the performance of a motor, and that in which one would speak of the performance of a person or actor (cf. Goffman, 1959, pp. 17–76, 'Performances') or of a cultural tradition (Singer, 1955; Wolff, 1964, pp. 75–6). Here the performance of a person is not identical with a behavioral record, or with the imperfect or partial realization of individual competence. It takes into account the interaction between competence (knowledge, ability for use), the competence of others, and the cybernetic and emergent properties of events themselves. A performance, as an event, may have properties (patterns and dynamics) not reducible to terms of individual or standardized competence. Sometimes, indeed, these properties are the point (a concert, play, party).

The concept of 'performance' will take on great importance, insofar as the study of communicative competence is seen as an aspect of what from another angle may be called the ethnography of symbolic forms— the study of the variety of genres, narration, dance, drama, song, instrumental music, visual art, that interrelate with speech in the communicative life of a society, and in terms of which the relative importance and meaning of speech and language must be assessed. The recent shift in folklore studies and much of anthropology to the study of these genres in terms of performances with underlying rules (e.g. Abrahams, 1967) can be seen as a reconstruction on an ethnographic basis of the vision expressed in Cassirer's philosophy of symbolic forms. (This reconstruction has a direct application to the communicative competence of children in American cities, where identification and understanding of differences in kinds of forms, abilities, and their evaluation is essential.)

The concept of 'performance' will be important also in the light of sociological work such as that of Goffman (cited above), as its concern with general interactional competence helps make precise the particular role of linguistic competence.

In both respects the interrelation of knowledge of distinct codes (verbal: non-verbal) is crucial. In some cases these interrelations will bespeak an additional level of competence (cf. e.g., Sebeok, 1959, pp. 141–2): 'Performance constitutes a concurrently ordered selection from two sets of acoustic signals—in brief, codes—language and music. . . . These are integrated by special rules. . . .'). In others, perhaps not, as when the separate cries of vendors and the call to prayer of a muezzin are perceived to fit by an observer of an Arabic city, but with indication of intent or plan.

The nature of research into symbolic forms and interactional competence is already influenced in important part by linguistic study of competence (for some discussion see Hymes, 1968b). Within the view of communicative competence taken here, the influence can be expected to be reciprocal.

Having stated these general recommendations, let me now review relations between the linguistic and other communicative systems, especially in terms of cultural anthropology. I shall consider both terminology and content, using the four questions as a framework.

1. Whether (and to what degree) something is formally possible

This formulation seems to express an essential concern of present linguistic theory for the openness, potentiality, of language, and to generalize it for cultural systems. When systemic possibility is a matter of language, the corresponding term is of course *grammaticality*. Indeed, language is so much the paradigmatic example that one uses 'grammar' and 'grammaticality' by extension for other systems of formal possibility (recurrent references to a cultural grammar, Kenneth Burke's *A Grammar of Motives*, etc.). For particular systems, such extension may well be the easiest course; it is much easier to say that something is 'grammatical' with respect to the underlying structure of a body of myth, than to say in a new sense that it is 'mythical'. As a general term, one does readily enough speak of 'cultural' in a way analogous to grammatical (Sapir once wrote of 'culturalized behavior', and it is clear that not all behavior is cultural). We may say, then, that something possible within a formal system is grammatical, cultural, or, on occasion, communicative (cf. Hymes, 1967b). Perhaps one can also say uncultural or uncommunicative, as well as ungrammatical, for the opposite.

2. Whether (and to what degree) something is feasible

The predominant concern here, it will be recalled, has been for psycholinguistic factors such as memory limitation, perceptual device, effects of properties such as nesting, embedding, branching, and the like. Such considerations are not limited to linguistics. A parallel in cultural anthropology is Wallace's hypothesis (1961a, p. 462) that the brain is such that culturally institutionalized folk taxonomies will not contain more than twenty-six entities and consequently will not require more than six orthogonally related binary dimensions for the definitions of all terms. With regard to the cultural, one would take into account other features of the body and features of the material environment as well. With regard to the communicative, the general importance of the notion of means of implementation available is clear.

As we have seen, question 2 defines one portion of what is lumped together in linguistic theory under the heading of performance, and, correspondingly, acceptability. Clearly a more specific term is needed for what is in question here. No general term has been proposed for this property with regard to cultural behavior as a whole, so far as I know, and *feasible* seems suitable and best for both. Notice, moreover, that the implementational constraints affecting grammar may be largely those that affect the culture as a whole. Certainly with regard to the brain there would seem to be substantial identity.

3. Whether (and to what degree) something is appropriate

As we have seen, appropriateness is hardly brought into view in the linguistic theory under discussion, and is lumped under the heading of performance, and, correspondingly, acceptability. With regard to cultural anthropology, the term *appropriate* has been used (Conklin,

Frake, etc.), and has been extended to language (Hymes, 1964, pp. 39–41). 'Appropriateness' seems to suggest readily the required sense of relation to contextual features. (Since any judgement is made in some defining context, it may always involve a factor of appropriateness, so that this dimension must be controlled even in study of purely grammatical competence (cf. Labov, 1966). From a communicative standpoint, judgements of appropriateness may not be assignable to different spheres, as between the linguistic and the cultural; certainly, the spheres of the two will intersect. (One might think of appropriateness with regard to grammar as the context-sensitive rules of sub-categorization and selection to which the base component is subject; there would still be intersection with the cultural.)

Judgement of appropriateness employs a tacit knowledge. Chomsky himself discusses the need to specify situations in mentalistic terms, and refers to proper notions of 'what might be expected from anthropological research' (1965, p. 195, n. 5). Here there would seem to be recognition that an adequate approach to the relation between sentences and situations must be 'mentalistic', entailing a tacit knowledge, and, hence, competence (in the usage of both Chomsky and this paper). But the restriction of competence (knowledge) to the grammatical prevails, so far as explicit development of theory is concerned. By implication, only 'performance' is left. There is no mention of what might contribute to judgement of sentences in relation to situations, nor how such judgements might be analysed. The lack of explicitness here, and the implicit contradiction of a 'mentalistic' account of what must in terms of the theory be a part of 'performance' show again the need to place linguistic theory within a more general sociocultural theory.

4. Whether (and to what degree) something is done

The study of communicative competence cannot restrict itself to occurrences, but it cannot ignore them. Structure cannot be reduced to probabilities of occurrence, but structural change is not independent of them. The capabilities of language users do include some (perhaps unconscious) knowledge of probabilities and shifts in them as indicators of style, response, etc. Something may be possible, feasible, and appropriate and not occur. No general term is perhaps needed here, but the point is needed, especially for work that seeks to change what is done. This category is necessary also to allow for what Harold Garfinkel (in discussion in Bright, 1966, p. 323) explicates as application of the medieval principle, *factum valet:* 'an action otherwise prohibited by rule is to be treated as correct if it happens nevertheless'.

In sum, the goal of a broad theory of competence can be said to be to show the ways in which the systemically possible, the feasible, and the appropriate are linked to produce and interpret actually occurring cultural behavior. [. . .]

* * *

[The areas of enquiry contributing directly or indirectly to communicative language teaching are many, and indeed Candlin (1976) lists no fewer than ten. Nevertheless it is possible, at least for the purposes of exposition, to consider these under three broad (and very often overlapping) headings: the sociological (sociolinguistic), the philosophical and the linguistic. Much of the recent work in these three areas shares the characteristic of studying language in relation to its uses. Under the first heading we include the work of Hymes, Gumperz, Goffman and many others in the fields of ethnography of speaking, ethnomethodology and anthropology. For examples of work being done in these fields see Laver & Hutcheson (1972), Turner (1974), Pride & Holmes (1972) and Robinson (1972).

The second area is philosophy. Work on the philosophy of language undertaken within the transformational framework (Katz, 1966 for example) is largely concerned with relating the considerable insights that framework provides to a general theory of knowledge: what the structure of language (as revealed in transformational linguistics) tells us about the structure of the mind. A quite separate set of problems concerns writers like Austin (1962) and Searle (1969), whose indirect influence on communicative language teaching has been considerable. These two philosophers explored the nature of 'speech acts'—acts performed when one uses language—and their general orientation is expressed in the question Searle poses in the opening sentence of his book. 'How', he asks, 'do words relate to the world?' As Sinclair and Coulthard (1975: 14) point out, Searle saw a theory of language as part of a theory of action, a view which finds a parallel in Halliday's paper, extracted below. For earlier discussion in this area, see e.g. Grice (1957) and Quine (1968). Within the field of linguistics, and as a direct reaction against the 'centrality of syntax' in Chomsky, a group of linguists including Ross, Fillmore and Lakoff developed a 'generative semantics' in which, as the label suggests, the semantic component plays a central part. The work of some of these linguists, and also that of Chafe (1970) finds direct parallel in language teaching through the attempts of applied linguists like Wilkins to specify syllabus content in semantic terms. For further discussion see Steinberg and Jakobovits (1971), Fillmore and Langendoen (1971), Fodor (1977).

Also directly relevant to language teaching is work in discourse analysis, and the recent upsurge of interest in this area is representative of the shift in emphasis we have been discussing. In the sixties many analyses of written or spoken text were based on the kinds of models discussed in Halliday *et al.* (1964) and Crystal and Davy (1969). These analyses characterized selected registers of English in terms of grammatical and lexical features. The answer to a question of the sort 'what is scientific English like' would be stated as a list of structures and lexical items (see Huddleston *et al.* 1968 for example). In discourse analysis the answers to similar questions are stated in functional terms. Sinclair and Coulthard (1975) for example analyse classroom interaction, and their answer to the question 'what is classroom interaction like?' is in terms of a hierarchy of categories with labels such as 'initiation', 'response', 'follow-up', 'evaluation', 'comment' and the like. For an introduction to discourse analysis, see Couthard (1977).

There are of course traditions within linguistics, especially British and European linguistics, which have always placed emphasis on meaning and use. The most influential linguist working within the British school is Halliday, and his paper 'Towards a sociological semantics' is extracted below. As this title suggests Halliday is here concerned with the way in which linguistics may help the sociologist in his 'search for explanations of social phenomena'. Since language is not always used in social contexts, this circumscribes the scope of the the study. But, as he says, if we consider language in relation to the contexts within which it is used, we shall certainly learn something about the way language operates as a system. It is interesting to compare the following quotation for what it implies concerning the aims and methods of linguistic study with the view of Hymes as expressed earlier. Both contrast sharply with Chomsky's standpoint. 'The more', Halliday says, 'we are able to relate the options in grammatical systems to meaning potential in the social contexts and behavioural settings, the more insight we shall gain into the nature of the language system, since it is in the service of such contexts and settings that language has evolved' (this volume, p. 39).

Halliday is concerned with three levels of analysis and the relationship between them. Each level is characterized as containing a set of options—a set of choices that the individual can make. At the level of behaviour, in any given context, the individual has various choices of action and Halliday calls this a 'behaviour potential'. They are choices as to what the individual 'can do', and one large set of options within this behaviour potential is linguistic. The individual can choose to say or write something. If he elects to do this, he is faced with a further set of choices on the level of semantics. This set of choices is the 'meaning potential'—what the individual 'can mean'. Then, once he has selected what to mean, there are more choices he has to make at the grammatical level. These choices represent the various ways the language system provides for expressing his meaning. We might say that at this level the individual has a choice as to what he 'can form' (though the term is not Halliday's).

Halliday illustrates the problem of relating these three levels of analysis—the behavioural, the semantic and the grammatical—by means of an example. A boy brings home an object which he has found on a building site. His mother wishes to express her disapproval. There are several 'behaviour options' open to her, including non-linguistic ones like smacking the child. If she decides on a linguistic option, scolding the boy in some way, there are various things she can say, and Halliday lists five of them.

There are, Halliday points out, two ways of analysing such utterances. On the behavioural level we can analyse them (much as a sociologist would) in terms of categories like 'threat of punishment' or 'emotional appeal' and so on. The alternative is a grammatical analysis in which we would treat the sentences as exemplifications of particular grammatical structures. But done in this way these two types of analysis—the behavioural and the grammatical—would be unrelated. The behavioural analysis would provide us with no information on how the various behavioural categories may be realized by the grammar of the language. It does not tell us for example *how* we 'threaten punishment' or 'appeal through emotion' in English. Similarly, the grammatical analysis makes no attempt to relate the grammatical features to the behavioural categories they realize. Neither analysis would, in Halliday's terminology, relate behaviour options to grammatical options.

If this relationship is to be specified we need what Halliday calls a 'semantic network' which analyses the sentences in terms of semantic options. He provides a provisional semantic network for the five sentences and, at the end of Section 2, indicates ways in which these semantic options may be realized in terms of grammar.]

* * *

Towards a sociological semantics[2]
M. A. K. Halliday

1. 'Meaning Potential' and semantic networks

We shall define language as 'meaning potential': that is, as sets of options, or alternatives, in meaning, that are available to the speaker-hearer.

At each of the levels that make up the linguistic coding system, we can identify sets of options representing what the speaker 'can do' at that level. When we refer to grammar, or to phonology, each of these can be thought of as a range of strategies, with accompanying tactics of structure formation.

There are also sets of options at the two interfaces, the coding levels which relate language to non-language. We use 'semantics' to refer to one of these interfaces, that which represents the coding of the 'input' to the linguistic system. The range of options at the semantic level is the potentiality for encoding in language that which is not language.

The term 'meaning' has traditionally been restricted to the input end of the language system: the 'content plane', in Hjelmslev's terms, and more specifically to the relations of the semantic interface, Hjelmslev's 'content substance'. We will therefore use 'meaning potential' just to refer to the semantic options (although we would regard it as an adequate designation for language as a whole).

Semantics, then, is 'what the speaker can mean'. It is the strategy that is available for entering the language system. It is one form of, or rather one form of the realization of, behaviour potential; 'can mean' is one form of 'can do'. The behaviour potential may be realized not only by language but also by other means. Behavioural strategies are outside language but may be actualized through the medium of the language system.

Let us take as an example the use of language by a mother for the purpose of controlling the behaviour of a child. This example is invented, but it is based on actual investigations of social learning—including, among a number of different contexts, that of the regulation of children's behaviour by the mother—carried out in London under the direction of Professor Basil Bernstein. In particular I have drawn on the work of Geoffrey Turner, who has undertaken much of the linguistic analysis of Professor Bernstein's material and shown how the networks of semantic options can serve as a bridge between the sociological and the purely linguistic conceptual frameworks (see Turner, 1973).

The small boy has been playing with the neighbourhood children on a building site, and has come home grasping some object which he has acquired in the process. His mother disapproves, and wishes both to express her disapproval and to prevent him doing the same thing again. She has a range of alternatives open to her, some of which are non-linguistic: she can smack him. But supposing she elects to adopt linguistic measures, the sort of thing she might say would be:

1. that's very naughty of you
2. I'll smack you if you do that again
3. I don't like you to do that
4. that thing doesn't belong to you
5. Daddy would be very cross

These represent different means of control, which might be characterized as (1) categorization of behaviour in terms of disapproval or approval on moral grounds; (2) threat of punishment linked to repetition of behaviour; (3) emotional appeal; (4) categorization of objects in terms of social institution of ownership; (5) warning of disapproval by other parent. And we could add others, e.g. (6) *you're making Mummy very unhappy by disobeying* (control through emotional blackmail, (7) *that's not allowed* (control through categorization of behaviour in terms of operation of rule), etc.

The mother's behaviour could also be described linguistically, in terms of grammatical systems of mood, transitivity and so on. For example, (1) is a relational clause of the attributive (ascription) type where the child's act is referred to situationally as *that* and has ascribed to it, in simple past tense, an attribute expressed by an attitudinal adjective *naughty*, the attribution being explicitly tied to the child himself by the presence of the qualifier *of you*. In (2) we have a hypotactic clause complex in which the main clause is a transitive clause of action in simple future tense with *smack* as process, *I* as actor and *you* as goal, the dependent clause being a conditional, likewise of the action type, with situationally-referring process *do that* and actor *you*.

But these two accounts of the mother's behaviour, the sociological and the linguistic, are unrelated, except in that they are descriptions of the same phenomena. In order to try and relate them, let us describe the mother's verbal behaviour in the form of a system of semantic options, options which we can then relate to the social situation on the one hand and to the grammatical systems of the language on the other.

Figure 1 is a first attempt at a semantic network for this context. It uses a simultaneous characterization of the opinions in terms of two variables: (i) the type of control adopted and (ii) the orientation of the control. System (ii) is redundant for the purpose of discriminating among the present examples, since all are uniquely specified in system (i); but it adds a generalization, suggesting other combinations of options to be investigated, and it specifies other features which we might be able to link up with particular features in the grammar.

2. Provisional version of a semantic network

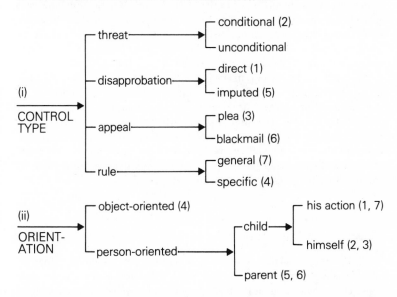

This is the simplest form of such a network, specifying merely options and sub-options. It reads: 'select threat *or* disapprobation *or* appeal *or* rule; *and either* object-oriented *or* person-oriented. *If* threat, *then either* conditional *or* unconditional,' and so on. Numbers in parentheses indicate how these options relate to the examples that were given above.

Now there is probably no category of 'threat' or 'blackmail' or 'object-oriented' to be found in the grammar of English. These are semantic not grammatical categories. But it may be possible to specify what are the grammatical realizations of semantic categories of this kind. For instance, 'threat' is likely to be realized as a transitive clause of action with *you* as Goal, and with a verb of a particular sub-class as Process, in simple future tense. The combination of 'disapprobation' and 'person-oriented: action' leads us to predict an attributive clause type, in which the action that is being censured is expressed as the 'attribuend' (the Goal of the attribution) and the Attribute is some adjective of the attitudinal class. Thus the semantic options are relatable to recognizable features in the grammar, even though the relationship will often be a rather complex one.

A semantic option may, in addition, have more than one possible realization in the grammar. For instance, 'threat' might be realized as a modalized action clause with *you* as Actor, e.g. *you'll have to stay indoors if you do that.* Where there are such alternatives, these are likely in the end to turn out to represent more delicate semantic options, systematic sub-categories rather than free variants (see Section 6 below). But until such time as a distinction in meaning (i.e. in their function in realizing higher-level options) is found, they can be treated as instances of diversification. This is the same phenomenon of diversification as is found in the relations between other pairs of strata.

We have not expressed, in the network, everything that was included in the description of the forms of control; there is no reference yet to the category of 'ownership', or to the fact that the disapproval is 'moral' disapproval. It is not yet clear what these contrast with; they might be fully determined by some existing option. But they are expressed in the same way, by realization in linguistic forms, and there is no difficulty in adding them as semantic options once their value in the meaning potential can be established. [. . .]

* * *

[Halliday now specifies the three requirements which a semantic network should meet if it is to be valid. The first is that it must be complete, accounting for all and only the 'well-formed selection expressions' for a given semantic area. At the same time (and as part of the first requirement) it should state the relationship between the various options it allows. There may, for example, be dependency relationships between the options, so that a given option can only be selected if another given option in a different part of the network is also chosen. The second requirement is that the semantic network should be relatable to a sociological analysis made in terms of behaviour options. Finally, as the third requirement, the semantic network must be relatable to a grammatical analysis. In this way the semantic network links behaviour options with grammatical options.

In Section 3 Halliday considers the first of these requirements only. He shows how a semantic network may specify the various semantic options within a restricted semantic area, and how the dependency relationships between these options may be indicated. He also considers how non-possible options can be excluded from the network, to meet the requirement that it should specify *only* as well as *all* possible options. Then, in Section 4 Halliday deals with his second requirement concerning the relationship between the semantic and behavioural levels of analysis.]

* * *

3. The semantic network as a statement of potential at that stratum

A network such as that in the previous section is a specification of meaning potential. It shows, in this instance, what the mother is doing when she regulates the behaviour of the child. Or rather, it shows what she *can* do: it states the possibilities that are open to her, in the specific context of a control situation. It also expresses the fact that these are *linguistic* possibilities; they are options in meaning, realized in the form of grammatical, including lexical, selections.

These networks represent paradigmatic relations on the semantic stratum (assuming a tri-stratal model of the linguistic system, with semantic, lexicogrammatical and phonological levels); so we shall refer to them as 'semantic networks'. A semantic network is a hypothesis about patterns of meaning, and in order to be valid it must satisfy three requirements. It has to account for the range of alternatives at the semantic stratum itself; and it has to relate these both 'upwards', in this instance to categories of some general social theory or theory of behaviour, and 'downwards', to the categories of linguistic form at the stratum of grammar.

In the first place, therefore, we are making a hypothesis about what the speaker can do, linguistically, in a given context: about what meanings are accessible to him. In order to do this we need not only to state the options that are available but, equally, to show how they are systematically related to one another. As has been pointed out earlier, this is the purpose of the system network. It is a general statement of the paradigmatic relations at the stratum in question, and therefore it constitutes, at one and the same time, a description of each meaning selection and an account of its relationship to all the others—to all its 'agnates', in Gleason's formulation.

From the network we can derive a paradigm of all the meaning selections. This is the set of 'well-formed selection expressions' from the network in question, and the network asserts that these and no others are possible.

The network is however open-ended in delicacy. We take as the starting point the total set of possible meaning selections, and proceed by progressive differentiation on the basis of systematic contrasts in meaning. It is always possible to add further specification; but it is never necessary to do so, so we can stop at the point where any further move in delicacy is of no interest. For instance, if for the purposes of a particular investigation the social theory places no value on the distinction between different types of 'appeal' in a control situation, there is no need to incorporate any sub-systems of 'appeal' into the semantic network.

We use the paradigm to test predictions about meaning selections that might be expected to occur. This can be illustrated from the same general context, that of parental regulation of child behaviour; but we will use a modified form of the network so that the illustration is kept down to a manageable size. Let us postulate the following network of options:

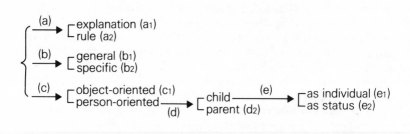

This specifies that the following meaning selections occur:

$(a_1 b_1 c_1)$	$(a_1 b_2 c_1)$	$(a_2 b_1 c_1)$	$(a_2 b_2 c_1)$
$(a_1 b_1 d_2)$	$(a_1 b_2 d_2)$	$(a_2 b_1 d_2)$	$(a_2 b_2 d_2)$
$(a_1 b_1 e_1)$	$(a_1 b_2 e_1)$	$(a_2 b_1 e_1)$	$(a_2 b_2 e_1)$
$(a_1 b_1 e_2)$	$(a_1 b_2 e_2)$	$(a_2 b_1 e_2)$	$(a_2 b_2 e_2)$

We can construct a set of possible exponents, one for each:

$(a_1 b_1 c_1)$ playing in that sort of place ruins your clothes
$(a_1 b_1 d_2)$ grown-ups like to be tidy
$(a_1 b_1 e_1)$ it's not good for you to get too excited
$(a_1 b_1 e_2)$ boys who are well brought up play nice games in the park
$(a_1 b_2 c_1)$ all that glass might get broken
$(a_1 b_2 d_2)$ Daddy doesn't like you to play rough games
$(a_1 b_2 e_1)$ you might hurt yourself

(a_1 b_2 e_2) you ought to show Johnny how to be a good boy
(a_2 b_1 c_1) other people's things aren't for playing with
(a_2 b_1 d_2) Mummy knows best
(a_2 b_1 e_1) you mustn't play with those kind of boys
(a_2 b_1 e_2) little boys should do as they're told
(a_2 b_2 c_1) that tin belongs to somebody else
(a_2 b_2 d_2) I told you I didn't want you to do that
(a_2 b_2 e_1) you'll get smacked next time
(a_2 b_2 e_2) you can go there when you're bigger

The paradigm seems to be valid. We have substituted just two types of control, 'by rule' and 'by explanation', each of which may be general or specific; and we have sub-divided 'child-oriented' into the more significant system of 'child as individual' versus 'child as status'.

As an example of a wrong prediction, if we kept the original network, which had 'child-oriented : child's action' versus 'child-oriented : child himself', and showed this system in free combination with the four types of control, we should almost certainly have found gaps. It is difficult to see how we could have the combination 'appeal' and 'child's action'; one can disapprove of an action, or give rules about it, but one can hardly appeal to it. The original network is thus wrong at this point, and would have to be rewritten.

Here is a rewritten version of it, corrected in respect of this error. In order to test it, we can write out the paradigm of meaning selections and, for each one, construct an example which would be acceptable as an exponent of it.

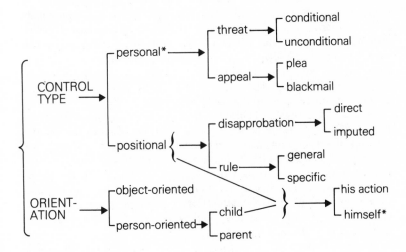

Here we have introduced two further conventions. The option *either* child's action *or* child himself' depends on the selection of *both* 'control type: positional' *and* 'orientation : child'; there is an intersection at this point in the network. Secondly, this system is characterized by the presence of an unmarked term, 'child himself', indicated by the asterisk. An unmarked option is always unmarked 'with respect to' some other option, here that of 'positional', also marked with an asterisk. The meaning is: 'if the speaker selects the "personal" control type, then if the orientation is to the child it must always be to the "child himself" '. The unmarked option is that which must be selected if one part of the entry condition is not satisfied, some other feature being selected which then determines the choice.

4. The semantic network as realization of behaviour patterns

In the second place, as is shown by what was said above, the semantic network is an account of how social meanings are expressed in language. It is the linguistic realization of patterns of behaviour.

We have stressed at various points that a linguistic description is a statement of what the speaker can mean; and that 'meaning', in its most general sense, includes both function within one level and realization of elements of a higher level. These 'higher level' elements will, at one point, lie outside the confines of what we recognize as language.

In the sociological context, the relevant extra-linguistic elements are the behaviour patterns that find expression in language. It is convenient to treat these under two headings: social, and situational.

First, there are the specifically social aspects of language use: the establishment and maintenance of the individual's social roles, the establishment of familiarity and distance, various forms of boundary maintenance, types of personal interaction and so on. These are largely independent of setting, but relate to generalized social contexts, such as those of mother and child already referred to.

The social contexts themselves are in turn dependent for their identification on a social theory of some kind, for instance Bernstein's theories of socialization and social learning. From such a theory, we are able to establish which contexts are relevant to the study of particular problems. The behavioural options are specific to the given social context, which determines their meaning; for example, 'threat' in a mother–child control context has a different significance from 'threat' in another social context, such as the operation of a gang. This may affect its realization in language.

Secondly, there are the situation types, the settings, in which language is used. These enable us to speak of 'text', which may be defined as 'language in setting'. Here we are concerned not with behaviour patterns that are socially significant in themselves but with socially identifiable units—transactions of various kinds, tasks, games, discussions and the like—within which the behaviour is more or less structured. Mitchell's classic study 'The language of buying and selling in Cyrenaica' provides an instance of a well-defined setting. The structure, in fact, may lie wholly within the text, as typically it does in a work of literature, or an abstract discussion; from the socio-logical point of view, these situation-independent uses of language are the limiting case, since the 'setting' is established within and through the language itself.

The behaviour patterns that we derive from social contexts and settings are thus intrinsic to sociological theory; they are arrived at in the search for explanations of social phenomena, and are independent of whatever linguistic patterns may be used to express them. The function of the semantic network is to show how these 'social meanings' are organized into linguistic meanings, which are then realized through the different strata of the language system. But whereas the social meanings, or behaviour patterns, are specific to their contexts and settings, their linguistic reflexes are very general categories such as those of transitivity, of mood and modality, of time and place, of information structure and the like. The input to the semantic networks is sociological and specific; their output is linguistic and general. [. . .]

This means that in sociological linguistics the criteria for selecting the areas of study are sociological. We investigate those contexts and settings that are socially significant, for instance those concerned with the transmission of cultural values. At the same time, it is not irrelevant that language has evolved in the service of social functions, so we may expect to take account of social factors in explaining the nature of language. There is therefore a clear *linguistic* motivation for studies of a socio-linguistic kind.

Here is an example drawn from a clearly-defined setting, the game of pontoon (vingt-et-un). This is a social context with closely circum-scribed behaviour patterns, namely the rules of the game. These define what the participant can do. The semantic network does not describe the rules of the game; it specifies what are the verbalized options in play—what the participant 'can mean', in our terms. [. . .]

* * *

[The section concludes with an example of language being used in one highly-restricted setting—to play a game of pontoon. Halliday's discussion (not reprinted below) concerns the problem of determining exactly where the behavioural analysis should end, and the semantic analysis begin.

Then, in Section 5, Halliday turns to his third requirement, that the semantic network should provide an 'input' to the grammar. There are cases, he says (and his example is greeting), where the semantic network leads directly to a set of fixed phrases. Such situations are rare, however, and in most cases the options in the semantic network will be related to and expressed through very general features of the language's grammar.

Halliday explores how the relationship between semantics and grammar may be specified, by looking at the areas of 'threatening' and 'warning'. He considers in some detail the grammatical features associated with these two fields, and it is at this point that the direct relevance of his paper to language teaching becomes clear. For what Halliday has done is to indicate how we may link 'function' and 'structure'. Indeed, 'threatening' and 'warning' are two of the categories of communicative function appearing in Wilkins' (1972a) specification for the Council of Europe's unit/credit system (see Trim in this volume p. 100). Halliday has in effect provided for us here a detailed list of the grammatical features associated with these functions. . . .]

* * *

5. The semantic network as realized in the grammatical system

In the third place, the semantic network is the 'input' to the grammar. The semantic network forms the bridge between behaviour patterns and linguistic forms.

We cannot, as a rule, relate behavioural options directly to the grammar. The relationship is too complex, and some intermediate level of representation is needed through which we express the meaning potential that is associated with the particular behavioural context. It is this intermediate level that constitutes our 'sociological' semantics. The semantic network then takes us, by a second step, into the linguistic patterns that can be recognized and stated in grammatical terms.

In some instances, the semantic network leads directly to the 'formal items'—to the actual words, phrases and clauses of the language. This is likely to happen only where there is a closed set of options in a clearly circumscribed social context.

Systems of greetings would often be of this kind. Here is a semantic network for a greeting system in middle-class British English:

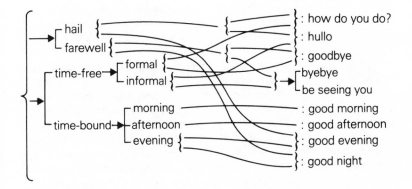

On the right are the items realizing the meaning selections; the colon is used *ad hoc* to show that these are on a different stratum.

[This display leaves out a number of facts, treating them by implication as behavioural (as 'rules of the game') and not semantic. There are severe limitations on the use of time-bound forms, other than *good night*, as valedictions; they are used mainly in the conclusion of trading transactions, and are probably disappearing. The form *how do you do?* is used only in the context of a new acquaintance, a time-bound form being required in the formal greeting of old acquaintances. Such factors could be incorporated into the network, if they are regarded as part of the 'meaning potential'; but for the present discussion it does not matter whether they are or not.]

In this instance, we can go straight from the options to the actual phrases by which they are realized, the 'formal items' as we have termed them. There is no need for any intervening level of grammatical systems and structures.

A number of more specific social contexts, and recurrent situation types, are likely to have this property, that the formal items, the words and phrases used, are directly relatable to the options in the semantic network. Apart from games, and greetings systems, which have already been exemplified, other instances would include musical terms (*adagio*, etc.), instructions to telephone operators, and various closed transactions such as buying a train or bus ticket. If we ignore the fact that the formal items are in turn re-encoded, or realized, as phonological items ('expressions'), which are in turn put out as speech (or the equivalent in the written medium), these are rather like non-linguistic semiotic systems, such as those of traffic signs and care labels on clothing, where the meanings are directly encoded into patterns in the visual medium. There is a minimum of stratal organization.

In language such systems are rather marginal; they account for only a small fraction of the total phenomena. In order to be able to handle systems of meaning potential which are of wider linguistic significance we have to consider types of setting which, although they may still be reasonably clearly circumscribed, are much more open and also much more general. In sociological linguistics the interest is in linguistic as well as in social phenomena, and so we need to explore areas of behaviour where the meanings are expressed through very general features, features which are involved in nearly all uses of language, such as transitivity in the clause.

In other words, for linguistic as well as for sociological reasons we should like to be able to account for grammatical phenomena by reference to social contexts whenever we can, in order to throw some light on why the grammar of languages is as it is. The more we are able to relate the options in grammatical systems to meaning potential in the social contexts and behavioural settings, the more insight we shall gain into the nature of the language system, since it is in the service of such contexts and settings that language has evolved.

This is no more than to recognize that there is a 'stratal' relation of the usual kind between grammar and semantics. In general the options in a semantic network will be realized by selections of features in the grammar—rather than 'bypassing' the grammatical systems and finding direct expression as formal items.

We have exemplified this already in discussing the realization of semantic categories such as that of 'threat'. Let us return to this instance, and add further examples. The following are some possible expressions of 'threat' and of 'warning' as semantic options in a regulatory context:

```
I'll smack you
Daddy'll smack you
you'll get smacked
I'll smack you        ⎫              ⎧ if you do that again
Daddy'll smack you    ⎬              ⎨ if you go on doing that
you'll get smacked    ⎭              ⎩
you do that again     ⎫                      ⎧ I'll smack you
you go on doing that  ⎬ and          ⎫       ⎨ Daddy'll smack you
don't you do that again ⎫  or        ⎬       ⎩ you'll get smacked
you stop doing that     ⎭             ⎭
I shall be cross with you
Daddy'll be cross with you
you'll fall down
you'll get hurt; you'll hurt yourself
you'll get dirty
```

you'll cut your hands; your hands'll get cut
you'll tear your clothes; your clothes'll get torn
your feet'll get wet
you'll get yourself hurt
you'll get your hands cut
you'll get your feet wet

We suggested earlier, as a generalization, that 'threat' could be realized by an action clause in simple future tense, having *you* either as Goal, or as Actor together with a modulation. We can now take this a little further, building up the network as we go.

The 'threat' may be a threat of physical punishment. Here the clause is of the action type, and, within this, of intentional or voluntary action, not supervention (i.e. the verb is of the *do* type, not the *happen* type). The process is a two-participant process, with the verb from a lexical set expressing 'punishment by physical violence', roughly that of § 972 (*punishment*) in Roget's *Thesaurus*, or perhaps the intersection of this with § 276 (*impulse*). The tense is simple future. The Goal, as already noted, is *you*; and the clause may be either active, in which case the agency of the punishment is likely to be the speaker (*I* as Actor), or passive, which has the purpose of leaving the agency unspecified. It is not entirely clear whether, if the Actor is other than *I*, the utterance is a threat or a warning; but it seems likely that in *Daddy'll smack you* the speaker is committing another person to a course of action on her behalf, so we will treat it as 'threat':

Any one of these threats may then be accompanied by a condition referring to the repetition or continuation by the child of whatever he was doing, and here we can specify almost the entire form of the clause: action verb substitute *do that*, Actor *you*, Conjunction *if*, and either auxiliary of aspect (*go on*) or aspectual adverb (*again*).

Probably all threats are conditional in this context, so the choice is between a condition that is explicit and one that is implicit. Note the alternative form of the condition—as an imperative clause (which must come first) in a paratactic: co-ordinate structure, either command with 'and' or prohibition with 'or'. (The prohibition also occurs by itself as a form of regulatory behaviour, e.g. *don't you do that again!*; but that is left out because it is not a threat.)

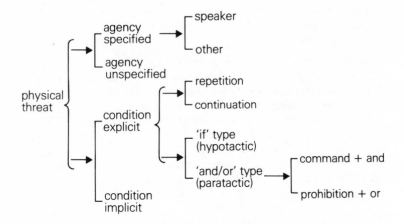

There are two other sub-categories of 'threat' among the examples given. One has a relational clause of the attributive type, having as Attribute an adjective expressive of anger or displeasure (Roget § 900 *resentment*) and *I* or a committed other person as Attribuend. The other is an action clause with the action modulated by necessity (e.g. *must, have to*), *you* as Actor and a wide range of punitive states of which little more can be specified. Contextually the former constitutes a threat of mental punishment, the latter a threat of restraint on the child's own behavioural options:

Next, there is the distinct category of 'warning'. This also is inherently conditional; we have given only examples without conditions but all could occur in an explicitly conditional form.

The warning specifies something that will happen to the child—something considered to be undesirable—if he does whatever it is he is being told not to do. The warning may relate to some process in which the child will become involved. Here the clause is of the 'action' type; it is, however, always 'superventive'—the child is involved against his own volition. The action in question may be one that is inherently unintentional, represented by a verb of the 'happen' type; in this case the meaning is 'do involuntarily' and the voice is active (e.g. *fall down*). Otherwise, if the action is inherently intentional, with a verb of the 'do' type (typically from a sub-set of Roget § 659 *deterioration*, or § 688 *fatigue*), the meaning is 'have done to one, come in for' and the voice is non-active: either passive: mutative (e.g. *get hurt*) or reflexive (*hurt yourself*), according to whether or not some unspecified agency is implied that is external to the child himself.

Alternatively, the warning may specify an attribute that the child will acquire. Here the clause is relational : attributive, also in the mutative form (i.e. *get* rather than *be*), and the attribute is an adjective of undesirable physical condition such as *wet, sore, tired, dirty* (in Roget § 653 *uncleanness*, § 655 *disease*, § 688 or elsewhere).

In all these clauses, there is only one participant, and it is always *you*. This may be Actor, Goal or Attribuend; but it always has the generalized function of Affected.

So far it has been assumed that the warning relates to the child himself. But it may relate instead to a part of his body or an item of his clothing (e.g. *you'll cut your hands, your clothes'll get muddy*). And finally the consequence has been represented as something that will happen to the child (or, again, to his person) without any specified agency: *you'll fall down, you'll get dirty, you'll get hurt, you'll hurt yourself, you'll cut your hands, you'll tear your clothes.* (Note that the last two are still superventive; *you'll tear your clothes* means 'your clothes will get torn', not 'you will tear your clothes deliberately'; cf. *you'll hurt yourself.*) But it may be represented instead as something which he will bring upon himself. In this case, the clause has the resultative form *you'll get your . . .* (*self*, part of the body or item of clothing) *hurt, dirty, torn* etc.; here *yourself, your clothes* etc. function as Affected and *you* as Agent.

Here is the network of warnings at this point:

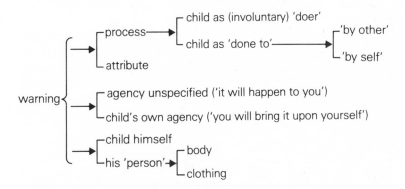

In this network we have shown the three options 'process, or attribute; agency unspecified, or child's own agency; the child himself, or his person' as being independent variables. This asserts that all logically possible combinations can occur, including those formed with the sub-options dependent on 'process' and on 'his person'; there is a total paradigm of 4 × 2 × 3 = 24 meaning selections. But only some of these are given in the examples, and this illustrates once again the point made earlier, that the paradigm defined by a system network provides a means of testing for all possibilities. If, when the paradigm is written out, it is found that not all combinations can occur, the network needs to be amended.

Here it will be found that the primary options are in fact independent. But the sub-option of 'child as doer, or child as done to', dependent on the selection of 'process', turns out to be at least partly determined in all environments except one, that of 'agency unspecified *and* child himself'. In the environment of 'child's own agency' it is fully determined—naturally: since the child is represented as bringing the consequence on himself, there is no distinction of how the process comes about. In the remaining environment, that of 'agency unspecified *and* child's person', it is partly determined: the opposition 'child as doer, or child as done to' is still valid, but the reflexive does not occur. This again is to be expected, since it is not the child himself but his person that is involved.

The final version of the network, showing both threat and warning, is therefore as follows:

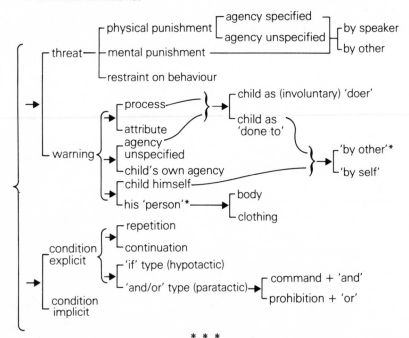

* * *

[Section 6 begins with a useful summary of the grammatical features associated with the 'threaten' and 'warn' networks:]

[. . .]

1. threat	clause: declarative
2. physical punishment	clause: action: voluntary (*do* type); effective (two-participant): Goal = *you*; future tense; positive; verb from Roget § 972 (or 972, 276)
3. agency specified	voice: active
4. agency unspecified	voice: passive
5. by speaker	Actor/Attribuend = *I*
6. by other	Actor/Attribuend = *Daddy*, etc.
7. mental punishment	clause: relational: attributive: Attribute = adjective from Roget § 900
8. restraint on behaviour	clause: action; modulation: necessity; Actor = *you*
9. warning	clause: declarative
10. process	clause: action: superventive (*happen* type)
11. attribute	clause: relational: attributive: mutative; Attribute = adjective from Roget § 653, 655, 688 etc.
12. agency unspecified	clause: non-resultative; Affected (Actor, Goal or Attribuend) = *you/yourself* or some form of 'your person'
13. child as 'doer'	voice: active; verb of involuntary action; Actor = *you*
14. child as 'done to'	voice: non-active; verb of voluntary action, from Roget § 659, 688 etc.
15. child's own agency	clause: resultative; Agent = *you*; Affected = *yourself* or some form of 'your person'
16. child himself	Affected = *you/yourself*
17. by 'other'	voice: passive: mutative
18. by 'self'	voice: reflexive
19. his 'person'	Affected: some form of 'your person'
20. body	'your person' = *your* + part of body
21. clothing	'your person' = *your* + item of clothing
22. condition explicit	clause complex; clause (1 or β): action: effective; anaphoric: verb substitute = *do that*; Actor = *you*
23. repetition	aspect: *again*
24. continuation	aspect: *go on/stop* (in negative) . . . *ing*

25. 'if' type   clause complex: hypotactic: clause β
                                   conditional: *if*

26. 'and/or' type   clause complex: paratactic: clause 1
                                   imperative

27. command + 'and'   clause 1 positive; *and*

28. prohibition + 'or'   clause 1 negative (including form with
                                   stop); *or*

29. condition implicit   (——)

[...]

[The final section of Halliday's paper contains a passage which both characterizes his approach and indicates its relationship to communicative language teaching (see Halliday, 1978, for further extension of these ideas):]

These networks are what we understand by 'semantics'. They constitute a stratum that is intermediate between the social system and the grammatical system. The former is wholly outside language, the latter is wholly within language; the semantic networks, which describe the range of alternative meanings available to the speaker in given social contexts and settings, form a bridge between the two.

Like any other level of representation in a stratal pattern, they face both ways. Here, the downward relation is with the grammar; but the upward relation is with the extra-linguistic context.

If we have tended to stress the instrumentality of linguistics, rather than its autonomy, this reflects our concern with language as meaning potential in behavioural settings. In investigating grammar and phonology, linguists have tended to insist on the autonomy of their subject; this is natural and useful, since these are the 'inner' strata of the linguistic system, the core of language so to speak, and in their immediate context they are 'autonomous'—they do not relate directly outside language. But they are in turn contingent on other systems which do relate outside language. Moreover we take the view that we can understand the nature of the inner stratal systems of language only if we do attempt to relate language to extra-linguistic phenomena. [...]

[Relating language to extra-linguistic phenomena what is links the work of Halliday and Hymes in a common tradition. And just as, for Halliday and Hymes, we can only *understand* language if we view it in this way, so it may be that we can only really *teach* language if we present and practise it in relation to the uses to which, as a communicative tool, it may be put. It is on this belief that communicative language teaching is based; a belief (to modify Halliday's phrase) in what amounts to 'the instrumentality of language teaching'.]

Notes

[1] This paper is revised from one presented at the Research Planning Conference on Language Development Among Disadvantaged Children, held under the sponsorship of the Department of Educational Psychology and Guidance, Ferkauf Graduate School, Yeshiva University, June 7–8, 1966. The original paper is included in the report of that conference, issued by the Department of Educational Psychology and Guidance (pp. 1–16). I wish to thank Dr Beryl Bailey and Dr Edmund Gordon of Yeshiva University for inviting me to participate and Dr Courtney Cazden, Dr John Gumperz, Dr Wayne O'Neill and Dr Vera John for their comments at that time.

Excerpts from D. H. Hymes, *On Communicative Competence*, Philadelphia: University of Pennsylvania Press, 1971: also published in Gumperz, J. J. and Hymes, D. (eds.) Directions in Sociolinguistics, Holt, Rinehart and Winston, 1970.

[2] Published in Explorations in the Functions of Language, Edward Arnold, 1973.

SECTION TWO

The Background to Teaching

The papers which appear in this section all explore ways in which the linguistic insights discussed in the first section are relevant to language teaching, particularly at the level of syllabus design. Widdowson, in the first two papers, outlines several arguments for giving discourse a much more prominent place in language teaching. Particularly, he argues that language teaching should move away from an emphasis on the properties of sentences in isolation to a concern for the use of sentences in combination. He insists in the first paper that discourse analysis should examine the *use* of sentences, and makes a distinction (expanded later in Widdowson, 1978: 24–29) between *cohesion* and *coherence*. The former involves overt, formal linguistic features in establishing the links in a piece of discourse, while the latter is concerned with the links which are established through the content of the message. Language teachers need to be concerned with both, and certainly need to understand what makes language coherent. The work of Labov and Searle, particularly, is discussed in order to establish a possible framework, and the paper concludes with some suggestions about what teachers can do to incorporate such ideas into their work. This paper, then, starts to answer some of the questions which are implicit in all the papers in this section, and most explicit in the Candlin paper, about the links between a grammar which is socially sensitive and a teaching grammar.

Widdowson's second paper is more technical. It explains the role of translation in relation to discourse as he defined it in the first paper. He concentrates on the establishment of what he calls 'pragmatic equivalence' between utterances in two languages. This relates to the use of the utterances as distinct from their meanings, and exploration of this concept raises important points about the relationship between the learning of language and the *content* of the language which is learnt. These points have still not been fully developed by language teachers, and deserve more consideration than they have so far received.

Candlin's paper covers similar ground to that of Widdowson's, and

illustrates the concern of a number of applied linguists in the early
1970s over the inadequacies of descriptive grammars for pedagogical
purposes. These issues are taken up more explicitly by Wilkins who,
in 'Grammatical, Situational and Notional Syllabuses', has formulated
the standard opposition to grammatical syllabuses and outlined a new
approach which has been extremely influential. The argument of this
paper is straightforward and needs no gloss, but it is worth pointing
out that the paper was originally presented as a speculative offering,
and that its rapid enshrinement as a source of firm doctrine goes against
the tone of much of Wilkins' other writings, as his second paper in this
volume illustrates. It is true that in his later book (Wilkins, 1976) a fairly
confident stance is maintained, but it is probably fair to remark that
the considerable effect of the original paper owes more to its success
in demolishing than in constructing. Certainly an argument is presented
which no language teacher can afford to ignore. Further, it is an argument which leads directly into many of the discussions of teaching
languages for specific purposes (cf., e.g. Holden, 1977; Mackay and
Mountford, 1978; Munby, 1978). Wilkins' second paper shows how a
'notional' approach may relate to the concept of a 'limited' grammar.

The five papers in this section all illustrate the state of argument in
syllabus design in the early 1970s. Out of this discussion has emerged
a great deal of valuable practical work, both in syllabus design and
teaching materials. Five years later there is (as should be expected
with any substantial innovation) some dissatisfaction with many of
these ideas. Such dissatisfaction cannot be expressed clearly, however,
unless an understanding of the original arguments has been achieved.

Directions in the teaching of discourse
H. G. Widdowson

The purpose of this paper is to suggest that there is a need to take discourse into account in our teaching of language, and to consider how far the attempts made by linguists and others to analyse discourse might help us to do this. In this paper I shall be concerned exclusively with English and with English teaching, but I believe that what I have to say has a more general application.

I think it is true to say that, in general, language teachers have paid little attention to the way sentences are used in combination to form stretches of connected discourse. They have tended to take their cue from the grammarian and have concentrated on the teaching of sentences as self-contained units. It is true that these are often presented in 'contexts' and strung together in dialogues and reading passages, but these are essentially settings to make the formal properties of the sentences stand out more clearly—properties which are then established in the learner's mind by means of practice drills and exercises. Basically, the language teaching unit is the sentence as a formal linguistic object. The language teacher's view of what constitutes knowledge of a language is essentially the same as Chomsky's: a knowledge of the syntactic structure of sentences, and of the transformational relations which hold between them. Sentences are seen as paradigmatically rather than syntagmatically related. Such a knowledge 'provides the basis for actual use of language by the speaker-hearer' (Chomsky, 1965: 9). The assumption that the language teacher appears to make is that once this basis is provided, then the learner will have no difficulty in dealing with the actual use of language: that is to say, that once the competence is acquired, performance will take care of itself.

There is a good deal of evidence to suggest that this assumption is of very doubtful validity indeed. It has been found, for example, that students entering higher education with the experience of six or more years of instruction in English at the secondary school, have considerable difficulty coping with language in its normal communicative use. So long as language is taught in a vacuum, as a set of skills which have no immediate utility, it is possible to believe that one is providing for some future use by developing a stock of grammatical competence which will be immediately converted into adequate performance when the need arises. It is only when language teaching has to be geared to specific communicative purposes that doubts as to the validity of this belief begin to arise. In many parts of the world the teaching of English has assumed the crucial auxiliary role of providing the means for furthering specialist education, and here it has become plain that a knowledge of how the language functions in communication does not automatically follow from a knowledge of sentences. As I have suggested elsewhere (Widdowson, 1971), this role for English requires a new orientation to its teaching.

What this orientation amounts to is a change of focus from the sentence as the basic unit in language teaching to the use of sentences in combination. Once we accept the need to teach language as communication, we can obviously no longer think of language in terms only of sentences. We must consider the nature of discourse, and how best to teach it. Language teaching materials have in the past been largely derived from the products of theoretical sentence grammars. We now need materials which derive from a description of discourse: materials which will effect the transfer from grammatical competence, a knowledge of sentences, to what has been called communicative competence (Hymes, 1970 and this volume, Campbell and Wales, 1970), a knowledge of how sentences are used in the performance of communicative acts of different kinds. Grammatical competence remains in a perpetual state of potentiality unless it is realized in communication. As Hymes put it 'There are rules of use without which the rules of grammar would be useless.' (Hymes, 1970: 14 and p. 15 this volume). We might hope, as applied linguists, that theoretical studies of discourse might indicate the nature of such rules, and give us some clues as to how we might approach teaching them.

I have referred to discourse as the use of sentences in combination. This is a vague definition which conveniently straddles two different, if complementary, ways of looking at language beyond the sentence. We might say that one way is to focus attention on the second part of my definition: *sentences in combination*, and the other to focus on the first part: *the use of sentences*. I think, it is important, from the applied linguistic point of view, to keep these two approaches distinct, though, as we shall see later, linguists have recently attempted to conflate them.

The study of discourse in terms of the combination or interconnection of sentences is, of course, exemplified in the work of Harris. 'Language' he observes, 'does not occur in stray words or sentences, but in connected discourse.' (Harris, 1952: 357), and he sets out to discover what the nature of this connection might be by applying his well-tried distributional method. By means of transformational adjustments to surface forms, he is able to establish equivalence classes of morphemes and to show that 'in many cases two otherwise different sentences contain the same combination of equivalance classes, even though they may contain different combinations of morphemes.' (Harris, 1952: 373). He is thereby able to discover a patterning in the discourse in terms of chains of equivalences. What he does, then, is to reduce different message forms to make them correspond to a common code pattern. The fact that the variation in the message form may have some significant communicative value is for him irrelevant. His concern is not to characterize discourse as communication, but to use it to exemplify the operation of the language code in stretches of text larger than the sentence. He himself recognizes the limited scope of his analysis.

> 'All this, however, is still distinct from an *interpretation* of the findings, which must take the meanings of morphemes into consideration and ask what the author was about when he produced the text. Such interpretation is obviously quite separate from the formal findings, although it may follow closely in the directions which the formal findings indicate.' (Harris, 1952: 382).

The notion that an understanding of the nature of discourse as communication may be dependent on a prior formal account is a significant one, pointing as it does towards a fundamental problem in linguistic description which has to do with the distinction I have made between the two approaches to the analysis of discourse. The notion is a common one among linguists of the transformational—generative persuasion. Thus, Chomsky himself:

> 'There seems to be little reason to question the view that investigation of performance will proceed only so far as understanding of underlying competence permits.' (Chomsky, 1965: 10).

The belief is that a native speaker's knowledge of the sentences of his language can be accounted for in terms of invariant rules of an algebraic kind. It is assumed that once the 'correct' grammar consisting of such rules is written, it will provide a basis for the study of performance as a whole, including the study of language in its social contexts of use. There have been objections to this neat isolation of competence as representing the sole concern of the linguist. Hymes (1970 and this volume) and Labov (1970), for example, have suggested that it is likely that an adequate description of the formal operation of language is dependent on an investigation into certain aspects of performance, and recent developments in generative grammar in fact give strong support to this suggestion. It is significant in the light of Harris's implication of the primacy of formal analysis that Labov should point to discourse analysis as being the very area of enquiry where such primacy cannot be established:

> 'There are some areas of linguistic analysis in which even the first steps towards the basic invariant rules cannot be taken unless the social context of the speech event is considered. The most striking examples are in the analysis of discourse.' (Labov, 1970: 206–7).

Since Harris has taken a considerable number of steps in the description of discourse, the question naturally arises as to how he has managed to do this without considering speech events and social contexts at all. The answer is, of course, that whereas Harris conceives of discourse in purely formal terms as a series of connected sentences, Labov is thinking of the way language forms are used to perform social actions:

> 'Commands and refusals are actions; declaratives, interrogatives, imperatives are linguistic categories—things that are said, rather than things that are done. The rules we need will show how things are done with words and how one interprets these utterances as actions: in other words, relating what is done to what is said and what is said to what is done. This area of linguistics can be called 'discourse analysis'; but it is not well-known or developed. Linguistic theory is not yet rich enough to write such rules, for one must take into account such sociological non-linguistic categories as roles, rights and obligations.' (Labov, 1969: 54–5).

Harris's work, well-known though it is, gets no mention; and it is clear that by this definition it has nothing to do with discourse analysis at all. We are confronted, then, with two quite different kinds of enquiry both contending for the same name. A terminological distinction seems to be called for. I propose that the investigation into the formal properties of a piece of language, such as is carried out by Harris, should be called text analysis. Its purpose is to discover how a text exemplifies the operation of the language code beyond the limits of the sentence, text being roughly defined, therefore, as *sentences in combination*. Changing the name of Harris's kind of enquiry is to some degree justified by the fact that he himself seems to use the terms *text* and *discourse* interchangeably, as in the following quotation: '. . . the formal features of the discourses can be studied by distributional methods within the text.' (Harris, 1952: 357).

We may now use the label *discourse analysis* to refer to the investigation into the way sentences are put to communicative use in the performing of social actions, discourse being roughly defined, therefore, as *the use of sentences*. Having distinguished these two areas of enquiry, I want now to consider what value their respective findings might have for the teaching of language both as text and as discourse. If we are to teach language in use, we have to shift our attention from sentences in isolation to the manner in which they combine in text on the one hand, and to the manner in which they are used to perform communicative acts in discourse on the other. What help can we get from the theorists?

Text analysis is exemplified most obviously by Harris. It is also exemplified, perhaps less obviously, in the work associated with Halliday, which comes under the headings of 'register analysis' and 'grammatical cohesion'. I will deal with each of these briefly in turn and indicate what relevance I think they have for the teaching of language. Although register analysis is not concerned with the way sentences are connected together in sequence, it falls within text analysis in that its purpose is to define varieties of language solely in terms of the occurrence of formal linguistic elements:

> 'It is by their formal properties that registers are defined. If two samples of language activity from what, on non-linguistic grounds, could be considered different situation-types show no differences in grammar or lexis, they are assigned to one and the same register . . .' (Halliday, McIntosh and Strevens, 1964: 89).

What has to be noted here is the deliberate rejection of the relevance of the 'sociological, non-linguistic categories' which, as we have seen, Labov represents as having a direct bearing on rules of discourse. Registers are, then, types of text, not types of discourse, since they are not defined in terms of what kind of communication they represent. The results of a register analysis of, say, a selection of scientific texts, will be a quantitative account of the frequency of occurrence of whichever formal elements were selected to be counted in the first place (see, for example, Huddleston *et al.* 1968). That is to say, it will indicate how the texts concerned exemplify the language code: it will tell us nothing directly (though we may hazard a few guesses) about the communicative acts which are performed in the use of such formal elements. Register analysis has been taken up, and in some extent taken further, by Crystal and Davy (1969) under the name of 'General Stylistics', but in spite of the refinements which they introduce into the analysis, it remains the analysis of text, as the following quotation makes clear:

> '. . . the procedures for approaching stylistic analysis are no different from those made use of in any descriptive exercise: the primary task is to catalogue and classify features within the framework of some general linguistic theory' (Crystal and Davy, 1969: 60).

Register analysis, or general stylistic analysis (in the sense of Crystal and Davy), is open to a number of rather serious theoretical objections, of which perhaps the principal one has to do with the difficulty of establishing when a formal difference is significant or not, when a certain linguistic feature is or is not stylistically distinctive. No two pieces of language are alike: but how non-alike do they have to be before they become stylistically distinct and specimens of different registers? But we are not at present concerned with theoretical issues but with deciding on what value such an approach to text analysis might have for language teaching. As I mentioned earlier, this approach does not seek to establish the way in which sentences are connected. On the contrary, the analysis is an atomistic one which breaks a piece of language down into its constituent linguistic elements. This procedure yields information about the relative frequency of different linguistic forms in the texts that have been examined. The question is: how can this information be used in language teaching? It provides some guide as to which linguistic elements to include in a course designed for students who are to deal with the kind of texts which provided the material for analysis, but it gives no indication at all as to how such elements are to be presented as text. What usually happens is that the findings of such an analysis are used to produce remedial courses in which the most frequent linguistic elements are presented within the framework of sentences. I think that the essential shortcoming of register/general stylistic analysis, as preached and practised by Halliday *et al.* and Crystal and Davy, is that it does not provide teachers with any directions as to how they might move from the sentence to the text. And yet the very reason for adopting the findings of such analysis is generally speaking to direct language teaching towards meeting the special needs of students, and to prepare them for their encounter with language in use as a medium for their specialist subjects. Register analysis may have its uses, but it seems to have very little value for the teaching of text, and none at all, of course, for the teaching of discourse.

The study of grammatical cohesion, on the other hand, does have direct relevance to the teaching of text, since it aims to discover 'the characteristics of a text as distinct from a collection of sentences.' (Hasan, 1968: 24). This aim is not very different from that of Harris, whose analysis begins with an observation which might easily have served as a rubric for Hasan's work:

> 'Language does not occur in stray words or sentences, but in connected discourse. . . . Arbitrary conglomerations of sentences are indeed of no interest except as a check on grammatical description.' (Harris, 1952: 357).

But although the aims of both are alike, their approaches towards achieving them are quite different. Whereas Harris sets out to establish patterns of formal equivalence, Hasan is concerned with the cohesive function of certain linguistic forms. Harris deals with formal elements like equivalence classes, whereas Hasan deals with such functional notions as anaphora and cataphora. The relevance of her work for language teaching lies in the fact that it indicates how language items take on particular values in context. For example, the lexical item *iron* stands in a relation of hyponymy to the lexical item *metal* in the semantic structure of English, but within a text they may have the value of synonymous expressions:

> In engineering it is rare to find *iron* used in its pure form. Generally the *metal* is alloyed with carbon and other elements to form wrought iron, steels and cast irons.

This is a simple instance of what Hasan refers to as 'substitution'. It is not always so easy to discover the referential value of items in a text. In the following, for example, the term *process* does not form a synonymous link with any preceding noun, and the term *ingredient* forms a link with a noun (i.e. *metal*) with which it has no semantic association in the code of the language at all:

> Most alloys are prepared by mixing *metals* in the molten state; then the mixture is poured into moulds and allowed to solidify. In this *process*, the major *ingredient* is usually melted first.

Similarly, items like the demonstrative pronoun *this* cause considerable difficulty in texts because of the very wide range of values they can have. As Hasan points out, *this* 'may have as referent not merely a nominal but any identifiable matter in the preceding text. Such matter may extend over a sentence, an entire paragraph or even longer passages.' (Hasan, 1968: 58).

The importance of the work on grammatical cohesion is that it is a description of the devices which are used to link sentences together to form text and as such provides the language teacher with an inventory of points he must incorporate into exercises to develop a knowledge of this aspect of language use.

Hasan makes a distinction between 'The internal and the external aspects of "textuality" ', the first having to do with cohesion, the second with the way language links meaningfully with the situation in which it is used. She speaks briefly about the external aspect of textuality in terms of register and her point seems to be that a piece of language can be recognized as text if its linguistic features can be plotted along a number of situational dimensions in such a way as to assign it to a specific register, even if cohesive links are missing. Similarly, Halliday defines the 'textual function' of language as having to do with 'making links with itself and with features of the situation in which it is used.' (Halliday, 1970a: 143), pointing out the cohesion is one aspect of the textual function as a whole (presumably that which relates to language 'making links with itself'). This function, says Halliday, 'enables the speaker or writer to construct "texts", or connected passages of discourse that is situationally relevant' (Halliday, 1970a: 143). Here, text and discourse are not kept terminologically distinct, but in my terms the external or situational aspects of 'text' or 'textuality' or 'texture' (Halliday, 1970a) have to do with discourse and are not concerned with *grammatical cohesion* between sentences but with *rhetorical coherence* of utterances in the performance of acts of communication.

The distinction between *cohesion* and *coherence* brings us to a consideration of discourse. Advances in our understanding of discourse have come not from linguistics as it is generally understood but from the two areas of enquiry which we might call the sociology of language on the one hand and the philosophy of language on the other. I do not propose to attempt a review of this work, but only to indicate briefly where I think these two approaches converge, and what relevance they have for the teaching of language.

We may take the distinction between cohesion and coherence as our starting point. Labov as we have already noted has pointed out that there are certain rules of discourse which cannot be described without reference to social context. That is to say, the description of such rules depends on reference to what Hasan calls 'external aspects of textuality', or what Halliday calls 'features of the situation'. Let us consider two pieces of dialogue:

A: Can you go to Edinburgh tomorrow?
B: Yes I can.
A: Can you go to Edinburgh tomorrow?
B: B.E.A. pilots are on strike.

In the first of these exchanges, we have a cohesive text in that B uses an eliptical form of the sentence 'Yes, I can go to Edinburgh tomorrow' (ellipsis being one of Hasan's categories of cohesion). In the second exchange, there is no cohesion between the sentences which are used. And yet the two utterances in combination made sense: we understand that B is saying that he cannot go to Edinburgh because the strike rules out what he considers to be the only reasonable means to getting there. It seems justifiable to claim, then, that the second exchange is coherent as discourse without being cohesive as text. The question is: can we support this claim by postulating rules of discourse which will account for the rhetorical connection between the two utterances in the second exchange?

Labov takes the view that discourse rules have to do with the sequence of actions which are performed in the issuing of utterances. As he puts it: 'Sequencing rules do not operate between utterances but between the actions performed by these utterances. In fact, there are usually no connections between successive utterances at all.' (Labov, 1970: 208). Labov is of course thinking primarily of spoken communication here. Written communication of its nature requires a much higher degree of interdependancy between cohesion and coherence. But it remains true for both media that discourse is characterized in terms of communicative actions and not in terms of linguistic forms. How, then, might we characterize the communicative actions performed in the second exchange? What Labov does is to specify a number of preconditions which have to be met for a given utterance to count as a particular communicative act. For an utterance to be seriously intended as an order, or a request for action, for example, the speaker, A, must believe the following:

1. That X, the action he refers to (e.g. going to Edinburgh), should be carried out for some purpose.
2. That the hearer, B, has the ability to do X.
3. That B has the obligation to do X.
4. That A has the right to ask B to do X.

The coherence of our second exchange is accounted for by the fact that each utterance focuses on the second of these preconditions. For A's utterance to be interpreted by B as an order, the other preconditions must be understood as obtaining by virtue of the situation, including, of course, the relationship between the two people. In these circumstances it is only necessary for the speaker to draw the hearer's attention to one precondition for the act of ordering to be performed, and only necessary for the hearer to refer to the same condition to decline to act upon the order.

The key to this approach to the analysis of discourse lies, then, in the understanding of what conditions must obtain for an utterance to count as a particular communicative act. An investigation into these conditions has been a feature of recent work in the philosophy of language. Searle (1969), following the lead of Austin (1962, 1963), has specified the conditions attendant upon the acts of promising, advising, warning, greeting, congratulating, and so on. We might expect that as this kind of work proceeds, and as we learn more about the relationship between what is said and what is done, we shall be able to describe a type of discourse in terms of the kind of communicative acts it represents, and the manner in which they are given linguistic expression. Thus we might hope that we shall be in a position to characterize varieties of usage not as registers or types of text, but as different ways of communicating. To take an example, scientific varieties of English are, as I have noted earlier, generally represented as types of text, exemplifying a high incidence of forms like the passive, certain modals, certain types of adverbial clause and so on. There seems no reason why they should not, in course of time, be represented as types of discourse consisting of certain combinations of such acts as definition, classification, generalization, qualification and so on, combinations which in many cases constitute larger communicative units like explanations, descriptions and reports, and which may be said to reflect the actual methodology of scientific enquiry. It should be noted that although it is convenient to consider acts of communication initially as corresponding with sentence-like stretches of language, there is no reason why such a correspondence should be assumed. In the case of acts like describing and reporting, for example, the conditions attendant on their performance in any particular type of discourse are likely to be communicative acts in their own right.

What I have tried to do in this paper is to distinguish two ways of looking at language beyond the limit of the sentence. One way sees it as text, a collection of formal objects held together by patterns of equivalances or frequencies or by cohesive devices. The other way sees language as discourse, a use of sentences to perform acts of communication which cohere into larger communicative units, ultimately establishing a rhetorical pattern, which characterizes the piece of language as a whole as a kind of communication. Both approaches to the description of language have their purposes, and if I have sometimes appeared to be recommending the latter at the expense of the former, this is only to restore the balance for language teaching, which should, in my view, be as much concerned with discourse as with text. What is important is that we should recognize the limitations of a particular approach to analysis, and not be too easily persuaded that it provides us with the only valid characterization of language in use. My reason for pointing to the limitations of register analysis and general stylistics (in the sense of Crystal and Davy) was that this approach has too often been represented as the only one to adopt when delimiting the language of a particular area of use. To be fair, and to maintain the balance, one might point to a similar atomistic approach to the description of discourse: the traditional rhetorical one which searches passages of prose for metaphor, litotes, oxymoron, synecedoche and so on, or to more recent studies in rhetoric which focus on the 'topic sentence' and describe the development of discourse only in terms of its referential function.

I have said that text analysis and discourse analysis are different but complementary ways of looking at language in use. I am aware that recent work in linguistics has attempted to integrate features of discourse into a unitary model of grammar by writing presuppositions, illocutionary act indicators and so on into the base component of a generative grammar (see, for example, Ross, 1970; Lakoff, 1970a). The result seems to have blurred the distinction between sentence and utterance and between semantics and pragmatics, and to create, in consequence, a good deal of confusion in linguistic description. One might point, for example, to the long discussion on the verb 'Remind' in recent editions of *Linguistic Inquiry*, initiated by Postal (1970), and to the corrective statements by Bar-Hillel (1971) and Bolinger (1971). It is interesting in this connection to see linguists tending towards the same error as beset linguistic philosophers of an earlier era (see Strawson, 1950). Both Postal (1970) and Karttunen (1970, 1971), for example, in their attempts to bring discourse features into grammar seem to me to be confusing what Strawson shows so clearly must be kept distinct: a sentence, and a use of a sentence (Strawson, 1950: 6), or, in my terms, text and discourse. Discourse must, of course, ultimately be accounted for in a total linguistic description, as both Hymes and Labov insist, but this does not necessarily involve incorporating it into a prescribed generative model of grammar.

There is, then, a good deal of turmoil in linguistics as a result of its attempts to account for the communicative properties of language. Meanwhile, the language teacher cannot wait for the dust to settle. I believe that it is urgent that he should incorporate text and discourse into his teaching. While the linguists are arguing among themselves, there is a great deal that can be done. We can set about devising exercises to develop a knowledge of grammatical cohesion. We can consider how far we can select and grade teaching material in terms of communicative acts rather than simply in terms of linguistic structures. We can, in short, be working out ways in which we can teach our students to use the foreign language to define, classify, generalize, promise, predict, describe, report, and so on; to make them aware of how the language is used for the particular kind of communication they are concerned with. Some ways of how this might be done are suggested in Allen and Widdowson (1974). In time we might hope that the linguists will provide us with more specific directions to follow. Meanwhile, the applied linguist, working, as it were, from the pedagogic end, can begin to specify the nature of different communicative acts, the way they are realized, the way they combine in different varieties of language use. These specifications may well develop from attempts to design language teaching materials which focus on the teaching of discourse. The applied linguist does not always have to wait, indeed, he cannot always wait, for the linguist to provide him with something to apply. He may follow his own path towards pedagogic application once the theorist has given a hint of the general direction. He may even, on the way, discover a direction or two which the theoretical linguist might himself explore with profit.

Note

Published in Corder, S. P., and Roulet, E. (eds.), Theoretical Linguistic Models in Applied Linguistics, AIMAV/Didier, 1973.

The deep structure of discourse and the use of translation
H. G. Widdowson

The purpose of this paper is to explore, in tentative fashion, different ways of looking at the process of translation with a view to discovering their potential utility for the teaching of foreign languages. The use of translation as a teaching technique has long been viewed with suspicion by language teachers and many, of course, proscribe it altogether as a matter of principle. I want to argue that translation, conceived of in a certain way, can be a very useful pedagogic device and indeed in some circumstances, notably those where a foreign language is being learned for 'special purposes' as a service subject, translation of a kind may provide the most effective means of learning.

As is pointed out in Catford (1965), the central problem in the theory and practice of translation is concerned with specifying the nature of equivalence in respect of two pieces of language. Clearly what counts as equivalence will be determined by the model of linguistic description which is being used in the translation process. Thus a model which accounts only for the surface structure of sentences will only be able to assign equivalence to two sentences from two languages if they both exemplify overt grammatical features which the model specifies in some way as being common to both language systems: such features might include, for example, tense, aspect, voice, and so on.

Let us suppose that English is the source language (SL) and French the target language (TL) and that we wish to make use of a taxonomic structuralist model to establish translation equivalents between the two languages. Such a model will assign different structural descriptions to the following sentences in the SL:

1. The postman opened the door.
2. The door was opened by the postman.

It will also assign different structural descriptions to the following sentences in the TL:

3. Le facteur ouvrit la porte.
4. La porte fut ouverte par le facteur.

Now, with reference to this model, one might say that 1. is equivalent to 3. and 2. to 4. on the grounds that these pairs exemplify common grammatical features: both 1. and 3. expound (to use Halliday's term) active voice and simple past tense whereas 2. and 4. expound the passive voice with the simple past tense. To say this, however, is to make certain assumptions which, on examination, are of very doubtful validity. To establish these equivalences one has to argue in the following way: in the system of English the simple past tense contrasts with the present perfect in the same way as the passé simple contrasts with the passé composé in the system of French, so that in Saussurean terms they have the same value (valeur) in their respective systems. The same argument would apply to the active and passive in the systems of the two languages. But although the terms may *appear* to be comparable, their value derives uniquely from the manner in which they contrast within each system and there is no principled way of establishing their equivalence across systems (for a more detailed discussion, see Van Buren, 1974).

One difficulty with the taxonomic structuralist model, then, is that it provides no way of establishing equivalent formal value of a Saussurean kind. Another difficulty is that it cannot account for communicative or functional value (see Widdowson, 1972 and p. 117 this volume). Even if one were able to set up a formal correspondence which established an equivalence relation between 1. and 3. and 2. and 4. to do this would be to ignore the fact that the passé simple is used very restrictively in French and does not have the same value in respect of range of use as the simple past in English. If one is thinking of equivalence in terms of communicative value then one would be inclined to reject 3. and 4. as translation equivalents of 1. and 2. in favour of the following:

5. Le facteur a ouvert la porte.
6. La porte a été ouverte par le facteur.

The kind of linguistic model we are considering, however, would be likely to invoke some measure of structural similarity to relate 5. and 6. not to 1. and 2. but to the following sentences in English:

7. The postman has opened the door.
8. The door has been opened by the postman.

Furthermore, of course, in some contexts 5. and 6. would indeed have the communicative value which would require 7. and 8. as equivalents and not 1. and 2.

If we are using a taxonomic structuralist grammar as a descriptive model, then there would appear to be no principled way in which we can account for the equivalence in terms of either formal or functional value. What such a model does, in effect, is to elevate a number of overt grammatical categories like tense and aspect to the status of universals and to assign formal equivalence by reference to some *ad hoc* measure of similarity in the realizations of these categories. Such a procedure yields the following equivalent pairs:

1. ...... 3.
2. ...... 4.
5. ...... 7.
6. ...... 8.

Let us now consider equivalence in relation to a transformational-generative grammar such as is outlined in Chomsky (1965). Such a model of description will represent 1. and 2./3. and 4. as equivalent in relation to a common deep structure. This will presumably allow us to say that 1. may be equivalent to 4. and 2. to 3. But (as is observed in Kac, 1969) a grammar of this kind will also represent a whole range of different surface structures as equivalent and these will include in the present case:

9. It was the postman who opened the door.
10. It was the door that was opened by the postman.

Similarly, one can cite sentences in French which might be said to represent different surface realizations of a common deep structure source. Thus one might regard the following as equivalent to 3. and 4.:

11. Ce fut le facteur qui ouvrit la porte.
12. Ce fut la porte qui fut ouverte par le facteur.

We have now, as it were, extended the range of equivalence, and it would be convenient if we could say that the underlying structure of 1–2 and 9–10 is equivalent to that of 3–4 and 11–12, so that any of the English sentences can count as equivalent to any of the French ones. Unfortunately to do so would be to make the same mistaken assumption as before: that is, that the categories which appear in the deep structure of a Chomsky (1965) model are realized in the same way in both languages.

At the same time, the fact that translation is possible at all suggests that it should be possible to arrive at a semantic base which would generate a proposition of which all of the sentences cited so far are alternative realizations. I do not wish (and in any case I do not feel competent) to discuss what form such a deep structure should take, but in principle it is possible to conceive of a deep structure which would serve as an underlying propositional reference for the sentences that we have been considering. We might call this (without, however, invoking temporal associations) a kind of 'proto-deep structure' and represent it as follows:

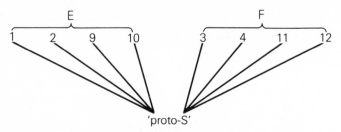

'proto-S'

Of course, each of these surface forms can be differentiated from the others by reference to the transformational rules required for its derivation, but they can all be regarded as linguistically equivalent at the deeper level of analysis in that they are all paraphrases of each other (see Katz and Postal, 1964: 157). It is, of course, the unique feature of this model of description that it provides for covert equivalence of this kind.

But although it is possible to claim that all of these sentences are equivalent in terms of basic grammatical properties, they clearly have different functional value: they are not in free variation as potential utterances. This difference can be accounted for in a number of ways. One can distinguish between different linguistic functions as Halliday does (Halliday, 1967/68, 1970b etc.) and say that these sentences are equivalent in respect of ideational function but not in respect of textual function. Alternatively, one might say that they are equivalent in that they all express the same propositional content, but not so in that they differ in topicalization (Fillmore, 1968) or in focus (Chomsky, 1968). In both cases what one is saying, essentially, is that the different forms are equivalent as sentences in isolation but not as utterances or kinds of message. I shall return to this point presently.

Meanwhile, let me recapitulate. A descriptive model which deals only in surface forms will only assign equivalence between sentences within and between languages if these sentences are held to expound (to use Halliday's terms) common ideational, inter-personal and textual features. A model which distinguishes between deep and surface levels of analysis will assign equivalence to sentences which exemplify common ideational and interpersonal features irrespective of their textual differences. The two models are alike, however, in that neither will allow equivalence to sentences which differ ideationally or inter-personally. As with the taxonomic model, it is difficult to see how the transformational-generative model can give explicit descriptive sanction to our feeling that 1. has the same general communicative value as 5., or provide us with any principled way of regarding them as translation equivalents. Clearly we cannot say that they derive from the same deep structure because to do so would be to conflate 1. and 7., which have different values, both from the communicative and grammatical points of view. We cannot simply add 5. and 7. as derivatives from our 'proto-S': the relationship between these sentences has to be represented differently:

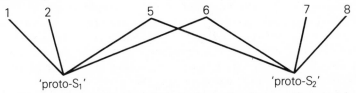

It would seem then that the transformational-generative model of description will assign grammatical equivalence to certain forms which have different communicative value and will deny equivalence to certain forms which have the same communicative value. Thus it will allow us to translate 1. as 4., 9. as 12. and so on, even when the context makes it inappropriate for us to do so, and it will prevent us from translating 1. as 5., 2. as 6. even when the context requires us to do so.

These observations suggest that we should distinguish between three kinds of equivalence. The first of these, which I will call structural equivalence, involves the correlation of the surface forms of sentences by reference to some *ad hoc* measure of formal similarity. The second, which I will call semantic equivalence, involves relating different surface forms to a common deep structure which represents their basic ideational and interpersonal elements. The third kind of equivalence is one which involves relating surface forms to their communicative function as utterances and this I will call pragmatic equivalence. Whereas semantic equivalence has to do with the propositional content of sentences, pragmatic equivalence has to do with the illocutionary effect of utterances. We may now say that 3. is a structural translation of 1. and 4. of 2., that either sentence from the English set 9–10 (and any other sentence relatable to the proto-S) is a semantic translation of either sentence from the French set 11–12, and that 5. can be (but is not invariably) a pragmatic translation of 1. and 6. of 2. We cannot, of course, by definition establish pragmatic equivalence by considering isolated sentences but only by considering what utterances count as in context.

I want now to place the foregoing discussion into broader perspective as a preliminary to relating it to pedagogic issues. When I say that pragmatic equivalence can only be established by considering what utterances count as in context what I mean is that the context, whether linguistic within the discourse or extra-linguistic within the situation, will provide the conditions whereby an utterance can be interpreted as representing a particular message or communicative act. I am not thinking of context in the raw state, as it were. I am not suggesting that the meaning of an utterance is discoverable directly by associating it with features of the context in which it occurs but that its value as a communicative act derives from its satisfying the kind of conditions specified in Searle (1969), Labov (1969, 1970) and which certain features of the context (though not all) provide for. Pragmatic meaning is therefore not the same thing as contextual meaning, as neo-Firthians appear to use this term, and by the same token, as I argue elsewhere (Widdowson, 1972 and p. 117 this volume) the communicative teaching of language is not the same thing as contextual language teaching as this notion is generally understood.

The distinction made in the previous paragraph enables us to characterize utterance types by reference to specific sets of conditions which are contextually realized rather than by reference to an unspecific (and unspecifiable) number of 'contexts of situation' *per se*. This allows us to set up communicative acts as utterance types which are defined independently of particular contexts and to provide a list of their most common linguistic realizations, either in relation to general use or in relation to particular universes of discourse (there is a crucial distinction here which I shall return to presently). Thus we can say, for example, that the following are pragmatically equivalent (though not equivalent in other respects) in the sense that they can all serve to perform the act of instruction:

13. Press the button twice.
14. The button must be pressed twice.
15. It is necessary to press the button twice.
16. The button is pressed twice.

Now there are differences in 'focus' here, and we may wish to speak of different kinds of instruction. But just as difference of focus does not prevent sentences 9–10/11–12 from being equivalent at a deeper grammatical level, so the differences here (which might be associated with Labov's 'modes of mitigation and politeness') need not be inconsistent with establishing pragmatic equivalence at a deeper rhetorical level. Notice that as with the case of 1. and 5. discussed earlier, not all of these potential utterances can be equated semantically, 16., for example, as a sentence can also be (and would usually be) formally linked with a sentence of the form:

17. (Someone) presses the button twice.

It would seem reasonable to say, then, that 16. is semantically equivalent to 17. but pragmatically equivalent to 13., 14. and 15. insofar as these utterances meet the necessary conditions. Other conditions can be specified which would establish 16. and 17. as pragmatically equivalent, as realizations of a different communicative act.

What I am proposing is that we might think in terms of two kinds of deep structure by means of which the two kinds of equivalence— semantic and pragmatic—can be established. Rhetorical deep structure, which accounts for pragmatic equivalence, is most naturally formulated as a set of conditions defining a particular communicative act such as Searle and Labov have made familiar. By reference to such a deep structure (as with the case of grammatical deep structure) we might proceed to set up equivalences across languages. Corresponding to the English set of utterances represented by 13–16 we might cite the following French equivalents:

18. Appuyer deux fois sur le bouton.
19. Appuyez deux fois sur le bouton.
20. Il faut appuyer deux fois sur le bouton.
21. On doit appuyer deux fois sur le bouton.

One might say that these are potential utterances which are representative of the communicative act of instruction and as such are pragmatically equivalent to 13–16 cited above (although, as with the English utterances, this does not preclude the possibility of making more 'delicate' distinctions).

Turning now to pedagogic issues, let us consider what implications can be drawn from the preceding discussion for the use of translation as a technique in language teaching. The objections to the use of translation seem generally to be based on the assumption that it must necessarily involve establishing structural equivalence. It is said, for example, that translation leads the learner to suppose that there is a direct one-to-one correspondence of meaning between the sentences in the TL and those in the SL. Another, and related, objection is that it draws the attention of the learner to the formal properties of the TL sentences and distracts him from the search for contextual meaning— that is to say, meaning which is a function of the relationship between sentences and appropriate situations. But if translation is carried out with reference to grammatical deep structure, as an exercise in establishing semantic equivalence, it is not open to the first of these objections; and if it is carried out with reference to rhetorical deep structure, as an exercise in establishing pragmatic equivalence, it is not open to the second of them.

There would appear to be a case for overtly relating surface forms in two languages to deep structure 'proto-forms' of both the semantic and the pragmatic kinds. What this might involve can be seen from a consideration of the type of syllabus proposed in Wilkins (1972a).

What Wilkins does, essentially, is to represent the content of a language teaching course as consisting of categories of what I have called grammatical and rhetorical deep structure. He gives them the super-ordinate label 'notional categories'. This label is (I venture to suggest) somewhat misleading since what he calls 'semantico-grammatical categories' are elements from grammatical deep structure and are quite distinct from his 'categories of communicative function' which are pragmatic in character and are elements of rhetorical deep structure. Wilkins invokes these notional categories as a principle of selection. The use of translation would invoke them as a principle of presentation. To do this would be to provide the learner with a representation of his existing knowledge and through this representation to link up what he already knows to what he has yet to learn.

We can think of translation then, in terms of three alternative processes, which might be shown diagramatically as follows:

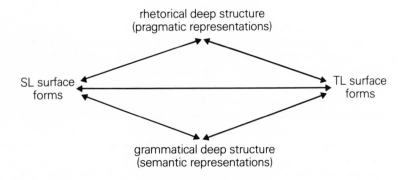

rhetorical deep structure
(pragmatic representations)

SL surface
forms

TL surface
forms

grammatical deep structure
(semantic representations)

If one follows the path through semantic representations one can demonstrate how sentences in the SL and TL relate to a common deep structure such as is, for example, partially realized in the common propositions of case grammar, deliberately grouping together sentences in the two languages which are structurally distinct at the superficial level of analysis. If one follows the path through pragmatic representations, one teaches communicative acts and shows how they may be realized in formally diverse ways in the SL and TL. Notice that although I have used the terms SL and TL, semantic and pragmatic translation (unlike structural translation) mediates neutrally between the linguistic forms which it relates: there is no 'direction' from one language to another since the translation is carried out with reference to conceptual patterns and social acts whose definition is independent of any particular linguistic structure.

Although such a deep structure approach to translation might seem plausible, there are, however, certain difficulties when it is applied on a large scale to relate two languages. To begin with, there is the assumption that conceptual patterns and social acts which are represented in the grammatical and rhetorical deep structures are invariant across and within speech communities. Now we do not have to embrace a strong form of the Whorfian doctrine to recognize that the fact of language variation itself points to considerable variation in cognition and social behaviour. It would be very odd indeed if language behaviour were the *only* thing that varied and the fact of language variation would be quite inexplicable. Within a single speech community there are groups of language users—scientists, for example—who acquire ways of structuring reality which are not shared by other users of the language, just as there are communicative acts like, for example, scientific explanation or the drawing up of certain legal forms of contractual agreement, which are restricted to specific kinds of social activity. In fact there is likely to be more in common between certain varieties in different languages than between different varieties within the same language. Scientific discourse expressed through one language, for example, is likely to be closer semantically and pragmatically to scientific discourse expressed in another than to other areas of discourse expressed in the same language. Hence, translating scientist-to-scientist discourse from an SL to a TL is likely to present far fewer problems than translating it into a different kind of discourse within the same language: that is to say, as far as scientific material is concerned at any rate, translation for peers is easier than simplification for a popular readership.

Let us explore this point a little further. In speaking of semantic and pragmatic equivalence I have made appeal to the notion of universals. This notion is a very tricky one to deal with. On the one hand the possibility of translation would appear to point to the existence of universals of one sort or another. On the other hand, universals have proved extremely elusive of definition. What I should like to suggest is that it may be that we have been looking for them in the wrong place. The grammarian's idealization of data allows him to postulate an abstract system which he represents as underlying the variation of actual language behaviour. Further abstraction leads him to postulate a universal base which he represents as underlying the variation of different language systems. I suggest that universals might be more readily discoverable not as properties of idealized abstractions but as properties of actualized language in certain areas of use, as features, in fact, which distinguish a particular universe of discourse independently of the different language systems which are used to realize it. What I am suggesting, then, is that there are universals of a communicative kind pertaining to certain universes of discourse which are independent not only of particular linguistic systems but also of any general system which underlies them at a deeper level of abstraction.

Let us, for example, consider the universe of discourse which we can, for present purposes, loosely describe as 'scientific'. From the grammarian's point of view, this can be regarded as a variety of the particular language he is concerned with and in consequence is idealized out by a process of standardization (see Lyons, 1972). But scientific discourse represents a way of conceptualizing reality and a way of communicating which must, if it is to remain scientific, be independent of different languages and different cultures. If one looks at scientific papers written in different languages one notices immediately that a considerable part of the information they convey is communicated by means of symbols, formulae and diagrams which are a part of the universal metalanguage of science. It seems reasonable to suppose that the verbal component of the discourse with which these non-verbal forms are related (both verbal and non-verbal elements being constituent parts of the discourse as a whole) must also represent concepts and methods which are universally recognized as the defining features of scientific enquiry.

It seems obvious that the learning of science must involve the acquiring of a 'superposed' knowledge of certain universal concepts and methods. The concepts constitute the grammatical deep structure and the methods the rhetorical deep structure of scientific discourse, whether this be superficially realized by Japanese, Russian, French, English or any other language. Thus, if any language is to serve the needs of scientific discourse it must have the means of expressing such deep structure concepts as, for example, the relationship between solids, liquids and gases or between acids, bases and salts, which are instances of the universal semantic structure of science. The semantic representations of such a universal base presumably would be expressible in terms of symbols, formulae and conventionalized diagrams which already have the status of an international metalanguage. Such non-verbal devices would, then, serve as the elements of grammatical deep structure of scientific discourse. The pragmatics of rhetorical deep structure would be represented by sets of conditions defining such communicative acts as classification, description, explanation and so on which constitute the basic methods of scientific investigation and exposition.

What I want to suggest is that semantic and pragmatic translation can be used as a teaching device for learners who need the TL as an additional medium for scientific communication. Its use involves the overt demonstration of how the surface forms in the TL and the SL are alternative realizations of scientific concepts and methods of enquiry which constitute the grammatical and rhetorical deep structure of scientific discourse and which are, by definition, neutral in regard to particular languages and cultures. I have taken science as the most obvious instance of a neutral area of language use but there are obviously several other domains of what I have called superposed knowledge which extend over cultural and linguistic boundaries and these would include most of the disciplines and technologies of tertiary education, that is to say, most of the special purposes for which a foreign language is learned as a service subject. Instead of thinking of the language use associated with these domains as being varieties of a particular language it would be more profitable (pedagogically at least) to think of them as universes of discourse which therefore provide universals of a semantic and pragmatic kind by reference to which superficially different realizations in two languages can be related.

In this paper I have been feeling my way, very tentatively, towards some clarification of what might be involved in the process of translation and of how this process might be pressed into pedagogic service. It has been an attempt to discover some rational grounds for two beliefs. The first (expressed in Widdowson, 1973a) is that the process of learning a foreign language should be presented not as the acquisition of new knowledge and experience but as an extension or alternative realization of what the learner already knows. The second is one which I have also expressed, not very satisfactorily, elsewhere (Widdowson, 1968): that language learning is more likely to be successful when it is associated with particular areas of use, or universes of discourse, which cut across linguistic and cultural boundaries.

Note

Published in Corder, S. P., and Roulet, E. (eds.), Linguistic Insights in Applied Linguistics, AIMAV/Didier, 1974.

The status of pedagogical grammars
Christopher N. Candlin

0.1   The purpose of this paper is to examine what might be understood by the term *'pedagogical grammar'* as a source and basis for language teaching materials on the one hand and pedagogical explanations on the other. I shall not be concerned here with taking a particular stance on psycholinguistic theories of second language learning, fundamental though this is to LT materials production; nor am I necessarily advocating, within the term 'pedagogical grammar', adherence to any particular grammatical model or theory of language.

0.2   The first section of this paper examines briefly the case for eclecticism in sources for LT materials; section two looks more closely at the status of pedagogic grammars with particular reference to their basis in a 'notional' or 'rhetorical' (Widdowson, 1971) understanding of communicative competence with references to the contribution of recent work in generative semantics; the final section refers further to the role of a pedagogical grammar as a basis for LT materials construction and classroom explanation.

1.1   The traditional reply to a question concerning the basis for LT materials is to examine the current state of linguistic theory, and attempt an illustrated restatement of existing formal descriptions. The criticisms which have then arisen have been less concerned with asking if any formal linguistic description can ever serve uniquely as such a basis than with discussing the relative merits for teaching purposes of one theory or one description over another.[1] Halliday, McIntosh, Strevens (1964) refer at length to the unclear categorizations, hetero-geneous criteria, fictions, conceptual formulations of traditional grammar; from the point of view of learning difficulties, from Jacobson (1966) the watershed lies between grammars with and grammars without a deep/surface distinction; and Mackey (1966) somewhat despairingly asks whose linguistics to apply. Nor can the problem be solved by sanguine appeals (Thomas, 1965) for application of the 'best available scientific grammar', since there remain the twin problems of (a) choice among several descriptions emanating from a single theoretical model (Marshall and Wales, 1966) and (b) the possibility of choosing different descriptions for different purposes (Halliday *et al.*, 1964). Following this suggestion of Halliday's, one might, in one's search for 'best' description, hold up *Aspects of the Theory of Syntax* as being 'good for' deep/surface distinctions, Prague School for theme/rheme and the semantics of surface structure, Fillmore and McCawley for the semantics of deep structure, and, presumably systemic grammar for estimating the 'weight' of particular systemic choices.

1.2   Attractive and necessary though this eclecticism is for LT one may still run foul of the God's Truth school, and the adequacy criteria:

> 'A grammar can be regarded as a theory of a language; it is descriptively adequate to the extent that it correctly describes the intrinsic competence of the idealized native speaker. The structural descriptions assigned to sentences by the grammar, the distinctions that it makes between well-formed and deviant, and so on, must, for descriptive adequacy, correspond to the linguistic intuition of the native speaker (whether or not he may be immediately aware of this) in a substantially and significant class of crucial cases.' (Chomsky, 1965, p. 24.)

and in Chomsky (1966) the constraints on observational, descriptive and explanatory adequacy, explicitness and simplicity. It is not necessary to enter the Rationalist/Empiricist controversy here but simply to make the obvious point, that there is no necessary isomorphism between linguistic categories and units and language learning categories and units,[2] and that since in any case any formal grammar underlying LT materials will be different in nature from those materials, an eclectic approach in materials is not subject to Chomsky's constraints; further, it is not necessary to stress that linguistic grammars find it difficult to meet his criteria anyway. A 'hocus pocus' view of linguistic data, given the variety of learning tasks and types of students, justifies itself for LT materials.

2.1   In Allen and van Buren (1971) three suggestions are made for reconciling 'formal' and in their terms 'practical' grammars[3]:

> '(1) bring about a reconciliation between the teaching grammar and the formal grammar by writing a transformational teaching text; (2) maintain a sharp distinction between the transformational competence model and the surface structure teaching model in the hope that the underlying rules will be inferred by the student without having to be overtly specified; (3) devise an eclectic teaching model by retaining the surface structure as the basic mode of presentation,

but incorporating deep structure insights whenever this can be done without incurring too many abstract rules.'

The implication in the third suggestion is that one method of developing LT materials is to match advances in formal grammar analysis with corresponding changes in LT materials. Allen and van Buren argue for an eclectic choice of sources among formal grammars, and if we accept the need for a filter between these formal grammars and the classroom, then the role of the pedagogic grammar is that of an interpreter between a number of formal grammars and the audience and situation-specific LT materials. The problem for a pedagogic grammar in such circumstances will be less one of measuring up to formal adequacy criteria (cf. 1.2 above), than of making a principled choice among a plethora of data. In practical terms, the task of applied linguistics might seem to be to take a grammatical topic, say relative clauses, and go to different formal grammars to discover what statements they have to offer; (for example, one analysis might lay stress on the role of the Wh-items, another on deep and surface distinctions, another on relationships between relative clauses and other types of modifier) and after examination with particular learners in mind the target is the production of LT materials stressing particular aspects of the grammatical topic in hand. Such an approach, with the difference of the pedagogic grammar seen here as an eclectic selector among a variety of formal models, seems to underlie Chomsky's statement (Chomsky, 1966) on the distinction between formal and pedagogic grammars:

'A grammar describes and attempts to account for the ability of the speaker to understand an arbitrary sentence of his language and to produce an appropriate sentence on a given occasion. If a pedagogic grammar it attempts to provide a student with this ability, if a linguistic grammar it aims to discover and exhibit the mechanisms that make this achievement possible.'

2.2   Useful though such an input from several linguistic grammars may be, the question begged is clearly that if pedagogic grammar is at the basis of LT materials, and if such materials have as their aim to lead the learner to 'knowledge' of the L_2, then they, and the pedagogic grammar, must be as concerned with rules of language *use* as they are with rules of grammaticality and well-formedness of sentences.

What is important in LT is to grasp the distinction between *sentence* and *utterance* (the former being a theoretical term referring to well-formed strings outputted from the grammar, and the latter units of discourse characterized by their use-value in communication) and if we understand pedagogics as being concerned with utterances, or linguistic competence realized, then it is necessary to introduce the notion 'communicative competence' (Hymes, 1970 and this volume) (Campbell and Wales, 1970) into the basis of LT materials, resting courses and syllabuses on this communicative base (Candlin, 1971, 1972). In doing so one is proposing that at the level of the semantics of utterances we can discover the relationships, dependencies and functionally important bonds (what Hymes calls 'the rules of use') which encode the speakers' attitudes, roles and purposes. In essence such relationships, deep down in the Grammar, are choice relationships: sociolinguistic systems of selections available to the user in different transactions and confrontations. Under utterances, if you like, are networks of choices within the grammatical system and behind these the complex network of social situation and encounter.[4] Clearly, then, an adequate pedagogic grammar cannot be limited to sentences but must act as interpreter of discourse, and as such its requirements are more onerous than existing linguistic grammars. It must deal not only with the grammaticality and acceptability of sentences but the pragmatics of language use.

2.3 Examining further this pragmatic requirement, a concentration on *utterances* has been linked by a number of applied linguists (Widdowson, 1971; Candlin, 1971; Wilkins, 1972a *inter alia*) to Searle's (1965, 1969) views on the nature of speech acts. According to Searle, utterances contain two not necessarily separate parts: a propositional element and a function indicating element; the latter element being termed an illocutionary act (cf. Austin, 1962): 'I may indicate the kind of illocutionary act I am performing by beginning the sentence with "I apologize", "I warn", "I state" ' (Searle, 1965 in Giglioli, 1972, p. 142). Following Searle's claim that the same proposition may be held in common to all kinds of illocutionary acts[5] the latter might be separated from the proposition and their linguistic realizations studied independently. Such a study would reveal sets of language functions such as asking questions, giving and responding to commands, greeting, advising, warning, etc. Illocutionarily related acts could be grouped[6]:

> explain, enquire, describe, instruct
> hypothesize, plan, analyse, compare, deduce, test
> choose, guess, deduct, infer
> invite, refuse, accept
> appreciate, praise
> persuade, conciliate, encourage, discourage, recruit, dissuade
> criticize, express opinions, reservations, contradictions, contrasts
> insult, antagonize, threaten, lie, cheat.

Two corollaries are important: that in LT materials one could declare that certain logical relationships were 'prior' to groups of semiotic acts indicated above, for example, cause/result/hypothesis/time, and that a variety of semiotic acts with their linguistic realizations could thus be grouped within the pedagogic grammar[7], and that, secondly, certain logico-grammatical concepts such as *comparison* might also have their alternative syntactic formulations grouped under such a heading in the pedagogic grammar rather than scattered on grounds of syntactic heterogeneity. Alternative approaches to language function exist: cf. Halliday (1969) where the concern is with 'different uses of language seen as realizing different intentions'—instrumental, regulatory, inter-actional, heuristic, imaginative, representational:

> 'Let us summarize the models in terms of the child's intentions, since different uses of language may be seen as realizing different intentions. In its instrumental function, language is used for the satisfaction of material needs; this is the "I want" function. The regulatory is the "do as I tell you" function, language in the control of behaviour. The interactional function is that of getting along with others, the "me and him" function . . . the personal is related to this = it is the expression of identity of the self, which develops largely *through* linguistic interaction; the "here I come" function, perhaps. The heuristic is the use of language to learn, to explore reality = the function of "tell me why", the imaginative is that of "let's pretend", whereby the reality is created, and what is being explored is the child's mind, including language itself. The representational is the "I've got something to tell you" function, that of communication of content.'

One obvious development within a pedagogical grammar would be to use Searle's illocutionary acts to fill in Halliday's 'relevant models of language'.

2.4   The arguments for a pedagogic grammar concerned with communicative competence suggest at very least that formal grammars with their centre in syntax will be insufficient as input and that LT materials writers will need to look further to grammars centred on generative semantics. Only those grammars which, as it were, begin with the semiotic act (cf. 2.3 above) and have as their aim the relating of different and disparate surface structures to centres in deep semantics, will be adequate as inputs to a pedagogic grammar. Recent articles, Boyd and Thorne (1969), Ross (1970), Fillmore (1969), Lakoff (1970), and lengthier treatments, Leech (1969), indicate ways of suitably organizing this communicative data. Fillmore in particular, characterizes the task of a pedagogic grammar when he poses the question (*op. cit.*, p. 274) 'what do I need to know in order to use this form appropriately and to understand other people when they use it?', while at the same time characterizing the question as one that linguistic semanticists to that point had not attempted to answer. Fillmore's partial answer, concerned with verbs of judging (accuse, blame, criticize, credit, praise, scold, confess, apologize, forgive, justify, excuse) is interesting, not merely because he related presuppositions to illocutionary acts, but also because he provides the semantic framework within which these varying realizations of the act of judging can be related in an organized fashion. Despite however, the clear possibility of extending Fillmore's list of verbs by further variant structures (scold: chide/tell off/tick off/ what on earth did you do that for? etc.) there remain important components of the communicative process which will not be accounted for in generative semantic terms—in particular, the need to incorporate information on what governs the appropriateness of transmitted messages; information on the nature of speaker/listener intentions, purposes, motivations and beliefs. Such information will not arise from displays of shared semantic properties among members of a 'field' of meaning, important though such deep structure links between disparate surface forms are for a pedagogic grammar; Lakoff (1969) makes the point that it is not grammaticality or acceptability in the interpretative semantic sense that decides between acceptable and non-acceptable utterances, but rather 'contextual acceptability':

> 'in other words in order to judge whether a sentence is correct in its context we must know something about the speaker's unstated belief about the world . . . it is important to realize that *no* grammatical rule, transformational or elsewhere, can be given here to enable the learner to make the correct distinction' (*op. cit.*, pp. 125–7).[8]

Correct distinctions of this kind stem from a knowledge of extra-linguistic preconditions for utterances, information on which will come, not so much from generative semantics but from discourse analysis supported by social-psychological experimentation into the implications of utterances. Discourse analysis in particular is now the subject of much interest from sociolinguists concerned with rule-writing for language variation in units of language beyond the sentence level. In his preliminary analyses, Labov suggests *inter alia* that such discourse analysis rules as he proposes (Labov, 1970) will need to account for the frequent 'lack of syntactic connection between successive utterances' (*op. cit.*, p. 81), as well as the variety of judgements which can be placed on an utterance. Preliminary work on the analysis of interview data of a non-psychotherapeutic kind suggest some of the problems that need to be faced; the unpredictability of response forms to

questions (in particular the unpredictability on the part of the inter-
viewee of the 'forms' of his response in relation to the message of the
interviewer[9]); examination of hesitation and juncture phenomena
relevant to our assessment of interruption/interjection forms, and
central to such assessments, and to the assessment of the implicational
meaning of utterances, a metalanguage sufficient for this extralinguistic
interpretation. Labov's point that the assessment of a speaker's utterances requires knowledge by the hearer of extralinguistic variables
such as age, class and status supports our plea for a communicative
competence basis to a pedagogic grammar. Experiments into the social
contexts of messages reported by Carswell and Rommetveit (1971)
indicate the complexity of these variable constraints indicated by
Labov, and the need for interpretation of utterances with reference to
the situation in which the utterances are spoken, their preceding
linguistic context and 'the hearer's knowledge of the speaker and the
topics which might be discussed with him'[10] (*op. cit.*, p. 5).

3.1 Because of the concentration of most current LT materials on the
sentence as a unit of structuralist grammar rather than the utterance
as a unit of discourse, foreign language learners are presented with
two major obstacles to the achievement of fluency: firstly that the
language they are learning from is unlike 'real' language because its
sentence-illustrating task excludes its proper communicative task as
an illustrator of speakers' roles and verbal purposes. (The point being
that the 'situations' of LT materials have largely served to mask the
reality of communication and have led to the common experience of
learners functioning successfully in the linguistically largely pre-
determined classroom environment while being much at a loss in the
less certain context of real encounters. Language learners' needs are
clearly not determined by a linguistic grammar but by their differing
communicative needs.) Secondly, that the organization of the linguistic
grammars underlying current LT materials has noticeably failed to
make the significant semantic generalizations between varieties of
surface structures which we have pointed to as one of the present
concerns of generative semantics. It is to be expected, as a result, that
learners intent on fluency have been met with severe obstacles in their
learning, both of an organizational and a communicative kind. Accepting
that a pedagogic grammar needs to be semantically-based (with the
extralinguistic additions put forward in 2.4 above), its principal
concern is to provide LT materials writers and foreign language
learners with the opportunity to view language as communication and
more particularly to provide in its explanations systematization under
language-function parameters to enable the learner to organize and
relate his often scattered and isolated knowledge of the language under

study. To enable the learner to relate, for example, under the heading *comparative* not merely the morphologically marked comparatives but all forms of the order:

1. John is taller than Mary.
2. I've got a bigger house than John has.
3. You need bigger boots than shoes.
4. He plays more elegantly than effectively.
5. It is more that he is careless than he is not intelligent.
6. A girl prettier than Mary would be hard to find. Etc.[11]

The practical consequence of this would be to reorganize LT materials on a communicative basis, with a variety of semiotic acts subsumed by more fundamental issues such as the language of comparison, hypothesis, cause and result on the one hand, and subsuming the inventory linguistic formulae employed as realizations of these semiotic acts on the other. One applied linguistic consequence is the devising of a rational and communicable metalanguage for the description of the utterances under study; not merely a linguistic metalanguage but one adequate to handle the social contexts of messages. As such we shall have to explore beyond linguistics in the narrow sense if we are to systematize and reorientate LT materials towards the teaching of communicative acts.

Notes

Published in Corder, S. P., and Roulet, E. (eds.), Theoretical Linguistics Models in Applied Linguistics, AIMAV/Didier 1973.

1. I do not want of course to ignore the point that a model shown wanting from a theoretical point of view may not retain much pedagogical value—structural linguistics being a case in point.
2. See Corder (1967) on the lack of equivalence between teaching syllabuses and learning syllabuses.
3. Allen and van Buren's term 'practical grammar' is used as a cover term for a variety of pedagogic material used by the teacher in his class. As such it is equivalent to Saporta's (1964) use of 'pedagogical grammar' to mean teaching materials used to 'develop a native-like ability to produce and recognize sentences appropriately in a L_2'. The use of 'pedagogic grammar' in this paper is somewhat different (cf. Section 2.2) where the point is made that such a pedagogic grammar lies between statements about communicative competence (including linguistic competence in the narrow sense) and specific practical materials themselves dependent on local learning conditions. This is not to say that local conditions can be (or ought to be) the only arbiter of course content—just as pedagogic

grammars in this sense are presumably dependent on communicative 'grammars' so they must 'condition' the form and content of practical LT materials.

4.The descriptive data for this communicative approach must come from sociolinguistic investigation into language variation and code-switching, social-pyschological studies of the implicative content of messages and semiotic analyses into the nature of the Speech Act. From such analyses as input material for a pedagogic grammar will arise the data for Hymes' 'existential adequacy'; language looking outward to social life and the actual realization of linguistic ability.

5.I am not ignoring here the important point (especially for LT materials) that any given utterances may have several illocutionary forces, or indeed the reverse that a single illocutionary force may have several linguistic realizations.

6.For such language functions integrated into a cyclic syllabus together with consideration of social role and attitude cf. Candlin (1972). For an application of a 'functional' analysis to LT materials cf. Levine (1972).

7.Cf. Candlin, Kirkwood, Moore (1971) for an approach to the application of this notion in LT materials in English for advanced students of technical/applied science and social science students with particular reference to study roles, study functions and study topics.

8.Cf. Lakoff's pair:
    1. Albert is a doctor in my neighbourhood.
    2. Albert is the doctor in my neighbourhood.
and the some/any series:
    1. Does someone want these sweets?
    2. Does anyone want these sweets?
    3. If he eats sweets, let me know.
    4. If he eats any sweets, let me know.

9.Q. 'Would any of you try to get there to see him? Is there any more at your school for someone else to go across?'
Double questions of this form may have their responses focused on a variety of points of information in the question, and are not predictably and uniquely answerable, despite the fact that the syntactic form of the response may mirror the syntax of the question (cf. Labov, 1970, p. 81). Clearly a variety of types of response to questions require fine awareness of the implicational significance of syntactic and intonational focus.

10.Cf. especially P. Henry: '*On Processing of Message Referents in Contexts*' for an analysis of the relationship between alternative connotatively different utterance formulations with the same denotative meaning; and R. M. Blakar and R. Rommetveit: '*Pro-*

cessing of Utterances in Contexts' on distinctions between implications and presuppositions.

11. I am grateful for these examples to David Wilkins. Note, also,
Corder's observation (1970) that disparate 'surface' errors may be
symptoms of a single 'deep' confusion, as, for example, when
scattered errors in surface determiners indicate a general underlying
unsureness of deixis as a whole.

Grammatical, situational and notional syllabuses
D. A. Wilkins

1. *Types of Syllabus.* It has been pointed out a number of times[1] that although many of the changes that have taken place in language teaching have been motivated by developments in linguistics, the changes have paradoxically taken place in the methods rather than the content of teaching. A glance at the history of language teaching reveals enormous diversity of methodology over the years but a remarkable stability in the principles underlying the choice of language to be taught and its arrangement. Whatever the method, it has been assumed that units of learning should be defined in grammatical terms, although the precise sequence in which they occurred would be influenced by pedagogic considerations. The theory that such an approach is based on, whether it is explicit or not, holds that splitting the language into parts determined by the grammatical categories of the language has psycholinguistic validity. That is, the task of learning a language is made easier if one is exposed to one part of the grammatical system at a time. *Mutatis mutandis* traditional grammar/translation, audio-lingual and structural methods, for example, are all applications of this principle. Changes in content, where they occur, are sometimes extremely superficial. For a while it was fashionable to label the content 'structures' rather than 'grammar', but the content changed little, apart from a greater concern with reducing the learning load in each unit. That the content of learning is still thought of in grammatical terms is indicated by the labels used to indicate the items to be learned: the definite article, the position of adjectives, the past tense, conditionals, comparative and superlative, and so on. It is fair to say, therefore, that, whether or not it is apparent, most textbooks have as their basis a *grammatical syllabus.*

The grammatical syllabus, however, is not without its critics. The criticisms come from a number of different directions. It is very difficult for many learners to appreciate the applicability of the knowledge they gain through such an approach. The process of being taken systematically through the grammatical system often reduces the motivation of those who need to see some immediate practical return for their learning. From another point of view, this approach might also be considered inefficient since its aim is to teach the entire system regardless of the fact that not all parts of the system will be equally useful for all learners. There is furthermore the danger that the learning of grammar will be identified with the learning of grammatical form and that grammatical meaning will be subordinated to this. Finally, there is the more recent criticism that the bringing together of grammatically identical sentences is highly artificial, since in real acts of communication it is sentences that are alike in meaning that occur together and not those that are alike in structure. The grammatical syllabus, it is argued, fails to provide the necessary conditions for the acquisition of communicative competence.

In recent years an alternative approach has been much discussed and this involves constructing not a grammatical, but a *situational syllabus*. According to this view language always occurs in a social context and it should not be divorced from its context when it is being taught. In any case, our choice of linguistic forms is frequently restricted by the nature of the situation in which we are using language. This suggests that it is possible for people to concentrate learning upon the forms of language that are most appropriate to their needs. This creates the possibility of a learner-based syllabus to replace the subject-based grammatical syllabus. (It should perhaps be made clear that reference is not being made here to a method of language teaching—sometimes called 'situational'—in which sentences are always presented in association with actions, mime, realia and visual aids. In practice this method is usually firmly rooted in a grammatical syllabus and the situations that are created are pedagogic, bearing little resemblance to natural language use.) The situational syllabus, therefore, is based upon *predictions of the situations in which the learner is likely to operate* through the foreign language. A set of parameters for the description of the significant features of situations is set up and a behavioural analysis is made in terms of these features. Learning units no longer have grammatical labels. Instead they are identified by situational labels. Such a syllabus focuses teaching upon what is most relevant to a particular group of learners and these learners, able to see the relevance of what they are doing, become more highly motivated. The resulting materials will, of course, be linguistically heterogeneous, since natural situations do not contain language of the uniformity of structure which characterizes a grammatical syllabus. How feasible is it to produce a complete syllabus according to situational criteria? In practice there are a number of problems. In the first place it is extremely difficult to define what a *situation* is. There are cases where the language we use is evidently very closely related to the physical context in which we produce it. But such cases are, if anything, atypical and we could not hope to cater for all a learner's language needs if we based our teaching on this type of situation alone. On the other hand, if the definition is widened to allow non-observable factors to be considered we reach the point where, 'the wish to describe a situation is basically the wish to describe the world, reality, life itself'[2]. Such a definition would clearly be inoperable. The conclusion must be that a situational syllabus is not suitable for a general language course, although it might be valuable in certain narrowly definable contexts of learning. In any case, the diversity of linguistic forms in any one situational unit makes the task of generalizing grammatical learning a difficult one and without it the learner may acquire no more than a set of responses appropriate to that one situation. He will be learning 'language-like behaviour'[3] rather than language.

The grammatical and situational approaches are essentially answers to different questions. The former is an answer to the question *how?* How do speakers of Language X express themselves? The latter is a response to the questions *when?* or *where?* When and where will the learner need the target language? There is, however, a more funda-mental question to be asked, the answer to which may provide an alternative to grammatical or situational organizations of language teaching, while allowing important grammatical and situational con-siderations to continue to operate. The question is the question *what?* What are the notions that the learner will expect to be able to express through the target language? It should be possible to establish what kind of thing a learner is likely to want to communicate. The restriction on the language needs of different categories of learner is then not a function of the situations in which they will find themselves, but of the notions they need to express. One can envisage planning the linguistic content according to the semantic demands of the learner. While there are, no doubt, some features of what may be communicated that are so general that no language learner can avoid acquiring the means to express them, others may be limited to people who will use the language only in certain fields. In this way the association of certain communication needs and certain physical situations is seen to be coincidental and those needs that cannot be related to situation can be handled just as easily as those that can. Furthermore, although there is no one-to-one relationship between grammatical structure and the notions they express, we should be able to take advantage of gram-matical generalizations wherever these provide important ways of meeting a particular communication need.

What is proposed, therefore, is that the first step in the creation of a syllabus should be consideration of the *content* of probable utterances and from this it will be possible to determine which *forms* of language will be most valuable to the learner. The result will be a *semantic* or *notional syllabus.* which establishes the grammatical means by which the relevant notions are expressed. The lexical content of learning is partly derivable from the notional analysis, but it may also be influenced by pedagogic and situational considerations. Here I am concerned only with the grammatical realizations.

2. *Background to the Present Study.* In order to construct a notional syllabus we must have a set of notional categories. The categories I am about to put forward are those which may, in my view, prove useful for the particular context in which they were developed. I should explain briefly what this context is.

There is a growing awareness that the process of education does not stop at the end of secondary or of higher education. In an increasingly complex economic world every individual must expect to adopt new or changing roles even well after his conventional education has finished. He will also need to be prepared for the greater leisure provided by modern working conditions. Education, therefore, far from ending as the individual reaches adulthood, will remain a continuing process. At the moment provision for *éducation permanente*, to use the French name, is, to say the least, haphazard. In West European countries, in which there has been a good deal of discussion of the concept of continuing education, adult education is in the hands of a multiplicity of state and private institutions, with the mass media often making a contribution inadequately integrated with that of educational establishments. Nowhere is this more apparent than in the field of languages. Adults who wish to learn a foreign language may attend one of several types of state institutions which provide full or part-time courses, or they may go to a private language school which may or may not be officially recognized; they may attend courses provided by their employer; they may receive private tuition; they may follow courses broadcast on radio or television or they may subscribe to one of the many self-instructional courses available on record or tape. In many cases no recognized system of language qualification is involved. In others learners obtain diplomas and certificates issued by a diverse set of state, private, official and unofficial bodies, few of which operate in more than one country. There is little comparability between the qualifications and no provision for mutual recognition of certificates.

To anyone seriously interested in providing *éducation permanente* such a situation seems almost anarchic. Over the past few years a number of studies have been made which are expected to contribute to the development of a more satisfactory system of continuing language education on a European scale. The work reported here is a part of these studies. Broadly, it is hoped to devise a system whereby an individual requiring any European language, probably for some specialized purpose, will be able to study a set of units which are particularly relevant to his needs and on completion of these, he will be awarded a number of credits. Initially there will be concentration on the most widely needed languages and on the most widely felt professional and personal needs. A conventional grammatical organization to such a system is obviously not suitable and the specialized units will probably have a behaviourial or situational basis. However, it is recognized that a common linguistic basis will need to be established and that, as has been shown above, not all language needs are predictable from an analysis of situational needs.

The notional framework which I am about to propose is intended to provide the means by which a certain minimum level of communicative ability in European languages can be set up. This minimum can then be taken for granted in the planning of the later, more situationally oriented units. It also provides the means of ensuring the inclusion in the syllabus of communicative functions which have no unique grammatical realizations and no unique situational occurrence. It is argued that a syllabus for the teaching of any European language can be derived from this approach and that a syllabus thus expressed in universalistic terms can be interpreted according to the forms of the different languages to be taught and in this way a high degree of comparability between schemes for the teaching of different languages can be achieved. In the context of this study such a result is highly desirable.

3. *The Categories of a Notional Syllabus.* It seems convenient to group the notional categories into two sections. The first is made up of what might be called semantico-grammatical categories. These are categories which, in European languages at least, interact significantly with grammatical categories. It is for this reason, of course, that they contribute to the definition of the grammatical content of learning. There are six of these categories, each of which may be further sub-categorized:

    1. *Time*
        a. Point of time
        b. Duration
        c. Time relations
        d. Frequency
        e. Sequence
        f. Age

    2. *Quantity*
        a. Grammatical number
        b. Numerals

    c. Quantifiers
    d. Operations

3. *Space*
    a. Dimensions
    b. Location
    c. Motion

(4. *Matter*)
Reference to the physical world is principally a matter of deciding the semantic fields within which the learner will operate. A notional analysis is less valuable than an analysis in terms of situation and/or subject-matter.

5. *Case*
    a. Agentive
    b. Objective
    c. Dative
    d. Instrumental
    e. Locative
    f. Factitive
    g. Benefactive

6. *Deixis*
    a. Person
    b. Time (see above)
    c. Place
    d. Anaphora

There is no time to comment in detail on each of these categories, but, to illustrate how syllabus decisions can be taken within this approach we can look briefly at two of them.[4] Let us take *time relations*, for example. It is common for events to be related to the moment of speech and to one another by use of the verbal system. Although the most obvious logical division of time might be into past, present and future, these concepts are scarcely ever realized uniquely by verb forms (tenses). In addition, far more subtle time distinctions are commonly indicated by verbal forms—before past, after past . . . and so on. In a situation in which one wished to teach a minimal operative system for communication, one might decide that in spite of the lack of iso-morphism* between logical and grammatical divisions, the aim should be at least to give the learner the means to express past, present and future time relations. In the case of English this raises further problems, since no verbal form is the only or the simple realization of these notions. Past events may be encoded in the past tense or in the present perfect **and the choice is made according to the speaker's emphasis and view**

similarity in appearance or structure of organisms belonging to different species or races

of events. In a minimal system the choice should probably go to the past tense, since its meaning is more easily acquired by most learners and in some dialects the past tense can be used in some places where other dialects use the present perfect. With regard to future time, there is no future tense in English. The choice lies between various forms, the use of each of which is stylistically or grammatically restricted. The choice of the form to be taught as the initial realization of future time relations may depend on the anticipated use of the minimal system. Where, in a colloquial course, the 'going to' form might be selected, in a more formal, written English course the construction with modal auxiliary 'will' might be preferred.

Looking more briefly at the category *case*, we can see that I am concerned with the type of relations described by Fillmore.[5] These notions help to define the fundamental syntactic relations within sentences. Some of them are absolutely essential to the most rudimentary communication. For example, it is necessary to be able to express the notion *Agent* and, at an early level, the only necessary realization of Agent is as Subject. Equally unavoidable is the notion *Objective* and in this case two realizations propose themselves for early learning, the Objective as Subject and as Object of an active sentence.

The second set of notional categories can be very broadly described as categories of communicative function. They relate to uses of language where there is at best a very untidy relationship between the function of the utterances and the grammatical categories through which these functions are realized. They are also concerned with expression of the speaker's intentions and attitudes. They are most easily understood by looking at the list of categories:

7. *Modality*—i.e. utterances in which the truth value of the propositional content is modified in some way
   a. Certainty
   b. Necessity
   c. Conviction
   d. Volition
   e. Obligation incurred
   f. Obligation imposed
   g. Tolerance

8. *Moral evaluation and discipline*—i.e. utterances involving assessment and judgement
   a. Judgement
   b. Release
   c. Approval
   d. Disapproval

9. *Suasion*—i.e. utterances designed to influence the behaviour of others
   a. Suasion
   b. Prediction

10. *Argument*—i.e. categories relating to the exchange of information and views
    a. Information asserted and sought
    b. Agreement
    c. Disagreement
    d. Denial
    e. Concession

11. *Rational enquiry and exposition*—i.e. categories relating to the rational organization of thought and speech
    e.g. Implication, hypothesis, verification, conclusion, condition, result, explanation, definition, cause, etc.

12. *Personal emotions*—i.e. expression of personal reactions to events
    a. Positive
    b. Negative

13. *Emotional relations*—i.e. expression of response to events usually involving interlocutor
    a. Greeting
    b. Sympathy
    c. Gratitude
    d. Flattery
    e. Hostility

14. *Interpersonal relations*—i.e. selection of forms appropriate to relationship of participants in the event
    a. Status (formality)
    b. Politeness

Once again I can only indicate briefly the issues subsumed under one or two of these headings. The category of *suasion*, for example, includes utterance functions such as: persuading, suggesting, advising, recommending, advocating, proposing, exhorting, begging and urging. Within suasion, *prediction* includes warning, threatening, instructing, directing and inviting. Within *modality*, *conviction* covers the whole range from absolute certainty about the truth of a proposition, expressed in the form of an unmodalized statement, through varying degrees of conviction and doubt, expressed through modal auxiliaries, lexical verb constructions and other devices, to complete lack of certainty. The point about all these categories is that these are the very things we use language for and yet they form only the smallest part of either the grammatical or the situational content of language courses. As yet, it is true, we do not fully understand how many of these functions are realized and it is certain that there is a good deal of linguistic diversity involved. Nonetheless the aim of language teaching is to teach learners to exploit their grammatical (and lexical) knowledge in creative acts of communication, so the possible difficulties involved in such an approach must be faced.

The value of the notional approach is that it forces one to consider the communicative value of everything that is taught. Items are not taught just because they are there. We aim progressively to expand the communicative competence of the learner. The set of categories just outlined provides us with a language for describing the communication needs of different sets of learners, whether their goal is a generalized or a specialized ability to use the language. Through this framework we can arrive at a set of learning priorities which is determined by the nature of the acts of communication in which the learner can be expected to participate. Information on the possible content of utterances will be of greater practical value than grammatical information and will be more complete than situational information. However, it will subsume both of these since each category has a particular set of grammatical realizations, and the aim of any syllabus would be, of course, to ensure that these were taught and situational language is just language in which particular notional categories occur with above-average frequency in association with defined physical situations. I believe that notional syllabuses will provide a path along which we can make new advances in defining the content of language curricula.

Notes

The work reported here was supported by the Council of Europe under Contract No. 84/71. Taken from Proceedings of the Third International Congress of Applied Linguistics, Copenhagen 1972, ed. by Association Internationale de Linguistique Appliquée (AILA), published by Julius Groos Verlag, Heidelberg, Germany.

1. See for example S. Saporta, 1966.
2. R. Richterich and H. Marchl, 1970.
3. B. Spolsky, 1966.
4. The framework presented here is more extensively discussed and exemplified in D. A. Wilkins, 1972.
5. C. J. Fillmore, 1968.

I should also like to acknowledge the contribution of H. G. Widdowson: The teaching of rhetoric to students of science and technology, in *Science and Technology in a Second Language*, London, CILT, 1971.

Notional syllabuses and the concept of a minimum adequate grammar
D. A. Wilkins

Anyone who has attended meetings of applied linguists in the last two or three years cannot fail to be very conscious of the fact that the current preoccupation in developing an adequate theory of second language learning is with the importance of the notion of communicative competence. The significance of the work of sociolinguists like Hymes and Labov for second language teaching has been readily accepted by applied linguists and more pedagogically oriented interpretations will presumably be disseminated to the wider language teaching profession as they reach a form suitable for publication.

Just what the new emphasis on communicative aspects of language will have to offer seems to me to remain in doubt. So far, observations about how language works in the social process of communication have been used principally to demonstrate the insufficiency of purely grammatical approaches to language teaching. At the same time informative but largely programmatic analyses have been proposed for particular communicative functions, so that usable but incomplete descriptions of particular aspects of language in use are becoming available. A more comprehensive framework for decision-making is offered by my own proposals for notional syllabuses, but this was designed with a particular situation in mind. Its generalizability remains to be shown and it is, in any case, lacking in linguistic detail and therefore no more than suggestive. In fact it is generally the case that our knowledge of the linguistic realizations of the communicative categories that we propose is decidedly superficial and is rarely the product of any observational research. In short, we have established a field that deserves our attention, but we do not yet know enough about it to see precisely the role it will play in the practical business of teaching languages.

As things stand our knowledge of the *grammatical* systems of language does provide us with a means to structure language learning in a systematic way. Since, it seems to me, language teaching is bound to proceed by means of significant generalizations, it is hardly surprising that, whatever the method, it is usual to adopt as a foundation for learning the approach that most readily makes such generalizations available, that is, a grammatical approach. It is, I think, readily recognized that a situational approach does not offer a genuine alternative to this, its value being limited to certain narrowly specifiable types of learning context. If a notional and functional approach is to be a serious alternative to either of these, it must be able to offer generalizations of equal or greater power. Language teachers would be rightly sceptical of abandoning the partly negotiable currency of the grammatical approach for the crock of gold at the end of the functional rainbow.

How useful then is a notional approach in most teaching situations? The facts of the teacher's life are met with most starkly in the context of the general language course—that is, typically, the school course where from three to five hours a week is devoted to the teaching of the foreign language and where behavioural or functional prediction is difficult, if not impossible. This is where the grammatical/structural syllabus, in whatever guise, has always dominated. How reasonable is it to suggest that because of what we now know about the nature of language in use, we should replace the grammatical syllabus by a notional/functional syllabus? In my view, such a suggestion is decidedly premature. We are quite simply woefully ignorant of the linguistic facts and will remain so for some time to come, so that we would risk causing a reaction against the communicative movement in language teaching by making greater claims for it than we can justify. I suspect that even when we are more knowledgeable about the pragmatics of language, we may still decide that the facts of use are not sufficiently generalizable for them to be suitable as the sole basis for the organization of the early stages of language learning. But that remains to be seen.

I would therefore be content if, for the present, notional and functional considerations were to be regarded as simply providing another dimension to the existing grammatical and situational parameters—a way of ensuring that general courses do not lose sight of the fact that linguistic forms provide a means to an end and that the end is communication. Greater concern should be given to seeing that what is learned has communicative value and that what has communicative value is learned, whether or not it occupies an important place in the grammatical system.

The new dimension could prove particularly valuable where the general course is largely remedial in aim.[1] Existing approaches to remedial teaching tend to be little more than a repetition of initial teaching procedures. A notional approach can provide a way of developing communicatively what is already known while, at the same time, enabling the teacher to fill the gaps in the learner's knowledge of the language. In either case the learner will have an awareness that he is doing something fresh.

I do not want to examine this any further here, nor do I wish to look at all closely at the idea of approaching the construction of specialized language courses through functional categories. Henry Widdowson has devoted himself particularly to this and is far better able than I am to demonstrate the practicability of a functional approach to courses of this type. Instead I want to devote the major part of this paper to a type of language learning situation where the notional/functional approach has immediate practical value and, indeed, where I believe it would be demonstrably superior to the grammatical syllabus, even though our knowledge of the appropriate language behaviour is inadequate.

High-Surrender Value

A characteristic of the general language course is that the learner commonly does not claim the return on his investment in learning until that learning has been proceeding for some years. He does not expect to be able to use the language communicatively as soon as the learning effort has begun, and since he or she is often in a situation where the occasion to use the language rarely arises, it does not really matter if the development of communicative ability is deferred. The case of the specialist language learner is often distinct in that a general grammatical competence is taken for granted as a starting-point. The specialization is then developed on this foundation.

There is, however, another context of language learning which is quite different from either of these. This is where the learner above all wants a communicative ability in the target language and wants it from the very day that he starts to learn. He will need a course where what he learns may be said to have *high surrender-value*.[2] There will be quite a number of types of language learners that share this characteristic: those attending crash courses of limited duration in a language of which they have no previous knowledge; those intending to develop an advanced proficiency, but not being prepared to wait for communicative capacity to appear towards the end of a long course; those who require only a limited functional capacity in the language and are prepared to stop short at this; learners in the field of continuing education who have something to gain from being able to use the language they are learning at the earliest opportunity; those learners who need the motivation of being able to see the practical, communicative value of the language being learned. If one accepts that there are such groups of language learners, one should ask how far their needs are satisfied if a course is given a conventional grammatical/structural organization.

The Content of Short-duration Intensive Courses

Let us imagine a group of graduate volunteers being given a three-week course in Malay in preparation for a year's work in Malaysia. Below is an outline of the content and sequence of one such course:

Grammatical Categories:	Demonstratives
	Pronouns
	Adjectives
	Possessives
	Question words
	Tag questions
	Numbers
	Quantitatives
Syntactic Structures:	Pronoun + Noun
	Pronoun + Adjective
	Pronoun + Pronoun
	Noun + Noun
	Noun modification
Sentence Types:	Statement, Question, Negative (throughout)
Functional Categories:	Greetings

Notice that up to this stage all sentences are of the copula type and there being no realization of the copula verb in Malay, the category of *verb* has not so far been met. The course then proceeds as follows:

Grammatical Categories:	Verbs
	Adverbials of time
	Time and aspect markers
	Prepositions of place
	Auxiliary verbs
Syntactic Structures:	Intransitive sentences
	Transitive sentences
	Preposition + noun
	Preposition + pronoun etc.
Sentence Types:	As above (continuing)
Functional Categories:	Commands
	Requests
	Invitations
	Prohibitions

If we assume that the three-week course is designed to produce a communicative capacity *at the end*, the exact sequence will not matter, but we can notice that *Greetings* apart, only at the final point do communicative categories get a mention. (By *Question* is really meant the grammatical category *Interrogative*.) The syllabus as such is clearly grammatical in organization and the sentences of the text demonstrate this:

Itu rumah	*That's a house*
Itu bukan kereta	*That isn't a car*
Rumah itu tidak besar	*That house isn't big*
Berapa jam?	*How many hours?*
Berapa hari?	*How many days?*
Berapa orang?	*How many people?*
Ada tiga orang di-sana	*There are three men over there*
Ali ada-kah?	*Is Ali there?*
Mereka tidak ada anak	*They have no children*

Sentences exemplify grammatical structures with some degree of acknowledgement that a useful vocabulary is needed. They rarely have much communicative verisimilitude and they certainly do not perform any communicative function for the individual learner. The communicative categories met at the end of the course provide some attempt to envisage language as a communicative process, but it is difficult to avoid treating the suggested devices as formulae, to be learned like lexical items:

Requests:

| Tolong buka pinta | *Open the door please* |
| Tolong berhenti di-sini | *Please stop here* |

It would seem that the learner's potential for communication at the end of such a course would be decidedly limited, since it has provided him with little opportunity to express the kind of thing that he must be expected to want to express in real communicative situations. With excellent teaching the learner's command of the grammatical systems will be good, but his command of those things *not* taught will be nil. It would be superfluous to list what is missing, but communication must be hampered, to say the least, when what is known is only part of the system. The problem lies in the fact that creative linguistic ability depends on knowing the rules of language and a *limited* linguistic ability is more accurately seen as a *partial* understanding of *many* rules than as a *thorough* understanding of a *few* rules. Just *what* someone can communicate, and with what purpose, when they have experienced only a part of the grammatical system is very hard to say. Generally, it is not true to say that certain parts of the grammatical system (rules) provide the means of producing certain types of message. It is possible for some things to have been learned very well and yet, because what is known is a decidedly limited part of the whole system, one's communcative capacity will have remained virtually at zero.

If, of course, the learners in their three-week course did not even get this far—and it is an ambitious programme for the time available— the communicative consequences are even more apparent: no auxiliaries, no prepositions, no markers of time . . .?

On the other hand if the structuring of language content had been notional and functional, then all language taught could have been of maximal communicative value. To take the categories suggested in my framework for a notional syllabus, one might have sought to include the following:

Time:	Points of time, days, hours, dates
	Time relations: past, present and future time
Quantity:	Numerals
	Limited range of quantifiers
Space:	Prepositions to express place and movement
Case:	A means of expressing notions of *agent*, *object*, *dative*, *locative*, also *predicative*
Deixis:	Person deixis (pronouns)
	Possibly place deixis
Modality:	Volition (intention, wish)
	Command, prohibition
	Permission
Discipline and evaluation:	Pardon (or forgiveness), apology
	Appreciation
Suasion:	Warning, directing, inviting
Argument:	Stating, questioning, requesting, agreeing (disagreeing?), negating, declining
Rational enquiry and exposition:	—
Personal emotions:	Pleasure
Emotional relations:	Greetings
	Gratitude
Interpersonal relations:	Consultative style
	Politeness

The aim is not so ambitious as may appear from the length of this list, since several of these categories may be realized within the same sentence/utterance. For example, a single sentence may have a pronoun subject (realizing *agent* and part of the category of *person deixis*), may indicate both *time* and *place*, may express an *intention* and may have the utterance function of *stating* or *reporting*. This does imply, of course, that individual pieces of language will contain far more that is new to the learner than is normally thought desirable in teaching and far greater diversity and heterogeneity in the course as a whole. What is gained is that the learner has means to express the most fundamental elements of propositional content and can perform some of the most urgent social functions of language.[3] His mastery of the grammatical devices he is using will, of course, be far from complete. The approach makes it almost inevitable that partial rather than whole systems are learned and that the full range of application of those forms that have been learned will not have been met. In a longer course greater grammatical generalization within such an approach can be provided for, but the three weeks assumed in the present example would make this rather difficult.

The Concept of a Minimum Adequate Grammar

Michael West talks about the possibility of a *Minimum Adequate Vocabulary*. This is a limited vocabulary that could be used particularly for defining purposes in a learner's dictionary. What is being suggested in this paper is what might be called a *Minimum Adequate Grammar*— that is to say a knowledge of the grammatical system of a language sufficient to meet fundamental and urgent communicative needs. To some extent this is also what *Basic English* aims to provide, only with too great a concern with vocabulary and too little awareness that grammatical and communicative competence are not identical. Obviously definition of an M.A.G. can only be arbitrary in that the size of the grammar to be learned is largely a function of the amount of time the learner has available. However, the procedures for determining the contents of an M.A.G. need not be entirely intuitive, given that we have some ideas of what might constitute semantic universals and that with the greater sociolinguistic sensibility that we now possess, we should be able to identify significant speech functions in the target language. Nor should the idea of an M.A.G. be beyond a fairly pragmatic assessment, since learners themselves will be in a position to judge whether it has accurately identified their most urgent communicative needs.

This paper argues therefore that the most valuable contribution to be expected from a notional approach to syllabus construction is in the provision of a Minimum Adequate Grammar for learners following short-term courses. Such courses and others where a high surrender-value for the language learned is important can benefit now from the semantic approach to course construction, whereas in the case of general language courses for those starting as complete beginners, it might be found that our knowledge of language in communication is too patchy for a thorough coverage of what would be needed.

Notes

Published in Corder, S. P., and Roulet, E. (eds.), Linguistic Insights in Applied Linguistics, AIMAV/Didier, 1974.

1. This was suggested to me by Keith Mitchell.
2. I first heard this term, derived from the field of insurance, applied to language teaching by Professor Corder some years ago in a lecture given in the Department of Applied Linguistics, University of Edinburgh.
3. Henry Widdowson made the point in discussion that it is precisely 'the most urgent social functions of language' that the learner is likely to acquire through his everyday contact with the language in use and that therefore this need not be the objective of an intro-ductory language course. I would accept that there is some truth in this. However, I would argue that even in a course that has a largely communicative orientation grammatical functions are not to be ignored. Unless learning of the grammatical system is begun, the learner will have no foundation on which further learning can be based once he is in the language community. It must be the aim, even of an introductory course, to create the conditions for communicative and grammatical facts to be learned simultaneously. In addition I think one can distinguish between what it is necessary that someone should learn and what it is desirable that he or she should learn. Since English is used as a second language in Malaysia, unavoidable Malay-medium social contacts may be rather few. Learning imposed by the situation may, therefore be strictly limited. It is obviously very desirable that any volunteer should have a communicative capacity that goes beyond this minimum. The best way to ensure this will be by means of a communicatively oriented course.

SECTION THREE

Applications and Techniques

The papers in this section are largely self-explanatory, and illustrate ways in which the ideas discussed in Part Two have been implemented. The first two papers illustrate the work of the Council of Europe. As the extract from Trim's paper makes clear (and the style of presentation is as significant as the contents), the development of language syllabuses responds partly to social and political pressures as well as to the demands of theory. A specification of language *uses* (a rather different concept from the language *use* which Widdowson is discussing) may be of great value in an educational system which wishes to categorize the various parts of its syllabus, either for the administration of teaching or of testing. The Trim extract indicates the main rationale for a unit/credit system (defined in 1.3.4 of the extract), and the chapters from van Ek's *Threshold Level* show the form which a statement of objectives might take. These two papers discuss syllabus design. In the next two Widdowson and Allen look at some methodological issues in relation to communication. These ideas have been taken up in a number of textbooks, and specifically in the series, *English in Focus*, which they edit. The final paper in this section, specially commissioned from Keith Morrow, explores the implications for testing of a communicative approach. There is a considerable risk that the gains in realism of a communicative test may be offset by losses in reliability. Morrow explores the extent to which formal tests can be constructed to evaluate the kind of teaching discussed elsewhere in this volume.

Draft outline of a European unit/credit system for modern language learning by adults
J. L. M. Trim

1.1.1. The divisive effect of language differences seems certain to prove to be one of the major obstacles to European integration over the next generation.

1.1.2. In recent times language-based nation states have provided a favourable environment for a steadily increasing scale of social organisation. The process has been greatly furthered by mass education and the spread of standard national languages, which make all citizens members of a freely interacting community and facilitate the further development of large-scale activities and institutions of all kinds.

1.2.1. Today, the internal consolidation of our countries is far advanced. However, the major developments of the last thirty years have progressively weakened the self-sufficiency of national cultures, even in day-to-day living. Mass travel for business and pleasure over continental motorway networks and air routes, electronic media, mass movements of immigrant labour and at managerial level in multinational corporations, supranational economic, cultural and political institutions, interdependence of imports/exports in an increasingly unified market, all conspire to render hard national frontiers within the Council for Cultural Co-operation area increasingly obsolete.

1.2.2. The discrete separation of national languages no longer provides a framework for increasing internal integration, but rather hindrances to an increasingly real and urgent wider unity. For children born today, who will spend the greater part of their lives in the third millennium, monolingualism will become increasingly out of date in a world where an active knowledge of an international *lingua franca* and some receptive acquaintance with one or two others, will be required over an unpredictably wide range of social situations. The effective teaching of languages in schools is thus a matter of great urgency, which, as so often in transitional situations, is widely underestimated.

1.2.3. Young adults, however, and the early-middle-aged, have completed their full-time education, in most cases (especially that of working-class children in the large monolingual countries) without acquiring any effective knowledge of any language save the standard form of the mother tongue. It is to be expected that very substantial numbers of them will find themselves at a disadvantage at some point in their future lives by an inability to communicate with fellow Europeans of a different mother tongue.

1.2.4. The extent of the disadvantage may range from the relatively trivial (inability to greet a visitor, to understand an entertainment film, to ask the time of a passer-by) to the disastrous (inability to summon help in sudden emergency, to retrieve a key piece of information from a publication, to negotiate a serious conflict of interest, to take employment in another country).

1.3.1. This situation gives particularly clear support to the general argument for a 'permanent education'. Modern life develops faster than educational planning can predict, or, having predicted, make effective provision for. A substantial proportion of educational resources should therefore be reserved for enabling the disadvantaged adult to acquire the knowledge and skills he now requires but which did not form part of his full-time education.

1.3.2. The knowledge and skills needed, often at short notice, by the adult will not, in most cases, be the highly generalised ones appropriate to the full-time education of the child and adolescent before the 'career watershed' is reached. Within a life and career the main lines of which are already laid down, the possibilities of action are limited. Adults rarely are able, or wish, to undertake the thorough study of an extensive new area of knowledge as a whole, in all its aspects. They rather require, on the basis of a sound grasp of necessary fundamental principles, to acquire quickly the factual knowledge and practical skills necessary for the immediate performance of urgent tasks with which they are faced in various aspects of their committed lives.

1.3.3. This is not to preach a narrow vocationalism. The recreational and liberating value of cultural studies is not to be underestimated. Even in these studies, however, the interests and motivations of the adult are generally more concentrated, related to a more defined pattern of past experience and future expectations.

1.3.4. Given such a concept of the nature and objectives of adult education, the transfer to this field of a pattern of generalised courses and global examinations developed for the schools is inappropriate. A better study framework can be provided if a given subject matter can be articulated into elements which can be grouped in different ways by different classes of learners in accordance with their needs and interests. Intelligent choice is then possible, and can perhaps be encouraged by recognising some coherent combinations of elements as constituting *units* of study. Where the mastery of such a unit is relevant to the acquisition of some formal qualification, *credits* can be awarded, allowing the qualification to be gained in a variety of ways appropriate to varying, but congruent, patterns of study and needs.

1.3.5.   A unit/credit system of this kind appears to offer a promising framework for guidance combined with freedom and flexibility in the at present badly understructured field of adult education.

2.1.   The aim of the European unit/credit system for modern language learning by adults is therefore to establish a framework for adult language learning, based upon the language needs of the learner and the linguistic operations required of him in order to function effectively as a member of the language community for the purposes, and in the situations, revealed by those needs.

2.2.   This aim is to be achieved by (*a*) an analysis of language use sufficiently rich for widely divergent learning objectives to be character-ised and (*b*) a set of principles according to which language learning units may be constructed corresponding to the communicative needs of the learner. Suggestions may then be made whereby 'credits' may be attached to such units, and given appropriate recognition on a European basis.

2.3.   The classification of language learning objectives is based upon an analysis of the language-using operations required of a member of a speech community. Each operation can be described in terms of (*a*) the behavioural input-output chain involved, (*b*) the communicative function performed, (*c*) the notional/semantic content expressed, (*d*) the formal linguistic resources employed (*e*) the situation in which it occurs.

[. . .]

Note

Published in *Systems Development in Adult Langauge Learning*, Council of Europe, Strasbourg, 1973.

The threshold level
J. A. van Ek

Language-learning objectives

Language-learning objectives, like other learning-objectives, are defined in terms of *behaviour*. The aim of learning is always to enable the learner to *do* something which he could not do at the beginning of the learning-process. This applies to physical ability, such as the ability to ride a bicycle, as well as to less directly observable abilities, such as the ability to appreciate the difference between a burgundy and a claret, or the ability to understand some scientific theory.

Moreover, as we saw in Chapter 1, learning-objectives must be geared towards learners' needs. This means that before defining an objective we must define the group of learners whose needs we wish to cater for, the target-group.

Once the target-group has been defined we try to determine as exactly as possible what they will need to do with, in our case, a foreign language.

It is not sufficient—not exact enough—to say that they 'want to speak the foreign language'. In the first place there is not much point, usually, in being able to *speak* a language if one cannot *understand* it as well. Moreover, when can one be said to 'speak a language'? When one can discuss the weather with casual acquaintances, or when one can address a formal meeting? It would seem that much depends on the kind of situations in which the learner may be expected to need the ability to use the foreign language. Will it be in the situation of an interpreter in a law-court or in that of a casual tourist?

In order to define the learning-objective for a target-group we first have to specify the *situations* in which they will need the foreign language. Specifying a situation means stating the *roles* a language-user has to play, the *settings* in which he will have to play these roles, and the *topics* he will have to deal with. More technically: by situation we mean the complex of extra-linguistic conditions which determines the nature of a language-act.

Once we have determined the situations in which the members of the target-group will want to use the foreign language we can try to specify just what they will have to be able to *do* in those situations.

First we specify the *language activities* the learner will be likely to engage in. These may be as comparatively 'simple' as understanding the weather-forecast on the radio or as complex as summarising orally in a foreign language a report written in one's native language. The traditional division of language-activities into four skills—speaking, listening, writing, reading—is not always fully adequate, as reflection on the last example will show.

Having determined the nature of the language activities we try to specify for what general purposes the learner will have to use the foreign language, what *language functions* he will have to fulfil. For instance, he may have to give information about facts, he may wish to express certainty or uncertainty, whether he considers something right or wrong, he may wish to express gratitude, he may wish to apologise.

But the learner will have to do more than fulfil such general language functions. He will not only have to give information in the abstract, but he will want to give information about *something*; he will wish to express certainty or uncertainty with respect to *something*; he will want to apologise for *something*. In other words, he will need the ability to refer to things, to people, to events etc., and to talk about them. In order to do all this he will have to be able to handle a large number of *notions* in the foreign language. What notions he will need depends to a large extent on the topics he will deal with. If he is dealing with the topic 'weather' he will have to handle notions such as *fair, sunshine, to rain, etc.*, when dealing with a menu the notions *meat, ice-cream, coffee* may be required. We can draw up lists of such notions for each topic if we ask ourselves just what the learners will want to be able to do with respect to each topic and what notions he will need in order to do this. There are also notions which are so general that they may be needed in any situation, when dealing with any topic. These are notions such as existence/non-existence, past/present, before/after, etc. Since such notions are not specifically related to any particular topic there is not much point in trying to derive them from a consideration of individual topics. Instead, they can be derived from a consideration of what, in general, people deal with by means of language. We may say, again in general, that people deal with:

1. entities (objects, persons, ideas, states, actions, events, etc.),
2. properties and qualities of entities,
3. relations between entities.

The entities themselves will be largely determined by the topics, whereas notions of properties and qualities, and those of relations, tend to be used more generally. In order to compose lists of these general notions we can set up a system of logically derived categories and subsequently determine what notions are likely to be used in each category.

When the specification of a language-learning objective has been completed up to this point we can determine what actual *language forms* (structures, words and phrases) the learner will have to be able to use in order to do all that has been specified. These forms are determined by considering each of the language-functions and the notions separately and establishing how they are realised in a particular language, in other words by establishing their *exponents*.

The final component of a language-learning objective is a statement about the *degree of skill* with which a successful learner will be expected to be able to do all that has been specified, in other words *how well* he will have to be able to do it. It is fairly easy to make such a statement in general terms but very difficult, if possible at all, to do it with anything approaching the degree of exactness we can achieve for the other components of the definition.

To sum up: Our model for the definition of language-learning objectives specifies the following components:

1. the situations in which the foreign language will be used, including the topics which will be dealt with;
2. the language activities in which the learner will engage;
3. the language functions which the learner will fulfil;
4. what the learner will be able to do with respect to each topic;
5. the general notions which the learner will be able to handle;
6. the specific (topic-related) notions which the learner will be able to handle;
7. the language forms which the learner will be able to use;
8. the degree of skill with which the learner will be able to perform.

The definition of the threshold level

Specification of situations

By *situation* we mean the complex of extra-linguistic conditions which determines the nature of a language-act (cf. Chapter 2). Properly speaking, situations are strictly personal and unique. One of the conditions is always the individual language-user himself with his unique background (the sum total of his experiences). For our purposes, however—the definition of a level of general language-ability will be an objective for a very large and heterogeneous population—we must ignore strictly individual conditions and we may concentrate on four components of situations, which, together, provide a sufficient basis for the further steps in our procedure. We shall, henceforward, distinguish four components of situations:

1. the *social rules* which the learner will be able to play;
2. the *psychological roles* which the learner will be able to play;
3. the *settings* in which the learner will be able to use the foreign language;
4. the *topics* which the learner will be able to deal with in the foreign language.

Social roles

The principal social roles for which T-level learners have to be prepared are:

1. *stranger/stranger*
2. *friend/friend*

This selection is made from a study by Richterich[1]; on the basis of the characteristics of the target-group (cf. Chapter 4). Various other roles are subsumed under 1, e.g.:

private person/official
patient/doctor, nurse, dentist

A role such as

asker/giver

may be subsumed under both 1 and 2.

 The inclusion of role 2 (*friend/friend*) has important consequences for the definition of the T-level. It raises this level above that required for purely physical survival in a foreign-language environment. It will prepare the learner for the establishment and maintenance of social relationships with foreign-language speakers. Only when this need is fulfilled can our level be called 'threshold level' in a meaningful way: it will enable the learner to cross the threshold into the foreign-language community.

Psychological roles

On the basis of the characteristics of the target-group we select from Richterich[2] the following roles:

1. neutrality
2. equality
3. sympathy
4. antipathy

These roles are the more 'neutral' roles and they are appropriate in a large variety of types of linguistic interaction.

Settings

On the basis of the characteristics of the target-group, we may draw up a long list of settings in which the learners may want to use the foreign language. The settings have been selected from lists provided by Richterich (op. cit.) and by Peck (private communication). In spite of its size this list is not to be considered exhaustive. It is assumed, however, that it is sufficiently comprehensive to produce—together with the other components of situation—specifications of language-ability which will enable the learners to behave adequately also in various settings which have not been listed (transfer).[3]

1. Geographical location:

1. foreign country where foreign language is native language
2. foreign country where foreign language is not native language
3. own country

2. Place:

2.1 Outdoors:

1. street
2. square
3. park, garden
4. terrace
5. countryside
6. beach
7. lake, sea
8. mountains
9. sports-field
10. open air swimming pool
11. camping site
12. bus stop
13. taxi stand
14. sights
15. market-place
16. car-park

2.2 Indoors

2.2.1 *Private life*:

1. house
2. apartment
3. room
4. kitchen

2.2.2 *Public life*:

2.2.2.1 *Purchases*

1. shop
2. supermarket

	3. multiple stores
	4. indoor market
2.2.2.2 *Eating and Drinking*:	1. restaurant
	2. café
	3. snack bar
	4. bar
	5. canteen
2.2.2.3 *Accommodation*:	1. hotel
	hotel room
	reception
	2. camping site
	3. holiday camp
	4. hostel
	5. boarding house
	6. farm house
2.2.2.4 *Transport*:	1. railway-station
	2. bus-station
	3. airport
	4. ferry terminal
	5. ticket office
	6. travel bureau
	7. information office
	8. lost property office
	9. customs and immigration
	10. garage
	11. petrol station
	12. indoor car-park
2.2.2.5 *Religion*:	1. church
2.2.2.6 *Physical services*	1. hospital
	2. doctor's/dentist's waiting-room
	3. surgery
	4. chemist
	5. public lavatory
	6. sauna
	7. hairdresser
2.2.2.7 *Learning*:	1. school
	2. language institute
	3. classroom
	4. library
2.2.2.8 *Displays*:	1. museum

2. art gallery
3. exhibition

2.2.2.9 *Entertain-*   1. theatre
ment: 2. cinema
3. concert-hall/opera
4. night-club

2.2.2.10 *Com-*   1. post-office
munication: 2. telephone-booth

2.2.2.11 *Finance*:   1. bank
2. money exchange office

2.2.2.12 *Work*:   1. office
2. workshop
3. factory

2.2.2.13 *Means of*   1. bus
transport: 2. tram
3. train
4. underground railway
5. boat/ferry
6. aeroplane
7. taxi
8. private car
9. bicycle

3. Surroundings (human)

1. family
2. friends
3. acquaintances
4. strangers

Topics

On the basis of the characteristics of the target-group, the following list of topics has been drawn up. A similar list provided by Peck has been used as the main source. In the composition of the list the social roles we have selected have been used as criteria for inclusion. With respect to this list the same remark applies which was made a propos of the list of settings: a certain measure of arbitrariness in the classification does not affect the value of the list as long as all the more important topics are included somewhere. Even this claim, however, cannot be upheld. No matter how carefully a list of this kind is composed, it is bound to be far from complete. However, this weakness is—to a certain extent—offset by the transfer-potential of linguistic ability. It may be assumed that a learner who is competent to deal with the topics listed will also be able to deal with several other topics for which he has not necessarily been prepared.

1. Personal identification

1. name
2. address
3. telephone number
4. date and place of birth
5. age
6. sex
7. marital status
8. nationality
9. origin
10. profession, occupation
11. employer
12. family
13. religion
14. likes and dislikes
15. character, temperament, disposition

2. House and home

1. types of accommodation
2. accommodation, rooms
3. furniture, bedclothes
4. rent
5. services
6. amenities
7. region
8. flora and fauna

3. Trade, profession, occupation

1. trades, professions, occupations
2. place of work
3. conditions of work
4. income
5. training
6. prospects

4. Free time, entertainment

1. hobbies
2. interests

3. radio, TV, etc.
4. cinema, theatre, opera, concerts, etc.
5. sports
6. intellectual pursuits
7. artistic pursuits
8. museums, galleries, exhibitions
9. press

5. Travel

1. travel to work, evening-class, etc.
2. holidays
3. countries and places
4. public transport
5. private transport
6. entering and leaving a country
7. nationalities
8. languages
9. hotel, camping-site, etc.
10. travel documents
11. fares
12. tickets
13. luggage
14. traffic

6. Relations with other people

1. friendship/aversion
2. invitations
3. correspondence
4. club-membership
5. political and social views

7. Health and welfare

1. parts of the body
2. positions of the body
3. ailments/accidents
4. personal comfort
5. sensory perception
6. hygiene
7. insurance
8. medical services
9. emergency services

8. Education

1. schooling
2. subjects
3. qualifications

9. Shopping

1. shopping-facilities
2. foodstuffs
3. clothes, fashion
4. smoking
5. household-articles
6. medicine
7. prices
8. weights and measurements

10. Food and drink

1. types of food and drink
2. eating and drinking out

11. Services

1. post
2. telephone
3. telegraph
4. bank
5. police
6. hospital, surgery, etc.
7. repairs
8. garage
9. petrol-station

12. Places

13. Foreign language

1. ability
2. understanding
3. correctness

14. Weather

1. climate
2. weather-conditions

[. . .]

Language Functions

This chapter specifies component 3 of the definition of the T-level. This will be done in non-language-specific terms: we shall list the various functions the learners will be able to fulfil at T-level, whatever language—here limited to those spoken in the member-countries of the Council of Europe—they have studied. In Chapter II we shall list for each function the actual language forms (grammatical and/or lexical) which we consider to be the most useful exponents for T-level English.

In setting up our list of language functions we have distinguished six main categories of verbal communication:

1. imparting and seeking factual information;
2. expressing and finding out intellectual attitudes;
3. expressing and finding out emotional attitudes;
4. expressing and finding out moral attitudes;
5. getting things done (suasion);
6. socialising

Each of these six main categories, and, indeed, each of the functions, may be realised separately in language-acts. Often, however, two or more of them will be combined in a single language-act. Thus, one may seek factual information while at the same time expressing surprise (emotional attitude). Yet, it is convenient to deal with each function separately and to specify just what each function involves by way of language-content.

The list of functions is far from exhaustive. In the first place it is unlikely that it is possible at all to draw up a complete list. Secondly, the list represents a deliberate selection for T-level. At higher levels more functions would be added.

It should be emphasised that the lists presented here and in other chapters are not to be regarded as final or definitive. They will—it is hoped—provide a sufficiently solid basis for practical applications of an experimental nature. The feedback from this experimental work will undoubtedly lead to numerous modifications in the lists.

Language functions for T-level

1.   *Imparting and seeking factual information*
1.1   identifying
1.2   reporting (including describing and narrating)
1.3   correcting
1.4   asking

2.   *Expressing and finding out intellectual attitudes*
2.1   expressing agreement and disagreement
2.2   inquiring about agreement or disagreement
2.3   denying something
2.4   accepting an offer or invitation
2.5   declining an offer or invitation
2.6   inquiring whether offer or invitation is accepted or declined
2.7   offering to do something
2.8   stating whether one remembers or has forgotten something or someone
2.9   inquiring whether someone remembers or has forgotten something or someone
2.10   expressing whether something is considered possible or impossible
2.11   inquiring whether something is considered possible or impossible
2.12   expressing capability and incapability
2.13   inquiring about capability or incapability
2.14   expressing whether something is considered a logical conclusion (deduction)
2.15   inquiring whether something is considered a logical conclusion (deduction)
2.16   expressing how certain/uncertain one is of something
2.17   inquiring how certain/uncertain others are of something
2.18   expressing one is/is not obliged to do something
2.19   inquiring whether one is obliged to do something
2.20   expressing others are/are not obliged to do something
2.21   inquiring whether others are obliged to do something
2.22   giving and seeking permission to do something
2.23   inquiring whether others have permission to do something
2.24   stating that permission is withheld

3.   *Expressing and finding out emotional attitudes*
3.1   expressing pleasure, liking
3.2   expressing displeasure, dislike
3.3   inquiring about pleasure, liking, displeasure, dislike
3.4   expressing surprise
3.5   expressing hope
3.6   expressing satisfaction
3.7   expressing dissatisfaction
3.8   inquiring about satisfaction or dissatisfaction
3.9   expressing disappointment
3.10   expressing fear or worry
3.11   inquiring about fear or worry

3.12 expressing preference
3.13 inquiring about preference
3.14 expressing gratitude
3.15 expressing sympathy
3.16 expressing intention
3.17 inquiring about intention
3.18 expressing want, desire
3.19 inquiring about want, desire

4. *Expressing and finding out moral attitudes*
4.1 apologising
4.2 granting forgiveness
4.3 expressing approval
4.4 expressing disapproval
4.5 inquiring about approval or disapproval
4.6 expressing appreciation
4.7 expressing regret
4.8 expressing indifference

5. *Getting things done (suasion)*
5.1 suggesting a course of action (including the speaker)
5.2 requesting others to do something
5.3 inviting others to do something
5.4 advising others to do something
5.5 warning others to take care or to refrain from doing something
5.6 instructing or directing others to do something

6. *Socialising*
6.1 to greet people
6.2 when meeting people
6.3 when introducing people and when being introduced
6.4 when taking leave
6.5 to attract attention
6.6 to propose a toast
6.7 when beginning a meal

[. . .]

Notes

Extracts from *The Threshold Level in a European Unit/Credit System for Modern Language Learning by Adults*. Council for Cultural Co-operation of the Council of Europe, Strasbourg, 1975.

1. R. Richterich, 1972.
2. R. Richterich, 1972.

3. It has been attempted to classify the settings in order to make the list more easily accessible as a check-list. This attempt has inevitably led to some rather arbitrary decisions of assignment to particular categories. It is felt, however, that the value of the list is not affected by this procedure provided all the more important settings are included somewhere.

The teaching of English as communication
H. G. Widdowson

What I should like to do in this short article is to consider a problem in the teaching of English which has come into particular prominence over the past few years, and to suggest a way in which it might be resolved.

The problem is that students, and especially students in developing countries, who have received several years of formal English teaching, frequently remain deficient in the ability to actually use the language, and to understand its use, in normal communication, whether in the spoken or the written mode.

The problem has come into prominence in recent years because, as a result of an enormous increase in educational opportunity, large numbers of students in developing countries are entering universities and technical institutions to take up subjects which can only be satisfactorily studied if the students are able to read textbooks in English efficiently. Efficient reading involves understanding how language operates in communication, and it is precisely this understanding which students appear not to acquire during their years of learning English in the secondary schools.

It seems generally to be assumed that the reason for this state of affairs is that secondary-school teachers do not do their job properly; they do not follow the approach to English teaching which is taught to them in training colleges and in-service courses, and which is embodied in the prescribed textbooks. The assumption is that if only teachers could be persuaded to put this approach into practice, then the problem would disappear. It is seldom that the validity of the recommended approach is called into question. What I want to suggest is that the root of the problem is to be found, in fact, in the approach itself.

In general, we might characterize the recommended approach as one which combines situational presentation with structural practice. Language items are presented in situations in the classroom to ensure that their meaning is clear, and then practised as formal structures by means of exercises of sufficient variety to sustain the interest of the learner and in sufficient numbers to establish the structures in the learner's memory. The principal aim is to promote a knowledge of the language system, to develop the learner's competence (to use Chomsky's terms) by means of controlled performance. The assumption behind this approach seems to be that learning a language is a matter of associating the formal elements of the language system with their physical realization, either as sounds in the air or as marks on paper. Essentially, what is taught by this approach is the ability to compose correct sentences.

The difficulty is that the ability to compose sentences is not the only ability we need to communicate. Communication only takes place when we make use of sentences to perform a variety of different acts of an essentially social nature. Thus we do not communicate by composing sentences, but by using sentences to make statements of different kinds, to describe, to record, to classify and so on, or to ask questions, make requests, give orders. Knowing what is involved in putting sentences together correctly is only one part of what we mean by knowing a language, and it has very little value on its own: it has to be supplemented by a knowledge of what sentences count as in their normal use as a means of communicating. And I do not think that the recommended approach makes adequate provision for the teaching of this kind of knowledge.

It might be objected, however, that the contextualization of language items by presenting them in situational settings in the classroom does provide for the communicative function of language. I do not think this is so. We need to draw a careful distinction between two different kinds of meaning. One kind of meaning is that which language items have as elements of the language system, and the other is that which they have when they are actually put to use in acts of communication. Let us, for convenience, call the first kind of meaning *signification* and the second kind *value*. What I want to suggest is that the contextualization of language items as represented in the approach we are considering is directed at the teaching of signification rather than value, and that it is for this reason that it is inadequate for the teaching of English as communication.

The distinction I am trying to make between these two kinds of meaning may be made clearer by an example. Let us suppose that we wish to teach the present continuous tense. The recommended approach will advise us to invent some kind of situation to demonstrate its meaning. One such situation might consist of the teacher walking to the door and saying *I am walking to the door* and then getting a number of pupils to do the same while he says *He is walking to the door, They are walking to the door*, and so on. Another might consist of the teacher and selected pupils writing on the blackboard to the accompaniment of comments like *I am writing on the blackboard, He is writing on the blackboard*, and so on. In this manner, we can demonstrate what the present continuous tense signifies and we can use the situations to develop 'action chains' so as to show how its meaning relates to that of other tense forms. But what kind of communicative function do these sentences have in these situations? They are being used to perform the act of commentary in situations in which in normal circumstances no commentary would be called for. Contextualization of this kind, then, does not demonstrate how sentences of this form are appropriately used to perform the communicative act of comment-ary. What is being taught is signification, not value.

The reaction of many teachers to this observation will be to concede that contextualization of this kind does not teach what I have chosen to call value, but to assert that in the restricted circumstances of the classroom, this is the only kind of meaning that can be taught. Further-more, they may feel that it is not necessary to teach value anyway; that the teaching of what I have referred to as signification provides learners with a basic knowledge of the essentials of the language, and that it is a simple enough matter for the learner to put this to use when it comes to communicating. As I have already implied, it seems to me that it is a radical mistake to suppose that a knowledge of how sentences are put to use in communication follows automatically from a knowledge of how sentences are composed and what signification they have as linguistic units. Learners have to be taught what values they may have as predictions, qualifications, reports, descriptions, and so on. There is no simple equation between linguistic forms and communicative functions. Affirmative sentences, for instance, are not always used as statements, and interrogative sentences are not always used as questions. One linguistic form can fulfil a variety of communicative functions, and one function can be fulfilled by a variety of linguistic forms.

What I should like to suggest is that we should consider ways of adapting the present approach to the teaching of English so as to incorporate the systematic teaching of communicative value. I would propose that in the process of limitation, grading, and presentation, we should think not only in terms of linguistic structures and situational settings, but also in terms of communicative acts.

Let us suppose, for example, that we wish to produce an English course for science students. Instead of selecting the language to be taught by reference to the frequency of linguistic forms like the universal present tense and the passive in scientific discourse, we might make a selection of those communicative acts which the scientist must of necessity most commonly perform: definition, classification, general-ization, deduction, and so on. When grading, we might consider ordering such acts according to the manner in which they normally combine to form larger communicative units: thus, for example, we might introduce the generalization before the observation since the latter serves as an illustration of the former, and they combine to form a very common unit of communication in scientific discourse. For example:

1. Metals expand when heated.
2. Railway lines get longer in hot weather.
3. Metals expand when heated. Railway lines, for example, get longer in hot weather.

The advantage of this kind of grading is that it quite naturally leads the learner beyond the sentence into increasingly larger stretches of discourse as one communicative act combines with another.

In presentation, we can make appeal to the kind of cognitive process which learners as students of science must develop anyway. Thus, for example, the value of certain sentences might be indicated by combining them into syllogisms like the following:

1. Metals expand when heated.
2. Iron is a metal.
3. Therefore iron expands when heated.

The difference between the teaching of value and the teaching of signification becomes clear when we compare the syllogism with action-chain sequences like the following:

1. I am going to write on the blackboard.
2. I am writing on the blackboard.
3. I have written on the blackboard.

Whereas the action-chain sequence relates sentence forms which do not combine to create a communicative unit, the syllogism represents a way of using language to perform the act of deductive reasoning. The syllogism is a particularly appropriate presentation device for the teaching of English to students of science since it reveals the inter-relationship between the subject and the language which is associated with it. One of the advantages of presenting language items by focusing on their communicative value is that the relevance of the language to the subject is more immediately apparent.

It would, of course, be a mistake to devote attention exclusively to communicative acts in the preparation and presentation of language-teaching materials. In the teaching of language, one has continually to make compromises and to adjust one's approach to the requirements of students and the exigencies of the teaching situation. It would be wrong to be dogmatic. All I wish to suggest in this article is that some adjustment to the approach generally recommended at present is needed in that it appears not to be adequate in its present form: it does not seem to provide for the teaching of the knowledge of how English is used to communicate. The suggestions I have put forward as to how this inadequacy might be made up for are only tentative and obviously need to be explored further before their validity can be assessed. At the same time, the problem which they bear upon urgently needs to be solved, and it may be that a shift in orientation from the formal to the communicative properties of language might lead us some way towards its solution.

Note

Published in English Language Teaching, XXVII, 1: 15–19, 1972.

Teaching the communicative use of English
J. P. B. Allen and H. G. Widdowson

English language teaching overseas is taking on a new character as a result of the need for many advanced students to use the language as a tool in the study of scientific and technical subjects. In this situation. the oral inductive methods of the conventional syllabus are no longer adequate. There is a need for a new approach to language teaching which will shift the focus of attention from the grammatical to the communicative properties of language, in order to show the student how the language system is used to express scientific facts and concepts. An English course at this level should be concerned both with discourse and with text. The first of these involves the ability to recognize how sentences are used in the performance of acts of communication and the second, the ability to manipulate the formal devices which are used to combine sentences in creating continuous passages of prose. Various types of exercise are suggested for the teaching of discourse. An approach to the teaching of grammar at an advanced or remedial level is discussed, together with a technique for guided paragraph building specifically designed for use in the context of scientific writing.

Introduction

In recent years, English language teaching overseas has taken on a new character. Previously it was usual to talk about the aims of English learning in terms of the so-called 'language skills' of speaking, under-standing speech, reading and writing, and these aims were seen as relating to general education at the primary and secondary levels. Recently, however, a need has arisen to specify the aims of English learning more precisely as the language has increasingly been required to take on an auxiliary role at the tertiary level of education. English teaching has been called upon to provide students with the basic ability to use the language, to receive, and (to a lesser degree) to convey information associated with their specialist studies. This is particularly so in the developing countries where essential textbook material is not available in the vernacular languages. Thus whereas one talked previous-ly in general terms of ELT, we now have such acronymic variants as ESP (English for Special Purposes) and EST (English for Science and Technology).

This association of English teaching with specialist areas of higher education has brought into prominence a serious neglect of the needs of intermediate and advanced learners. Most of the improvements in language teaching methodology brought about during the last two decades have concentrated on the elementary syllabus. The reason for this is fairly clear: in any attempt to improve language teaching materials the logical place to start is at the beginning. Moroever, this approach ensures that the problems of organizing language data are reduced to a minimum, since the course writer has a comparatively small number of words and structures to deal with in the early stages. The large amount of time and money that has been spent in developing elementary language teaching materials has produced impressive results, and a wide range of courses is now available to cater for the needs of students who are still in the process of acquiring a stock of basic vocabulary and simple grammatical structures. The teaching method which has proved most effective for this purpose contains two main ingredients: a step-by-step technique of structural grading, and a battery of intensive oral drills. Both features are based on the behaviourist doctrine that language learning consists primarily in establishing a set of habits, that is, a set of responses conditioned to occur with certain stimuli which may be either situations or words in a syntactic frame. Unfortunately, however, the generous provision of basic courses has coincided with a striking lack of new material specially designed for intermediate and advanced students. As a result, students who have become accustomed to an orderly progression of graded materials, simple explanations and easily-manipulated drills during the first two or three years of language learning find that these aids are suddenly withdrawn when they reach the end of the basic course, and that they are left to fend for themselves with little or no guidance at a time when the language is rapidly becoming more difficult. On the one hand we have an abundant supply of basic language courses, and on the other hand we have advanced teaching techniques (essay writing, report making, comprehension of complex reading material, etc.) designed for students who have a near-native competence in handling the target language, but there are virtually no materials to help the learner effect an orderly transition between these two extremes.

The general English instruction which is provided in secondary schools has in most cases proved to be inadequate as a preparation for use which students are required to make of the language when they enter higher education. In consequence, many technical institutions and universities in developing countries provide courses with titles like 'Functional English', 'Technical English' and 'Report Writing', the purpose of which is to repair the deficiencies of secondary school teaching. However, such courses seldom recognize that a different approach may be needed to match the essentially different role which English assumes in higher education. They continue to treat English as a subject in its own right. It is true that there is some recognition of the auxiliary role it now has to play in that the selection of grammatical structures and lexical items to be taught are those which are of most frequent occurrence in the specialist literature with which the students are concerned. But the emphasis is still squarely on separate grammatical structures and lexical items, and such courses do little more than provide exercises in the manipulation of linguistic forms. The approach to English teaching is basically the same as that of the schools, and the assumption seems to be that it is likely to be more effective only because it is practised more efficiently. In fact, there is little evidence that such remedial courses are any more effective than the courses which they are intended to rectify.

The purpose of this paper is to suggest that what is needed is a different orientation to English study and to outline an approach which departs from that which is generally taken. Broadly, what is involved is a shift of the focus of attention from the grammatical to the communicative properties of the language. We take the view that the difficulties which the students encounter arise not so much from a defective knowledge of the system of English, but from an unfamiliarity with English use, and that consequently their needs cannot be met by a course which simply provides further practice in the composition of sentences, but only by one which develops a knowledge of how sentences are used in the performance of different communicative acts. The approach which we wish to outline here, then, represents an attempt to move from an almost exclusive concern with grammatical forms to at least an equal concern with rhetorical functions.

One might usefully distinguish two kinds of ability which an English course at this level should aim at developing. The first is the ability to recognize how sentences are used in the performance of acts of communication, the ability to understand the rhetorical functioning of language in use. The second is the ability to recognize and manipulate the formal devices which are used to combine sentences to create continuous passages of prose. We might say that the first has to do with the rhetorical coherence of *discourse*, and the second with the grammatical cohesion of *text*. In practice, of course, one kind of ability merges with the other, but in the form and function approach we are presenting here we focus on each of them in turn, while at the same time allowing for peripheral overlap.

The use of language in discourse

Language considered as communication no longer appears as a separate subject but as an aspect of other subjects. A corollary to this is that an essential part of any subject is the manner in which its 'content' is given linguistic expression. Learning science, for example, is seen to be not merely a matter of learning facts, but of learning how language is used to give expression to certain reasoning processes, how it is used to define, classify, generalize, to make hypotheses, draw conclusions and so on. People who talk about 'scientific English' usually give the impression that it can be characterized in formal terms as revealing a high frequency of linguistic forms like the passive and the universal tense in association with a specialist vocabulary. But to characterize it in this way is to treat scientific discourse merely as exemplification of the language system, and does little or nothing to indicate what kind of communication it is.

The first principle of the approach we propose, then, is that the language should be presented in such a way as to reveal its character as communication. Let us consider how this principle might be put into practice. We will suppose that we are to design an English course for students of science in the first year of higher education.[1] We make two basic assumptions. Firstly, we assume that in spite of the short-comings of secondary school English teaching the students have acquired considerable dormant competence in the manipulation of the language system. Secondly, we assume that they already have a knowledge of basic science. Hitherto, these two kinds of knowledge have existed in separation: our task is to relate them. We do this by composing passages on common topics in basic science and presenting them in such a way as to develop in the student an awareness of the ways in which the language system is used to express scientific facts and concepts. The passages are composed rather than derived directly from existing textbooks for two reasons. Firstly, we are able to avoid syntactic complexity and idiosyncratic features of style which would be likely to confuse students fresh from their experience of controlled and largely sentence-bound English instruction in schools, and/or deflect their attention from those features of use which we wish them to concentrate on. Our intention is to make linguistic forms as unobtrusive as possible. At the same time we wish to make their communicative function as obvious as possible, and this is the second reason for composing passages: we are able to 'foreground' features of language which have particular communicative value. It might be objected that the passages are not therefore representative of scientific writing. The answer to this is that they are representative of what we conceive to be certain basic communicative processes which underlie, and are variously realized in, individual pieces of scientific writing, and that they have been designed expressly to bring such processes more clearly into focus.

Each passage is provided with comprehension questions, but since we want to bring the student's attention to bear on his own reading activity as a process which involves a recognition of how language functions to convey information, the questions are not given at the end of the passage, as is the common practice, but are inserted into the passage itself. Furthermore, to ensure that the student is made aware of how the functioning of the language and his own understanding are related, solutions are provided for each comprehension question. These solutions are explanations in the sense that they make overt the kind of reasoning which underlies the ability to give the correct answer to the comprehension questions with which they are associated. Reasoning procedures such as are represented in these solutions might be said to be an essential element in any area of scientific enquiry, and their use here is intended to show the relevance of language to the study of science and to make appeal to the particular cognitive bent of science students.

The following is a sample of a passage composed and presented as described above. The sentences are numbered for ease of reference in the solutions, and in the exercises, which we shall discuss directly.

Matter and Volume

[1]Matter is the name given to everything which has weight and occupies space. [2]It may usually be detected by the senses of touch, sight or smell.

[3]Matter may exist in three states: solid, liquid and gas. [4]All substances, except those which decompose when heated, like wood, may be changed from one state into another. [5]A substance in the solid state may be changed into a liquid substance, and one in the liquid state may be changed into a gaseous substance. [6]Conversely, changes can take place in the reverse order: gases may be changed into liquids and liquids into solids. [7]A solid substance such as ice may be changed into the liquid state, or liquefied, to become water; and this may be changed into the gaseous state, or evaporated, to become steam. [8]Steam may also be converted into water and water into ice.

a)	Matter can usually be seen, smelt or touched.
b)	Matter can be seen, smelt and touched.
c)	All substances can be changed from one state into another.
d)	A liquid can be changed either into a gas or into a solid.

Solutions

a) may = can
   may usually be detected by the senses of touch, sight or smell (2)
   = can usually be touched, seen or smelt

∴ | Matter can usually be seen, smelt or touched. |

b) touched, seen or smelt.
   = *either* touched *or* seen *or* smelt.
   i.e. Some matter can be seen but not touched (e.g. visible gases)
   Some matter can be smelt but not seen (e.g. some invisible gases), etc.
   Matter can be seen, smelt and touched.
   = *All* matter can be seen *and* smelt *and* touched.
   ∴ *It is NOT TRUE that matter can be seen, smelt and touched.*

c) All substances, *except those which decompose when heated*, may be changed from one state to another. (4)
   ∴ Some substances cannot (= may not) change from one state to another.
   ∴ *It is NOT TRUE that all substances can be changed from one state to another.*

d) A substance in the liquid state may be changed into a gaseous substance. (5)
   i.e. A liquid can be changed into a gas.
   gases may be changed into liquids and liquids [may be changed] into solids. (6)

∴ | A liquid can be changed *either* into a gas *or* into a solid. |

The purpose of the comprehension 'check' questions and the solutions is to draw the reader's attention to the process by which a piece of language is interpreted as discourse. The notes are meant to relate surface language forms to logical operations, and so to point to their communicative function in the passage concerned. It is likely that the student will know the meanings of such forms as elements of the language code: this kind of meaning, which we will call *signification*, can be exemplified by isolated sentences and is usually learned by pattern practice. What the student is less likely to recognize is the *value* which such items take on in utterances occurring within a context of discourse. For example, in the case of the passage just quoted, the student may know the signification of items like the articles, the quantifier *all* and the adverb *usually*. What the comprehension questions and solutions are intended to draw out is the value such terms have in the making of statements of different kinds: generalizations, qualifications and so on, which set up implicational relations with other parts of the discourse. When a qualification is signalled by the use of *usually*, for example, we need to recognize not only that the sentence in itself has a particular rhetorical value, but also that it has a rhetorical relation with preceding and succeeding sentences.

This focus on communicative value is also a feature of the exercises which follow the notes. The first of these draws the student's attention to anaphoric devices. Such devices, of course, are capable of a very wide range of values. The so-called 'demonstrative pronouns' *this* and *these*, for example, are generally given an 'ostensive' signification which associates them with singular and plural noun phrases: in the early lessons of an English course they occur in sentences such as 'This is a book' 'These are books' and as pro-forms they usually make no further appearance in the course. In actual discourse, however, it is not always easy to recognize which noun phrase, or phrases, such pro-forms are to be related to since they do not appear in neat equative sentences such as are presented in the early English lessons. The reader has to select the appropriate value from a number of alternatives, all of which are grammatically possible. Furthermore, it commonly happens that *this* does not relate to a noun phrase at all, but to some superordinate notion which is not given overt expression as such in the discourse. Thus, it may take on the value 'the fact X', 'the set of facts X, Y, Z', 'the idea X', 'the set of ideas X, Y, Z', 'the argument X', 'the set of arguments X, Y, Z' and so on, where X, Y, Z are elements in the preceding discourse. To recognize the value of *this* in such cases the reader has to understand the communicative intention expressed through the choice of particular surface forms.

The passage cited above would be an early one in the course we have in mind and so contains no instance of the use of *this* to refer to a superordinate notion. It is better to lead up to the 'superordinate' use of *this* by getting the student to recognize first the simpler operations of anaphora. One way of doing this (where *this* = 'the ability to recognize the simpler operations of anaphora'!) is by drawing the student's attention directly to features of anaphora in the passage by means of an exercise of the following kind:

Exercise A: Pronoun Reference

1. In sentence 2, *It* refers to:
   a) Weight
   b) Space
   c) Matter

2. In sentence 5, *one* refers to:
   a) A substance
   b) A substance in the solid state
   c) A liquid substance
3. In sentence 7, *this* refers to:
   a) A solid substance
   b) Water
   c) Ice

Another difficulty which learners have in understanding discourse is in recognizing when different expressions have equivalent contextual value. Learners may have their attention drawn to the way different forms function as expressions in a particular passage by means of an exercise of the following kind:

Exercise B: Rephrasing

Replace the expressions in italics in the following sentences with expressions from the text which have the same meaning.

1. *A substance in the solid state* may be changed into *a liquid substance*.
2. *Gases* may be changed into *liquids* and *liquids* may be changed into *solids*.
3. A solid may be *changed into the liquid state*.
4. A liquid may be *changed* into a gas.

So far we have been principally concerned with getting the learner to recognize the communicative value of expressions which correspond with sentence constituents. We may now introduce exercises which focus on the way sentences themselves function as communicative acts within the discourse. Our interest now is in the illocutionary force of the sentences which are used. (See Austin, 1962; Searle, 1969.) We want to get the learner to see that understanding a passage of English involves the recognition of what illocutionary acts are performed in it. One way of doing this is to ask him to insert expressions into the sentences of the passage which make explicit what their illocutionary function is. Thus in a sentence which is being used as an illustrative statement, *for example* can be inserted; in one which serves as a classification, one can insert the performative verb *classify*, and so on. An exercise of this kind based on the passage given might be as follows:

Exercise C: Relationships between Statements

Place the following expressions in the sentences indicated. Replace and re-order the words in the sentence where necessary:

a) can be defined as (1)
b) for example (4)
c) thus (5)
d) also (6)
e) thus (6)
f) for example (7)
g) then (7)
h) conversely (8)

The three types of exercise which have been proposed are graded in the sense that they are designed to make increasing demands on the learner's own writing ability. Exercise A, like the comprehension check questions, involves no writing at all. Exercise B is a simple copying exercise, the purpose of which is to reinforce the reader's perception of certain discourse functions. Exercise C requires the reader to use his knowledge of the language productively: he has to insert the given expressions in the correct places and to make structural alterations where necessary in the sentences concerned. This grading is intended to effect a gradual transfer from receptive awareness to productive ability.

We may now continue to provide writing practice based on the reading passage. But we wish to do this not as a meaningless manipulation of sentence patterns, but as a use of English in the performance of different communicative acts relevant to the learner's special subject of study. We want to preserve the rhetorical orientation we have adopted, and keep the learner's attention focused on language in use. In Exercise C our purpose was to get the learner to make acts like defining and illustrating explicit. Now we want to get him to perform such acts himself. This might be brought about by an exercise of the following kind, which combines control with the sort of scope for mental activity which might be expected to appeal to the kind of learner we are concerned with, and which brings the language being learnt into close association with the subject for which it serves as medium. The exercise is based on the continuation of the reading passage quoted above, which provides the information necessary to complete the diagram.

Exercise D: Statements based on Diagrams

1. Write out a complete version of the following diagram by filling in the spaces.

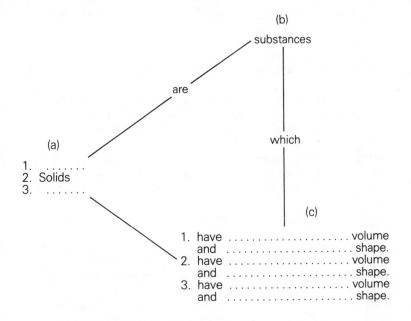

2. Use the completed diagram to:

(i) Write definitions, by using boxes (a), (b) and (c)
Example:
Solids are substances which have a definite volume and a definite shape.

(ii) Write generalizations, by using boxes (a) and (c)
Example:
Solids have a definite volume and a definite shape.

Exercise D reflects the importance we attach to the presentation of language as an essential aspect of the scientific subject which the learner is studying. The purpose of the approach we are illustrating here is to get the learner to recognize how the language and 'subject matter', commonly considered in isolation, are interrelated in acts of communication. We may promote this purpose further by following up Exercise D with exercises which present a problem requiring reference to knowledge of both language and of 'subject matter' for its solution. One might, for example, get the learner to produce definitions and generalizations relating to another content area by asking him first to reduce the essential information to tabular form. Again, one could get him to draw a simple diagram of a machine, or a flow-chart of a process as a preliminary to providing a verbal description. Given any scientific or technical field, it is not difficult to think of relevant problems which would serve to integrate the student's knowledge of language and 'subject matter', and which would be a logical extension of exercises based on reading passages.

So far our business has been to draw the attention of the learner to the way English is used to communicate. We have been concerned with rhetorical function, although this has naturally involved consideration of the formal operation of language. We now shift our emphasis from discourse to text, and focus on the formal properties of language in use. We assume, of course, that the previous exercises will have provided the learners with a meaningful communicative framework to which they will relate their learning of the way language forms combine in the composition of texts.

The use of language in text

In considering the formal properties of language in use, we must first decide on what attitude to adopt to the teaching of grammar. What factors do we have to take into consideration in designing a model of grammar for advanced or remedial language teaching? We may assume, firstly, that a pedagogic grammar for advanced learners must provide the student with fresh and stimulating material. As was suggested earlier in this paper, there is no point in presenting a remedial English class at the University level with a speeded-up version of the secondary school syllabus, for the class will rapidly become bored and resentful even if they show evidence of not having fully mastered the material. The rejection by students of the rapid repeat technique of remedial teaching is a familiar experience in higher education, and should occasion no surprise. Not only do advanced learners have a natural reluctance to cover familiar ground for the second or third time, they have, in fact, reached a stage in their studies when they may no longer be able to benefit from the oral, inductive type of teaching employed at a more elementary level. As was pointed out earlier, it is this fact that prompts us to propose an approach which gives recognition to the real needs of advanced students. It must be stressed that the task for the advanced learner is not simply to experience more language material, but to develop a complex set of organizational skills over and above those which he needed to cope with the elementary syllabus, and to learn to put these to use in serving a variety of communicative purposes. One difference between elementary and advanced courses lies in the fact that students at an advanced level have had a good deal of instruction in grammar and, as was suggested earlier, are likely to possess considerable dormant competence in English. It follows that one of the principal aims of advanced language teaching should be to activate this competence, and to extend it, by leading the student to relate his previously-acquired linguistic knowledge to meaningful realizations of the language system in passages of immediate relevance to his professional interests or specialized field of studies.

A second consideration is that the information in a pedagogic grammar must be relevant to a learner's needs. In order to ensure this we must insist on a clear distinction between linguistic and pedagogic grammars. A linguistic grammar is concerned with a specification of the formal properties of a language, while the purpose of a pedagogic grammar is to help a learner acquire a practical mastery of a language. There is no reason for supposing that the two types of statement will bear any overt resemblance to one another. It is particularly important that this principle should be clearly stated at a time when many teachers and textbook writers are turning to linguistics as a source of ideas about how to handle language in the classroom. In general, we expect that knowledge of linguistic grammars will provide teachers with pedagogically useful insights into language structure, but we do not expect that the content of a linguistic grammar will be reflected in any direct or systematic way in a pedagogic grammar based on it. A further principle is that pedagogic grammars are typically eclectic. By this we mean that the applied linguist must pick and choose among formal statements in the light of his experience as a teacher, and decide what are pedagogically the most appropriate ways of arranging the information that he derives from linguistic grammars. Thus, we expect that the insights incorporated in a pedagogic grammar will be drawn from a number of linguistic models, and that the teaching materials will be judged solely in terms of whether or not they promote quick and efficient learning in the student.

As already stated, we assume that the students have some knowledge of how the language works, which derives from pedagogic grammar. We also assume that this knowledge will be consolidated as the students experience language used in meaningful contexts. For these reasons we have not attempted to provide a detailed review of English grammar. Instead, the grammar exercises are designed to focus on points which are particularly important in scientific writing, especially those which may represent continuing 'trouble spots' for many students. Wherever possible we aim to avoid the more mechanical types of substitution drill. The whole approach we adopt in this paper is based on the assumption that the students will be people whose minds are directed towards rational thought and problem-solving, and the grammar exercises are designed to take this fact into account. Wherever possible, we have here, as elsewhere, used exercises which we hope will require the same kind of thinking that science students would naturally be engaged in as part of their specialist studies. The following examples show how we have attempted to provide grammar practice in a meaningful way, and without losing sight of the natural communicative use of language.

Exercise E: Definitions in scientific discourse

Definitions in scientific discourse often take the following forms:

1. A $\begin{Bmatrix} \text{is/are} \\ \text{may be defined as} \end{Bmatrix}$ B which C

E.g.   A thermometer *is* an instrument *which* is used for measuring temperatures.
A thermometer *may be defined as* an instrument *which* is used for measuring temperatures.

2. B which C $\begin{Bmatrix} \text{is/are called} \\ \text{is/are known as} \end{Bmatrix}$ A

E.g.   An instrument *which* is used for measuring temperatures *is called* a thermometer.
An instrument *which* is used for measuring temperatures *is known as* a thermometer.

Expand the following into full definitions. Write each sentence twice, using any of the patterns illustrated above.

1. metamorphosis/ the physical transformation/ is undergone by various animals during development after the embryonic state.
2. metals/ the class of chemical elements/ are characterized by ductility, malleability, lustre and conductivity.

Exercise F. Formation of the impersonal passive

Write down the passive version of all the active sentences. Then combine the passive sentences, following the clues provided in the box.

Active: we may show the expansion of a gas
Passive: the expansion of a gas – – – – – – – – – – – – – –
Active: we heat the gas
Passive: the gas – – – – – – – – –
Active: we demonstrate an apparatus in Figure 41
Passive: an apparatus – – – – – – – – – in Figure 41

> The expansion of a gas when it – – – – – – – – may – – – – –
> – – – – – – by the apparatus – – – – – in Figure 41

Exercise G: Time expressions

Rewrite the sentences, selecting one of the time expressions and putting it at the beginning of the sentence. The time expression you select should be the one which corresponds most closely to the meaning of the words in italics, which should be omitted.

1. the water vapour condenses to water *as a result* it is able to fall downwards as rain or snow (when, before).
2. the aluminium is in the measuring cylinder *during this time* we may measure the volume of water displaced (as soon as, while).
3. *first* the water is forced out of the ballast tanks by compressed air *before this* the submarine is not able to rise to the surface (until, when).

Compare the following sentences with your answer in Part (i). If the sentences have approximately the same meaning, put a tick in the box; if not, put a cross.

1. Water vapour can fall as rain or snow but the vapour must condense to water first. ☐
2. A volume of water is displaced and as a result we can put the aluminium in the measuring cylinder. ☐
3. A submarine is not able to rise to the surface while the ballast tanks are full of water. ☐

It may seem to some that exercises based on a surface structure approach constitute a return to outmoded principles. There is an important issue at stake here, which we touched on earlier in our discussion of the distinction between linguistics and pedagogic grammars. A number of recent publications have shown a tendency to assume that the latest developments in linguistic theory should at all costs be reflected in language teaching materials. But it is not always the latest linguistic model which provides the most satisfactory basis for the preparation of teaching materials. For example, the relevant treatment of trans-formations for our purpose appears to be that of Zellig Harris rather than Chomsky. For Harris, transformational analysis is a logical extension of constituent analysis, and is based on the same criteria of form and distribution. Transformations are set up formally as a relation between text-sentences, and not in the form of instructions for gener-ating sentences, as in Chomsky's theory. A pedagogically useful con-sequence is that we can distinguish well-established transformations from those which are barely acceptable or used only in particular linguistic environments. Moreover, Harris's transformational rules are relevant to the notion of communicative competence, and therefore seem to be a more suitable basis for teaching material than Chomsky's transformations, which operate without reference to context.

Methods of teaching the writing skill

In the classroom it is not always easy to devise situations which call for genuine written communications, so that students can express themselves in a natural way in response to a real need. One method of making writing meaningful is to get the learner to 'talk to himself' on paper. This approach, generally known as 'creative writing', has been widely advocated in L1 teaching situations as a substitute for formal essays which fail because the task is boring and artificial. Creative writing clearly has a general educational value, but its usefulness is limited in that it tends to produce an intensely personal style, in fact a type of literature, which has little or no social function. Advocates of this approach believe that the skill developed in creative writing carries over into institutional writing without the need for further instruction, but this claim is not substantiated by the evidence so far available. On the face of it, it seems unlikely that a student who has been encouraged to express himself through the medium of prose poems will be able to turn his hand readily to the production of business correspondence or an academic treatise, without some explicit instruction in the conventions which govern these particular styles of writing. A second limitation is that the creative writing approach is restricted to an L1 learning situation. If an L2 student wishes to express himself 'creatively' he will normally turn to his mother tongue. He needs the target language in order to read textbooks, write summaries and reports, and participate in routine professional or social conversations, all of which are examples of the institutional use of language, which require a mastery of the appropriate conventions.

A variation of the creative writing approach is found in many American textbooks designed for use with freshman composition classes. These books devote much space to the discussion of such traditional principles of rhetoric as coherence, unity and emphasis, the classical structure of the oration and an analysis of the various types of discourse (exposition, argument, description, narration, etc.). The authors of some composition handbooks include the rudiments of formal logic, in the belief that patterns of proof can be used as an aid in the organization of paragraphs and in checking for weak points in an argument once it has been written. Such books are based on the assumption that it helps a learner if he understands the potentialities of written language and is familiar with some of the rhetorical devices that fluent writers habitually use. However, it is doubtful whether an *analysis* of other people's writing can in itself produce fluent writers. What the learner needs, especially in an L2 situation, is a form of exercise which will help him to achieve a *synthesis* of many disparate grammatical and lexical elements in the form of a coherent composition of his own. One problem in achieving this type of synthesis in the classroom is to find the right combination of freedom and control: enough control to ensure that the student's composition does not degenerate into a mass of mistakes, and enough freedom for the student to exercise his own judgement and thereby to learn something instead of merely copying. Various attempts have been made to provide guided practice developing into free composition. The materials available fall into four main categories, and we will examine a representative example from each category.

Substitution in frames. Example: K. W. Moody (1966). Moody's frames are akin to the familiar substitution table in which interchangeable elements are grouped in columns, but whereas most substitution tables represent the structure of a single sentence, in this case the frames are arranged in a series, so that a succession of choice from left to right will result in a paragraph, letter or short composition. The selection of alternatives is not entirely automatic; the structural patterns are fixed but the choice of lexical items is determined by the student. When he begins this series of exercises the student does not have to worry about the choice of grammatical patterns or the way in which sentences interrelate, but he has to think about the meaning of what he is writing and he must ensure that his lexical choices produce a composition that makes sense. The exercises are arranged in four stages to give the student progressively more freedom of choice. At the first stage the sets of alternatives in the frames are written out in full, and the student's problem is mainly one of lexical collocation. Each exercise at Stage 1 is matched with a Stage 2 exercise in which the frame is repeated but with a number of blanks. The purpose of this is to give the learner some opportunity of using his own choice of words, once he has achieved control over the structural patterns of the paragraph. At Stage 3 the student has even more freedom of choice, since only a few words are retained from the original frame. At Stage 4 he is asked to write a paragraph of his own, along the lines suggested by the earlier exercises, but without the frame to guide him. At the final stage, therefore, the student has a free choice of words and structures, but he has been led into free composition gradually and he should retain a clear idea of the paragraph outline from earlier stages of the practice.

Sample composition with selective structure practice. Example: T. C. Jupp and John Milne (1968). As in the case of Moody, the aim is to provide students who are learning composition writing with detailed guidance in language and subject matter, but at the same time to leave them with the opportunity for personal expression. With this second approach, however, the element of control is more relaxed and the student is encouraged to make his own selection of words and structures throughout the practice. The Jupp and Milne sequence is arranged in four stages. Stage 1 consists of a statement of the subject of the composition, e.g.: 'Write about a very important examination, interview or meeting which you once went to. Carefully describe your feelings and thoughts, and say what happened.' Stage 2 consists of oral and written structure practice, the aim of which is to make students proficient in the use of those structures which he is likely to need in order to write about the set topic. A few new patterns are introduced in each unit, but most of the structure practice consists of a revision of patterns which have been previously learned. It is a feature of this material that the structures practised are grouped according to topic rather than being determined by an abstract linguistic scheme of grading. At Stage 3, having been well primed by class discussion and by structure drills, the student reads a sample composition in which the set topic is handled in a context familiar to the authors (in this case, an account of an entrance examination at Cambridge). The structures that the students have been practising are exemplified in the sample composition. Finally, at Stage 4, the student is instructed to (a) write down some sentences from the structure practice; (b) carefully re-read the sample composition, noting examples of relevant structures; (c) write a composition of his own, referring if necessary to the sample composition and making sure that he uses examples of the practised structures; (d) give the finished composition to a friend to read.

Modification of model paragraphs. Example: Dykstra, Port and Port (1966). These materials consist of a collection of 42 passages all concerned with the adventures of Ananse the spider, a character in West African folklore. Using these passages as a basis, the student is required to perform a series of operations, including structural modification and lexical insertion, in a series of graduated steps, beginning with relatively mechanical operations and proceeding as quickly as possible to the most advanced steps, which represent free creative composition. The materials are arranged in such a way that they represent a roughly programmed course which can be useful to students who have attained different levels of control over writing in English. The following instructions, all quoted from the text, show the types of activity involved. The numbers indicate grading in difficulty on a scale 1–58. The operations listed can be performed on any of 42 passages, and usually more than one operation is performed on a single passage.

1. Copy the passage.
4. Rewrite the entire passage changing *Ananse* to *the spiders*. Change the pronouns where necessary.
14. Rewrite the entire passage in the active voice.
36. Rewrite the entire passage adding adjective clauses beginning with *who*, *which* or *that* after the following words: *young*, *man*, *mother*, *village*, etc.
58. Create a folktale of your own about Ananse the spider. Use between 100 and 150 words in your tale.

The three types of guided composition exercise summarized above are all based on the notion of parallel texts. This approach is successful so long as the student's writing is restricted to short letters, folktales, personal histories or other stereotyped formulas. However, the parallel text approach tends to break down if the student has to handle scientific subjects, since in this type of writing the arguments are highly specific and each text must be regarded as unique. The guided composition method discussed below involves the intensive study of a single text, and is suitable for use in the context of scientific writing where parallel texts are difficult to devise.

Guided paragraph building. The exercise is done in four stages. At the first stage the student examines various groups of words and combines each group into a sentence by following the clues provided. Some sentences are easy to write, some are more difficult; this reflects the situation in actual writing, where simple sentences alternate with more complex structures according to the nature of the message the writer wishes to convey. At the second stage the student creates a coherent paragraph by rewriting the sentences in a logical order, adding various 'transitional' features where necessary. Thirdly, the student checks his work against a version of the paragraph incorporated into a free reading passage elsewhere in the book. The paragraph writing is designed to allow some scope for the student to exercise his own judgement, so there is no reason why the student's version should be identical to the one in the book. If the paragraphs differ, the student should try to evaluate the relative merits of the two versions. At the fourth stage the student writes the paragraph again in a free style of his own devising, based on a set of notes which are similar to the rough jottings made by an author when he is sketching out a plan for a paragraph. Thus the student is led by stages to the point where he should be able to write a paragraph of his own, in a way which seeks to imitate some of the processes of real-life composition.

The following paragraph writing exercise illustrates this procedure.

A. Join each of the groups of words below into one sentence, using the additional material in the box. Words in italics should be omitted. Number your sentences and begin each one with a capital letter.

1. an acid will *affect* litmus
   an acid will react with washing soda
   it will give off carbon dioxide

turn/red/and/it/,/giving

2. the metal disappears
   hydrogen is liberated

> and

3. one class of bases *is* called alkalis
   they will dissolve in water
   they will form solutions
   they will *affect* red litmus

> special/,/,/and/which/turn/blue

4. an acid is a compound
   it will attack some metals
   it will liberate hydrogen
   magnesium is dissolved in it

> containing hydrogen/which/and/when

5. alkalis form solutions
   they feel soapy
   they will dissolve substances
   they are used in various cleaning processes

> which/and which/oily and greasy/,/and for this reason/
> frequently

6. acids *burn* substances
   wood paper cloth human skin

> have a burning effect on/like/,/,/and

B. Create a coherent paragraph by rewriting the eleven sentences in a logical order.[2] Before you write the paragraph, add the following material to the sentences.

> 2. in the latter case
> 6. a further characteristic of acids is that they

C. When you have written your paragraph, re-read it and make sure that the sentences are presented in a logical order. Give the paragraph a suitable title. Check with the version given in the back of the book and correct if necessary. (It is possible to write this paragraph in more than one way.)

D. Read through the paragraph again. Make sure you know all the words, using a dictionary if necessary. Without referring to your

previous work rewrite the paragraph using the following clues:
  compounds—divided—acids—bases—salts
  acid—compound of hydrogen—attack metals—liberate hydrogen
  —magnesium dissolved
  acid—litmus red—washing soda—carbon dioxide
  burn substances—wood, paper, etc.
  base—oxides, hydroxides—neutralize acids—salt-like substances
  alkalis—solutions—soapy—dissolve oil—grease—cleaning
  salt—product, acid neutralized—metal dissolved
  metal disappears—hydrogen liberated
  salt—substance—metal takes place of hydrogen

Conclusion

In this paper we have suggested an approach to the teaching of English which recognizes that the acquisition of receptive and productive knowledge of a language must involve the learning of rules of use as well as rules of grammar. Many students who enter higher education have had experience only of the latter and are consequently unable to deal with English when it is used in the normal process of communication. What we have attempted to do is to show how rules of use might be taught, both those which have to do with the communicative properties of discourse and those which have to do with the formal properties of texts. We make no claim that the kind of exercises which we have illustrated here are in any sense definitive: other, and no doubt more effective, exercises might be devised. We believe, however, that such exercises should take into account the needs of the students and the nature of the abilities which must be developed to meet them, and be related therefore to the kind of theoretical considerations within the context of which we have placed the exercises presented here. There are signs that linguists are now turning their attention to the communicative properties of language and the functioning of language in social contexts. We have said that it is a mistake for the language teacher to assume that he must automatically adjust his pedagogy to conform to the latest linguistic fashion, but in this case it is necessary for the language teacher to emulate the linguist by considering communicative functions as well as, and in relation to, linguistic forms. Such a shift in focus is warranted not by the practice of the linguist but by the essential needs of the language learner.

Notes

Published in International Review of Applied Linguistics, 12, 1: 1–21, 1974.

1. Such a course has, in fact, been designed, and appears under the title *English in Physical Science*. This is the first of a series entitled 'English in Focus', published by Oxford University Press. The examples of teaching material which appear in this paper are from a draft version of *English in Physical Science*. [See also p. 225 in this volume.]
2. Five groups of words have been omitted.

Communicative language testing: revolution or evolution?
Keith Morrow

Introduction

Wilkins (1976) concludes with the observation that, 'we do not know how to establish the communicative proficiency of the learner' (p. 82) and expresses the hope that, 'while some people are experimenting with the notional syllabus as such, others should be attempting to develop the new testing techniques that should, ideally, accompany it' (*loc. cit.*). In the two years that have passed since the publication of this book, the author's hope on the one hand has been increasingly realized, and if his observation on the other is still valid, there are grounds for believing that it will not be so for much longer.

At the time of writing, it is probably true to say that there exists a considerable imbalance between the resources available to language teachers (at least in E.F.L.) in terms of teaching materials, and those available in terms of testing and evaluation instruments. The former have not been slow to incorporate insights into syllabus design, and increasingly methodology, deriving from a view of language as communication; the latter still reflect, on the whole, ideas about language and how it should be tested which fail to take account of these recent developments in any systematic way.[1]

This situation does seem to be changing, however. A number of institutions and organizations have set up working parties to assess the feasibility of tests based on communicative criteria, and in some cases these have moved on to the design stage.[2] It therefore seems reasonable to expect that over the next five years new tests and examinations will become available which will aim to do precisely the job which Wilkins so recently held up as a challenge, i.e. to measure communicative proficiency.

This paper, then, will be concerned with the implications for test design and construction of the desire to measure communicative proficiency, and with the extent to which earlier testing procedures need to be reviewed and reconsidered in the light of this objective. But it is a polemical paper. The assumption which underlies it is that the measurement of communicative proficiency is a job worth doing, and the task is ultimately a feasible one.

The Vale of Tears

A wide range of language tests and examinations are currently in use, but most belong to a few key types. Spolsky (1975) identifies three stages in the recent history of language testing: the pre-scientific, the psychometric-structuralist, and the psycholinguistic-sociolinguistic. We might characterize these in turn as the Garden of Eden, the Vale of Tears and the Promised Land, and different tests (indeed different parts of the same test) can usually be seen to relate to one or other of these stages. The historical perspective offered by Spolsky is extremely relevant to the concerns of this paper. While critiques of the 'pre-scientific' approach to testing are already familiar (Valette, 1967), it seems useful to take some time here to clarify the extent to which current developments relate to what has more immediately gone before through a critical look at some of the characteristics of psychometric-structuralist testing. The point of departure for this is Lado (1961).

Atomistic

A key feature of Lado's approach is the breaking down of the complexities of language into isolated segments. This influences both what is to be tested and how this testing should be carried out.

What is to be tested is revealed by a structural contrastive analysis between the target language and the learner's mother tongue. Structural here is not limited to grammatical structure—though this is of course important. Contrastive analyses can be carried out of all the levels of structure (syntactic down to phonological) which the language theory encompasses, and test items can be constructed on the basis of them.

The same approach is adopted to the question of how to test. Discrete items are constructed, each of which ideally reveals the candidate's ability to handle one level of the language in terms of one of the four skills. It soon became recognized that it was in fact extremely difficult to construct 'pure' test items which were other than exceedingly trivial in nature, and thus many tests of this sort contain items which operate on more than one level of structure.

The clear advantage of this form of test construction is that it yields data which are easily quantifiable. But the problem is equally clearly that its measurement of language proficiency depends crucially upon the assumption that such proficiency is neatly quantifiable in this way. Indeed the general problem with Lado's approach, which attaches itself very firmly to certain very definite views about the nature of language, is that it crumbles like a house of cards as soon as the linguistic foundation on which it is constructed is attacked. This is not the place to develop a generalized linguistic attack, but one particular assumption is worth picking up, since it is so central to the issue under discussion.

An atomistic approach to test design depends utterly on the assumption that knowledge of the elements of a language is equivalent to knowledge of the language. Even if one adopts for the moment a purely grammatical view of what it is to know a language (cf. Chomsky's definition in terms of the ability to formulate all and only the grammatical sentences in a language), then it seems fairly clear that a vital stage is missing from an atomistic analysis, viz. the ability to synthesize. Knowledge of the elements of a language in fact counts for nothing unless the user is able to combine them in new and appropriate ways to meet the linguistic demands of the situation in which he wishes to use the language. Driving a car is a skill of a quite different order from that of performing in isolation the various movements of throttle, brake, clutch, gears and steering wheel.

Quantity v. Quality

In the previous section it was the linguistic basis of tests such as Lado's which was questioned. Let us now turn to the psychological implications. Following the behaviourist view of learning through habit formation, Lado's tests pose questions to elicit responses which show whether or not correct habits have been established. Correct responses are rewarded and negative ones punished in some way. Passing a test involves making a specified proportion of correct responses. Clearly language learning is viewed as a process of accretion.

An alternative view of the psychology of language learning would hold, however, that the answers to tests can, and should, be considered as more than simply right or wrong. In this view learners possess 'transitional competence' (Corder, 1975) which enables them to produce and use an 'interlanguage' (Selinker, 1972). Like the competence of a native speaker, this is an essentially dynamic concept and the role of the test is to show how far it has moved towards an approximation of a native speaker's system. Tests will thus be concerned with making the learner produce samples of his own 'interlanguage', based on his own norms of language production so that conclusions can be drawn from it. Tests of receptive skills will similarly be concerned with revealing the extent to which the candidate's processing abilities match those of a native speaker.

The clear implication of this is that the candidate's responses need to be assessed not quantitatively, but qualitatively. Tests should be designed to reveal not simply the number of items which are answered

correctly, but to reveal the quality of the candidate's language performance. It is not safe to assume that a given score on the former necessarily
allows conclusions to be drawn about the latter.

Reliability

One of the most significant features of psychometric tests as opposed
to those of 'pre-scientific' days is the development of the twin concepts
of reliability and validity.

The basis of the reliability claimed by Lado is objectivity. The
rather obvious point has, however, not escaped observers (Pilliner, 1968;
Robinson, 1973) that Lado's tests are objective only in terms of actual
assessment. In terms of the evaluation of the numerical score yielded,
and perhaps more importantly, in terms of the construction of the
test itself, subjective factors play a large part.

It has been equally noted by observers that an insistence on testing
procedures which can be objectively assessed has a number of implications for the data yielded. Robinson (*op. cit.*) identifies three areas of
difference between testing procedures designed to yield data which can
be objectively assessed and those which are open to subjective assessment.

1. The amount of language produced by the student. In an objective
   test, students may actually produce no language at all. Their role
   may be limited to selecting alternatives rather than producing
   language.
2. Thus the type of ability which is being tested is crucially different.
   In a subjective test the candidate's ability to produce language is
   a crucial factor; in an objective test the ability to recognize
   appropriate forms is sufficient.
3. The norms of language use are established on different grounds.
   In an objective test the candidate must base his responses upon
   the language of the examiner; in a subjective test, the norms
   may be his own, deriving from his own use of the language.
   Thus an objective test can reveal only differences and similarities
   between the language norms of the examiner and candidate; it
   can tell us nothing of the norms which the candidate himself
   would apply in a use situation.

The above factors lead to what Davies (1978) has called the reliability–
validity 'tension'. Attempts to increase the reliability of tests have led
test designers to take an over-restrictive view of what it is that they are
testing.

Validity

The idea that language test designers should concern themselves with
validity—in other words that they should ask themselves whether they

are actually testing what they think they are testing, and whether what they think they are testing is what they ought to be testing—is clearly an attractive one. But unfortunately, because of the 'tension' referred to above, designers working within the tradition we are discussing seem to have been content with answers to these questions which are less than totally convincing.

Five types of validity which a language test may claim are traditionally identified (cf. Davies, 1968).

Face	the test looks like a good one.
Content	the test accurately reflects the syllabus on which it is based.
Predictive	the test accurately predicts performance in some subsequent situation.
Concurrent	the test gives similar results to existing tests which have already been validated.
Construct	the test reflects accurately the principles of a valid theory of foreign language learning.

Statistical techniques for assessing validity in these terms have been developed to a high, and often esoteric level of sophistication. But unfortunately, with two exceptions (face, and possibly predictive) the types of validity outlined above are all ultimately circular. Starting from a certain set of assumptions about the nature of language and language learning will lead to language tests which are perfectly valid in terms of these assumptions, but whose value must inevitably be called into question if the basic assumptions themselves are challenged. Thus a test which perfectly satisfies criteria of content, construct or concurrent validity may nonetheless fail to show in any interesting way how well a candidate can perform in or use the target language. This may occur quite simply if the construct of the language learning theory, and the content of the syllabus are themselves not related to this aim, or if the test is validated against other language tests which do not concern themselves with this objective. There is clearly no such thing in testing as 'absolute' validity. Validity exists only in terms of specified criteria, and if the criteria turn out to be the wrong ones, then validity claimed in terms of them turns out to be spurious. *Caveat emptor.*

Comments

The criticisms, implicit and explicit, made in the preceding sections apply to a theory of testing which has hardly ever been realized in the extreme form in which Lado presented it. Certainly in the U.K. a mixture of pragmatism and conservatism has ensured that much of the institutionalized testing of foreign languages owes as much to the 1920's as to the 1960's. This does not mean though, that there is anything chimerical about the ideas put forward by Lado. Their influence has been recognized by writers on language testing ever since the first publication of his book. But it is as representation of theory that the ideas are most significant. In practice, as Davies (1978) remarks, there is very often a gap between what Lado himself does and what he says he does.

But this gap is often of detail rather than principle. Even if the totality of Lado's views have been more often honoured in the breach than in the observance, the influence of his work has been tremendous. Of the ideas examined above, very few have failed to find implicit acceptance in the majority of 'theory-based' tests developed over the last 15 years. The overriding importance of reliability (hence the ubiquitous multiple-choice), the acceptance of validity of a statistical rather than necessarily of a practical nature, the directly quantifiable modes of assessment—these are all ideas which have become common currency even among those who would reject many of the theories of language and language learning on which Lado based his approach.

Only in one area has a consistent alternative to Lado's views been argued, and that is the development of 'integrated' tests/test items[3] as opposed to Lado's arguments (at least in principle) in favour of 'pure' discrete items.[4] A clear statement of an 'integrated' position is made by Carroll (1968):

'. . . since the use of language in ordinary situations calls upon all these aspects [of language], we must further recognize that linguistic performance also involves the individual's capability of mobilizing his linguistic competences and performance abilities in an integrated way, i.e. in the understanding, speaking, reading or writing of connected discourse.' (p. 58).

This implies a view of language which runs directly counter to a key assumption which we have earlier examined in Lado's work. It denies the atomistic nature of language as a basis for language testing. To this extent, Carroll's contribution is extremely important, but even here it must be observed that in practical terms he was doing no more than providing a post-hoc rationalization. For the purely practical reasons alluded to earlier, very few 'pure' items had found their way into tests; in a sense, Carroll was merely legitimizing the existing situation.

Less casuistically, it must be observed that attempts to develop more revolutionary integrated tests (Oller, 1971, 1973) have left out of account a crucial element in the original formulation, viz. 'the use of language in ordinary situations'.

Both cloze and dictation are fundamentally tests of language competence. Both have their uses in determining the basic level of language proficiency of a given candidate. (More accurately, they enable the level of language proficiency to be assessed relative to that of other people who take exactly the same test under the same conditions.) Oller claims that both test basic language processing mechanisms (analysis by synthesis); both sample a wide range of structural and lexical items in a meaningful context. But neither gives any convincing proof of the candidate's ability to actually use the language, to translate the competence (or lack of it) which he is demonstrating into actual performance 'in ordinary situations', i.e. actually using the language to read, write, speak or listen in ways and contexts which correspond to real life.

Adopting this 'use' criterion might lead us to consider precisely why neither discrete point nor integrative tests of the type we have considered are able to meet it.

Let us look in a rather simple way at some of the features of language use which do not seem to be measured in conventional tests.

Interaction–Based: in the vast majority of cases, language in use is based on an interaction. Even cases such as letter writing, which may seem to be solitary activities, can be considered as weak forms of interaction in that they involve an addressee, whose expectations will be taken into account by the writer. These expectations will affect both the content of the message and the way in which it is expressed. A more characteristic form of interaction, however, is represented by face-to-face oral interaction which involves not only the modification of expression and content mentioned above but also an amalgam of receptive and productive skills. What is said *by* a speaker depends crucially on what is said *to* him.

Unpredictability: the apparently trivial observation that the development of an interaction is unpredictable is in fact extremely significant for the language user. The processing of unpredictable data in real time is a vital aspect of using language.

Context: any use of language will take place in a context, and the language forms which are appropriate will vary in accordance with this context. Thus a language user must be able to handle appropriacy in terms of:

context of situation	e.g. physical environment
	role/status of participants
	attitude/formality
linguistic context	e.g. textual cohesion

Purpose: a rather obvious feature of communication is that every utterance is made for a purpose. Thus a language user must be able to recognize why a certain remark has been addressed to him, and be able to encode appropriate utterances to achieve his own purposes.

Performance: What Chomsky (1965) described as 'competence', leaving out of account:

> 'such grammatically irrelevant conditions as memory limitations, distractions, shifts of attention and interest, and errors (random or characteristic)'

has been the basis of most language tests. Such conditions may or may not be 'grammatically irrelevant', but they certainly exist. To this extent the idealized language presented in listening tests fails to measure the effectiveness of the candidate's strategies for receptive performance. Similarly, the demand for context-free language production fails to measure the extent to which features of the candidate's performance may in fact hamper communication.

Authenticity: a very obvious feature of authentic language should be noted in this context, i.e. with rare exceptions it is not simplified to take account of the linguistic level of the addressee. Thus measuring the ability of the candidate to, e.g. read a simplified text tells us nothing about his actual communicative ability, since an important feature of such ability is precisely the capacity to come to terms with what is unknown.

Behaviour–Based: the sucess or failure of an interaction is judged by its participants on the basis of behavioural outcomes. Strictly speaking no other criteria are relevant. This is an extreme view of the primacy of content over form in language and would probably be criticized by language teachers. Nevertheless, more emphasis needs to be placed in a communicative context on the notion of behaviour. A test of communication must take as its starting point the measurement of what the candidate can actually achieve through language. None of the tests we have considered have set themselves this task.

These then are some of the characteristics of language in use as communication which existing tests fail to measure or to take account of in a systematic way. Let us now turn to an examination of some of the implications of building them into the design specification for language tests.

The Promised Land

We can expect a test of communicative ability to have at least the following characteristics:

1. It will be criterion-referenced against the operational performance of a set of authentic language tasks. In other words it will set out to show whether or not (or how well) the candidate can perform a set of specified activities.
2. It will be crucially concerned to establish its own validity as a measure of those operations it claims to measure. Thus content,

construct and predictive validity will be important, but concurrent validity with existing tests will not be necessarily significant.

3. It will rely on modes of assessment which are not directly quantitative, but which are instead qualitative. It may be possible or necessary to convert these into numerical scores, but the process is an indirect one and recognized as such.

4. Reliability, while clearly important, will be subordinate to face validity. Spurious objectivity will no longer be a prime consideration, although it is recognized that in certain situations test formats which can be assessed mechanically will be advantageous. The limitations of such formats will be clearly spelt out, however.

Designing a test with these characteristics raises a number of interesting issues.

Performance Tests

Asking the question, 'What can this candidate do?' clearly implies a performance-based test. The idea that performance (rather than competence) is a legitimate area of concern for tests is actually quite a novel one and poses a number of problems, chiefly in terms of extrapolation and assessment. If one assesses a candidate's performance in terms of a particular task, what does one learn of his ability to perform other tasks? Unless ways of doing this in some effective way can be found, operational tests which are economical in terms of time are likely to run the risk of being trivial. Problems of assessment are equally fundamental. Performance is by its very nature an integrated phenomenon and any attempt to isolate and test discrete elements of it destroys the essential holism. Therefore a quantitative assessment procedure is necessarily impractical and some form of qualitative assessment must be found. This has obvious implications for reliability.

Given these problems, the question obviously arises as to whether communicative testing does necessarily involve performance tests. This seems to depend on what the purpose of the test is. If the purpose is proficiency testing, i.e. if one is asking how successful the candidate is likely to be as a user of the language in some general sense, then it seems to me incontrovertible that performance tests are necessary. The reasons for saying this should by now be clear, but at the risk of labouring the point let me re-state the principle that in language use the whole is bigger than the parts. No matter how sophisticated the analysis of the parts, no matter whether the parts are isolated in terms of structures, lexis or functions, it is implausible to derive hard data about actual language performance from tests of control of these parts alone. However, if the test is to be used for diagnostic purposes rather than proficiency assessment, a rather different set of considerations may apply. In a diagnostic situation it may become important not simply to know the degree of skill which a candidate can bring to the performance of a particular global task, but also to find out precisely which of the communicative skills and elements of the language he has mastered. To the extent that these can be revealed by discrete-point tests and that the deficiencies so revealed might form the input to a teaching programme, this might be information worth having. (The form that such tests might take is discussed in Morrow, 1977.) But one more point must be made. It might be argued that discrete-point tests of the type under discussion are useful as achievement tests, i.e. to indicate the degree of success in assimilating the content of a language learning programme which is itself based on a communicative (notional) syllabus. This seems to me misguided. As a pedagogic device a notional syllabus may specify the elements which are to be mastered for communicative purposes. But there is little value in assimilating these elements if they cannot be integrated into meaningful language performance. Therefore discrete-point tests are of little worth in this context.

The clear implication of the preceding paragraphs is that by and large it is performance tests which are of most value in a communicative context. The very real problems of extrapolation and assessment raised at the beginning of this section therefore have to be faced. To what extent do they oblige us to compromise our principle?

Let us deal first with extrapolation. A model for the performance of global communicative tasks may show for any task the enabling skills which have to be mobilized to complete it. Such a model is implicit in Munby (1978) and has been refined for testing purposes by B. J. Carroll (1978). An example of the way this might work is as follows:

Global Task

Search text for specific information

Enabling Skills

e.g. Distinguish main point from supporting details

Understand text relations through grammatical cohesion devices

Understand relations within sentences

Understand conceptual meaning

Deduce meaning of unfamiliar lexis

The status of these enabling skills vis-à-vis competence: performance is interesting. They may be identified by an analysis of performance in operational terms, and thus they are clearly, ultimately performance-based. But at the same time, their application extends far beyond any one particular instance of performance and in this creativity they reflect an aspect of what is generally understood by competence. In this way they offer a possible approach to the problem of extrapolation.

An analysis of the global tasks in terms of which the candidate is to be assessed (see later) will usually yield a fairly consistent set of enabling skills. Assessment of ability in using these skills therefore yields data which are relevant across a broad spectrum of global tasks, and are not limited to a single instance of performance.

While assessment based on these skills strictly speaking offends against the performance criterion which we have established, it should be noted that the skills are themselves operational in that they derive from an analysis of task performance. It is important that the difference between discrete-point tests of these enabling skills and discrete-point tests of structural aspects of the language system is appreciated.

Clearly, though, there exists in tests of enabling skills a fundamental weakness which is reminiscent of the problem raised in connection with earlier structural tests, namely the relationship between the whole and the parts. It is conceivable that a candidate may prove quite capable of handling individual enabling skills, and yet prove quite incapable of mobilizing them in a use situation or developing appropriate strategies to communicate effectively. Thus we seem to be forced back on tests of performance.

A working solution to this problem seems to be the development of tests which measure both overall performance in relation to a specified task, and the strategies and skills which have been used in achieving it. Written and spoken production can be assessed in terms of both these criteria. In task-based tests of listening and reading comprehension, however, it may be rather more difficult to see just how the global task has been completed. For example, in a test based on the global task exemplified above and which has the format of a number of true/false questions which the candidate has to answer by searching through a text, it is rather difficult to assess why a particular answer has been given and to deduce the skills and strategies employed. In such cases questions focusing on specific enabling skills do seem to be called for in order to provide the basis for convincing extrapolation.

If this question of the relationship between performance and the way it is achieved, and the testing strategy which it is legitimate to adopt in order to measure it seems to have been dealt with at inordinate length in the context of this paper, this reflects my feeling that here is the central distinction between what has gone before and what is now being proposed.

Admitting the necessity for tests of performance immediately raises the problem of assessment. How does one judge production in ways which are not hopelessly subjective, and how does one set receptive tasks appropriate for different levels of language proficiency?

The answer seems to lie in the concept of an operational scale of attainment, in which different levels of proficiency are defined in terms of a set of performance criteria. The most interesting work I know of in this area has been carried out by B. J. Carroll (Carroll, 1977). In this, Carroll distinguishes different levels of performance by matching the candidate's performance with operational specifications which take account of the following parameters:

Size ⎫ Complexity ⎭	of text which can be handled
Range	of, e.g. enabling skills, structures, functions which can be handled
Speed	at which language can be processed
Flexibility	shown in dealing with changes of, e.g. topic
Accuracy ⎫ Appropriacy ⎭	with which, e.g. enabling skills, structures, functions, can be handled
Independence	from reference sources and interlocutor
Repetition ⎫ Hesitation ⎭	in processing text

These specifications (despite the difficulties of phrasing them to take account of this in the summary given) are related to both receptive and productive performance.

It may well be that these specifications need to be refined in practice, but they seem to offer a way of assessing the quality of performance at different levels in a way which combines face validity with at least potential reliability. This question of reliability is of course central. As yet there are no published data on the degree of marker reliability which can be achieved using a scheme of this sort, but informal experience suggests that standardization meetings should enable fairly consistent scorings to be achieved. One important factor is obviously the form which these scores should take and the precise basis on which they should be arrived at.

It would be possible to use an analytic system whereby candidates' performance was marked in terms of each of the criteria in turn and these were then totalled to give a score. More attractive (to me at least) is a scheme whereby an overall impression mark is given with the marker instructed simply to base his impression on the specified criteria. Which of these will work better in practice remains to be seen, but the general point may be made that the first belongs to a quantitative, analytic tradition, the second to a qualitative, synthetic approach.

Content

We have so far considered some of the implications of a performance-based approach to testing, but have avoided the central issue: what performance? The general point to make in this connection is perhaps that there is no general answer.

One of the characteristic features of the communicative approach to language teaching is that it obliges us (or enables us) to make assumptions about the types of communication we will equip learners to handle. This applies equally to communicative testing.

This means that there is unlikely to be, in communicative terms, a single overall test of language proficiency. What will be offered are tests of proficiency (at different levels) in terms of specified communicative criteria. There are three important implications in this. First, the concept of pass:fail loses much of its force; every candidate can be assessed in terms of what he can do. Of course some will be able to do more than others, and it may be decided for administrative reasons that a certain level of proficiency is necessary for the awarding of a particular certificate. But because of the operational nature of the test, even low scorers can be shown what they have achieved. Secondly, language performance can be differentially assessed in different communicative areas. The idea of 'profile reporting' whereby a candidate is given different scores on, e.g. speaking, reading, writing and listening tests is not new, but it is particularly attractive in an operational context where scores can be related to specific communicative objectives.

The third implication is perhaps the most far-reaching. The importance of specifying the communicative criteria in terms of which assessment is being offered means that examining bodies will have to draw up, and probably publish, specifications of the types of operation they intend to test, the content areas to which they will relate and the criteria which will be adopted in assessment. Only if this is done will the test be able to claim to know what it is measuring, and only in this way will the test be able to show meaningfully what a candidate can do.

The design of a communicative test can thus be seen as involving the answers to the following questions:

1. What are the performance operations we wish to test? These are arrived at by considering what sorts of things people actually use language for in the areas in which we are interested.
2. At what level of proficiency will we expect the candidate to perform these operations?
3. What are the enabling skills involved in performing these operations? Do we wish to test control of these separately?
4. What sort of content areas are we going to specify? This will

affect both the types of operation and the types of 'text'[5] which are appropriate.

5. What sort of format will we adopt for the questions we set? It must be one which allows for both reliability and face validity as a test of language use.

Conclusion

The only conclusion which is necessary is to say that no conclusion is necessary. The rhetorical question posed by the title is merely rhetoric. After all it matters little if the developments I have tried to outline are actually evolutionary or revolutionary. But my own feeling is that those (e.g. Davies, 1978) who minimize the differences between different approaches to testing are adopting a viewpoint which is perhaps too comfortable; I think there is some blood to be spilt yet.

Notes

Specially written for this volume.

1. Exceptions to this are the two oral examinations promoted by the Association of Recognized English Language Schools: The ARELS Certificate and the ARELS Diploma, as well as the Joint Matriculation Board's Test in English for Overseas Students. But without disrespect to these, I would claim that they do not meet in a rigorous way some of the criteria established later in this paper.

2. My own work in this field has been sponsored by the Royal Society of Arts who have established a Working Party to re-design their range of examinations for foreign students. The English Language Testing Service of the British Council is developing communicative tests in the area of English for Academic Purposes, and a similar line is likely to be followed soon by the Associated Examining Board.

3. Note that the word 'integrated' is used in different ways by different writers. For some it is possible to conceive of individual items which test integration of various elements of the language; for others the very isolation of separate items means that full integration is not being achieved.

4. Earlier it was implied that Lado himself very rarely used items of a totally pure kind. See Davies (1978) for an interesting discussion of integrated v. discrete-point testing. Davies argues that they are at different ends of the same continuum rather than in different universes.

5. Use of the term 'text' may mislead the casual reader into imagining that only the written language is under discussion. In fact the question of text type is relevant to both the written and the spoken language in both receptive and productive terms. In the written mode it is clear that types of text may be specified in terms such as 'genre' and 'topic' as belonging to a certain set in relation to which performance may be assessed; specifying spoken texts may be less easy, since the categories that should be applied in an analysis of types of talking are less well established. I am at present working in a framework which applies certain macro-functions (e.g. ideational, directive, interpersonal) to a model of interaction which differentiates between speaker-centred and listener-centred speech. It is hoped that this will allow us to specify clearly enough the different types of talking candidates will be expected to deal with. More problematical is the establishing of different role-relationships in an examination context and the possibility of testing the candidates' production of anything but rather formal stranger:stranger language. Simulation techniques, while widely used for pedagogic purposes, may offend against the authenticity of performance criterion we have established, though it is possible that those who are familiar with them may be able to compensate for this.

SECTION FOUR

Methodological Perspectives

As will be apparent from earlier discussion, the major emphases in application have been on syllabus design and materials development. In this section a more explicit attempt has been made to link the general discussion to broader educational perspectives. One attractive methodological solution to problems of communication is to reduce the extent of teacher involvement in and direction of the process of language use in the classroom. The first two papers in this section have been influential in this movement. Newmark's paper poses a number of problems which have not been solved in the decade since its publication, but that interest in this line of approach has not subsided is indicated by the widespread enthusiasm with which Allwright's paper was received. Two further papers, specially written for this book, attempt to link classroom practice, syllabus design and educational principles in a discussion of current preoccupations of methodologists and teachers. There is some feeling in the teaching profession that theory has outrun practice, perhaps because its base has for several years been the discipline of applied linguistics rather than the practice of teaching. If the connection with the classroom is to be renewed, it will only come from a synthesis of linguistic principle with educational theory and practical intuition. Such a synthesis would seem to be the task of the next few years.

How not to interfere with language learning
Leonard Newmark

In the applied linguistics of the past twenty years much has been made of the notion of first-language interference with second-language learning. Our dominant conception of languages as structures and our growing sophistication in the complex analysis of these structures have made it increasingly attractive to linguists to consider the task of learning a new language as if it were essentially a task of fighting off an old set of structures in order to clear the way for a new set. The focal emphasis of language teaching by applied linguists has more and more been placed on structural drills based on the linguist's contrastive analysis of the structures of the learner's language and his target language: the weight given to teaching various things is determined not by their importance to the user of the language, but by their degree of difference from what the analyst takes to be corresponding features of the native language.

A different analysis of verbal behavior has been motivated in psychology by reinforcement theory; the application of this analysis has led, of course, to programmed instruction, step-by-step instruction based in practice on the identification of what are taken to be the components of the terminal verbal behavior. What could be more natural than the marriage of linguistics and psychology in the pro-grammed instruction of foreign languages, with linguistics providing the 'systematic specification of terminal behaviors' and psychology providing 'the techniques of the laboratory analysis and control' of those behaviors.[1]

If the task of learning to speak English were additive and linear, as present linguistic and psychological discussions suggest it is, it is difficult to see how anyone could learn English. If each phonological and syntactic rule, each complex of lexical features, each semantic value and stylistic nuance—in short, if each item which the linguist's analysis leads him to identify had to be acquired one at a time, pro-ceeding from simplest to most complex, and then each had to be connected to specified stimuli or stimulus sets, the child learner would be old before he could say a single appropriate thing and the adult learner would be dead. If each frame of a self-instructional program could teach only one item (or even two or three) at a time, programmed language instruction would never enable the students to use the language significantly. The item-by-item contrastive drills proposed by most modern applied linguists and the requirement by programmers that the behaviors to be taught must be specified seem to rest on this essentially hopeless notion of the language learning process.

When linguists and programmers talk about planning their textbooks, they approach the problem as if they had to decide what structural features each lesson should be trying to teach. The whole program will teach the sum of its parts: the student will know this structure and that one and another and another. . . . If the question is put to him directly, the linguist will undoubtedly admit that the sum of the structures he can describe is not equal to the capability a person needs in order to use the language, but the question is rarely put to him directly. If it is, he may evade the uncomfortable answer by appealing to the intelligence of the user to apply the structures he knows to an endless variety of situations. But the evasion fails, I think, against the inescapable fact that a person, even an intelligent one, who knows perfectly the structures that the linguist teaches, cannot know that the way to get his cigarette lit by a stranger when he has no matches is to walk up to him and say one of the utterances. 'Do you have a light?' or 'Got a match?' (Not one of the equally well-formed questions, 'Do you have fire?' or 'Do you have illumination?' or 'Are you a match's owner?'.)

In natural foreign language learning—the kind used, for example, by children to become native speakers in a foreign country within a length of time that amazes their parents—acquisition cannot be simply additive; complex bits of language are learned a whole chunk at a time. Perhaps by some process of stimulus sampling[2] the parts of the chunks are compared and become available for use in new chunks. The possible number of 'things known' in the language exponentiates as the number of chunks increases additively, since every complex chunk makes available a further analysis of old chunks into new elements, each still attached to the original context upon which its appropriateness depends.

It is not that linguists and psychologists are unaware of the possibility of learning language in complex chunks or of the importance of learning items in contexts. Indeed it would be difficult to find a serious discussion of new language teaching methods that did not claim to reform old language teaching methods in part through the use of 'natural' contexts. It is rather that consideration of the details supplied by linguistic and psychological analysis has taken attention away from the exponential power available in learning in natural chunks. In present psychologically oriented programs the requirement that one specify the individual behaviors to be reinforced leads (apparently inevitably) to an artificial isolation of parts from wholes; in structurally oriented textbooks and courses, contrastive analysis leads to structural drills designed to teach a set of specific 'habits' for the well-formation of utterances, abstracted from normal social context.

Our very knowledge of the fine structure of language constitutes a threat to our ability to maintain perspective in teaching languages. Inspection of language textbooks designed by linguists reveals an increasing emphasis in recent years on structural drills in which pieces of language are isolated from the linguistic and social contexts which make them meaningful and useful to the learner. The more we know about a language, the more such drills we have been tempted to make. If one compares, say, the Spoken Language textbooks devised by linguists during the Second World War with some of the recent textbooks devised by linguists,[3] he is struck by the shift in emphasis from connected situational dialogue to disconnected structural exercise.

The argument of this paper is that such isolation and abstraction of the learner from the contexts in which that language is used constitutes serious interference with the language learning process. Because it requires the learner to attach new responses to old stimuli, this kind of interference may in fact increase the interference that applied linguists like to talk about—the kind in which a learner's previous language structures are said to exert deleterious force on the structures being acquired.

Consider the problem of teaching someone to say something. What is it we are most concerned that he learn? Certainly not the mere mouthing of the utterance, the mere ability to pronounce the words. Certainly not the mere demonstration of ability to understand the utterance by, say, translation into the learner's own language. Even the combination of the two goals is not what we are after: it is not saying *and* understanding that we want but saying *with* understanding. That is, we want the learner to be able to use the language we teach him, and we want him to be able to extend his ability to new cases, to create new utterances that are appropriate to his needs as a language user.

Recent linguistic theory has offered a detailed abstract characterization of language competence; learning a finite set of rules and a finite lexicon enables the learner to produce and interpret an infinite number of new well-formed sentences. Plausible detailed accounts also abound in the psychological and philosophical literature to explain how formal repertoires might be linked referentially to the real world. But the kinds of linguistic rules that have been characterized so far (syntactic, phonological, and semantic) bear on the question of well-formedness of sentences, not on the question of appropriateness of utterances. And the stimulus-response or associational- or operant-conditioning accounts that help explain how *milk* comes to mean 'milk' are of little help in explaining my ability to make up a particular something appropriate to say about milk—such as *I prefer milk*—in a discussion of what one likes in his coffee, and even less my ability to ignore the mention of milk when it is staring me in the face. An important test of our success as language teachers, it seems reasonable to assert, is the ability of our students to choose to say what they want. It has been difficult for linguists and psychologists to attach any significance to the expression 'saying what you want to say'; our inability to be precise about the matter may well have been an important reason for our neglect of it in language teaching. But importance of a matter is not measured by our ability at a given moment to give a precise description of it: we can be precise about the allophones of voiceless stops in English after initial /s/, but it seems absurd to claim that it is basically as important— some textbooks imply *more* important—to teach students to make these allophones properly as it is to teach them, for example, how to get someone to repeat something he has just said.

The odd thing is that despite our ignorance as experts, as human beings we have always known how to teach other human beings to use a language: use it ourselves and let them imitate us as best they can at the time. Of course, this method has had more obvious success with children than with adult learners, but we have no compelling reason to believe with either children or adults that the method is not both necessary and sufficient to teach a language.

If we adopt the position I have been maintaining—that language is learned a whole act at a time rather than learned as an assemblage of constituent skills—what would a program for teaching students to speak a foreign language look like?[4]

For the classroom, the simple formulation that the students learn by imitating someone else using the language needs careful development. Since the actual classroom is only one small piece of the world in which we expect the learner to use the language, artificial means must be used to transform it into a variety of other pieces: the obvious means for performing this transformation is drama—imaginative play has always been a powerful educational device both for children and adults. By creating a dramatic situation in a classroom—in part simply by acting out dialogues, but also in part by relabeling objects and people in the room (supplemented by realia if desired) to prepare for imaginative role-playing—the teacher can expand the classroom in-definitely and provide imaginatively natural contexts for the language being used.

The idea of using models as teachers is hardly new in applied linguistics, and nothing could be more commonplace than the admonition that the model be encouraged to dramatize and the student to imitate the dramatization of the situation appropriate to the particular bit of language being taught. The sad fact is, however, that the drill material the model has been given to model has intrinsic features that draw the attention of the student away from the situation and focus it on the form of the utterance. Instead of devising techniques that induce the model to act out roles for the student to imitate, the applied linguist has devised techniques of structural drill that put barriers in the way of dramatic behavior and a premium on the personality-less manipulation of a formal repertoire of verbal behavior.

If what the learner observes is such that he cannot absorb it completely within his short-term memory, he will make up for his deficiency if he is called on to perform before he has learned the new behavior by padding with material from what he already knows, that is, his own language. This padding—supplying what is known to make up for what is not known—is the major source of 'interference,' the major reason for 'foreign accents.' Seen in this light, the cure for interference is simply the cure for ignorance: learning. There is no particular need to combat the intrusion of the learner's native language—the explicit or implicit justification for the contrastive analysis that applied linguists have been claiming to be necessary for planning language-teaching courses. But there is need for controlling the size of the chunks displayed for imitation. In general if you want the learner's imitation to be more accurate, make the chunks smaller; increase the size of the chunks as the learner progresses in his skill in imitation. We do not need to impose arbitrary, artificial criteria for successful behavior on the part of the learner. If we limit our demand for immediate high quality of production, we may well find that his behavior is adequately shaped by the same *ad hoc* forces that lead a child from being a clumsy performer capable of using his language only with a terribly inaccurate accent, and in a limited number of social situations, to becoming a skillful native speaker capable of playing a wide variety of social roles with the appropriate language for each.

To satisfy our requirement that the student learn to extend to new cases the ability he gains in acting out one role, a limited kind of structural drill can be used: keeping in mind that the learning must be embedded in a meaningful context, the drill may be constructed by introducing small variations into the situation being acted out (e.g., ordering orange juice instead of tomato juice, being a dissatisfied customer rather than a satisfied one, changing the time at which the action takes place) which call for partial innovation in the previously learned role. In each case the situation should be restaged, re-enacted, played as meaning something to the student.

The student's craving for explicit formulization of generalizations can usually be met better by textbooks and grammars that he reads outside class than by discussion in class. If discussion of grammar is made into a kind of dramatic event, however, such discussion might be used as the situation being learned—with the students learning to play the role of students in a class on grammar. The important point is that the study of grammar as such is neither necessary nor sufficient for learning to use a language.

So far, I have been talking about the use of live models in language classrooms. How can such techniques be adapted for self-instruction? The cheapness and simplicity of operation of the new videotape recorders already make possible a large portion of the acquisition of a language without the presence of a model; it has been shown convincingly that under the proper conditions it is possible for human students to learn—in the sense of acquiring competence—certain very complex behaviors by mere observation of that behavior in use.[5] Acquiring the willingness to perform—learning in a second sense— seems to depend to a greater extent on reinforcement of the student's own behavior and is thus not quite so amenable to instruction without human feedback at the present time. However, extension of techniques (originally developed to establish phonological competence in step-by-step programmed instruction)[6] for self-monitoring to cover whole utterances with their appropriate kinetic accompaniment may suffice in the future to make the second kind of learning as independent of live teachers as the first and thus make complete self-instruction in the use of a language possible.

Notes

Published in International Journal of American Linguistics, 32, I, II, 1966.

1. Harlan Lane, 1964.
2. I take the term and notion from W. K. Estes, 'Learning Theory' *Annual Review of Psychology*, 13. 110, 1962.
3. For example, see Dwight L. Bolinger, *et al.*, 1960; L. B. Swift, *et al.*, 1962; John J. Gumperz and June Rumery, 1962.
4. I shall restrict myself here to the question of teaching a spoken foreign language. How one teaches people to read and write a foreign language depends on their literacy in another language and on their mastery of the spoken language in which they are

learning to be literate. The problems involved would take me too far afield of the subject I am discussing here.

5. For an excellent discussion of the roles of imitation and reinforcement in the acquisition and performance of complex behaviur, see Albert Bandura and Richard H. Walters, 1963.

6. For example, the techniques used in Stanley Sapon's *Spanish A*, in the TEMAC series for Encyclopedia Britannica Films, 1961

Language learning through communication practice
Richard Allwright

In defence of a minimal language teaching strategy

It has been accepted for many years that 'communication' is the proper aim for language teaching. More recently increasing attention has been paid to what this might mean if taken seriously.[1] The implied charge that only lip-service has normally been paid to the aim of communication is difficult to prove, but perhaps not so difficult to accept, given that it does seem generally accepted that language teaching, globally, has not led to a satisfactory level of communicative skill in the vast majority of cases. Inspection of textbooks and national syllabuses (as well as of actual teaching) suggests that this failure could be blamed on the apparent failure to ensure that communicative skill is adequately represented in language courses. Textbooks and national syllabuses, typically, and for obvious reasons, present an analysis of language rather than of communicative skill. To put the position very simply, 'communication' has become fully accepted as an essential and major component of the 'product' of language teaching, but it has not yet been given more than a token place (with some very honourable exceptions of course[2]), as an essential and major component of the 'process'. A logical extension of the argument would suggest that if communication is THE aim, then it should be THE major element in the process. The question could be put:

Are we teaching *language* (for communication)?

or

Are we teaching *communication* (via language)?

Most teachers would probably quickly respond that they are first and foremost *language* teachers, by training and also by inclination, and they might at the same time object to the question, since it suggests that the two possibilities are mutually incompatible. My point is somewhat different. The two are not directly incompatible of course, but there is a logical relationship between them that demands attention. It is the same relationship as that which holds between linguistic competence and communicative competence. A diagram will make the point more clearly.

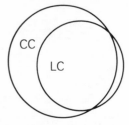

CC = Communicative Competence

LC = Linguistic Competence

The diagram implies that some areas of linguistic competence are essentially irrelevant to communicative competence,[3] but that, in general, linguistic competence is a part of communicative competence. This modified part-whole relationship implies, in turn, that teaching comprehensively for linguistic competence will necessarily leave a large area of communicative competence untouched, whereas teaching equally comprehensively for communicative competence will necessarily cater for all but a small part of linguistic competence. If this way of specifying the relationship is generally correct, then, if we really have communication as the major aim of our (language) teaching, we would be well advised to focus on communicative skills, in the knowledge that this will necessarily involve developing most areas of linguistic competence as an essential part of the product rather than focus on linguistic skills and risk failing to deal with a major part of whatever constitutes communicative competence.

What might it mean, however, to reorient language teaching towards a major focus on communicative skills? In discussing and attempting to answer this question I shall use a macro-analysis of language teaching that identifies three basic elements (for a full discussion see Allwright, 1976[4]):

1. *Samples* of the target language.
   These may or may not be intended as 'model' samples and they may come in spoken form or written form, from teachers, or learners, or teaching materials. They may simultaneously function as 'guidance' (see below).

2. *Guidance* concerning the nature of the target language.
   Three main types of guidance are suggested:
   a. *Rules*, more or less explicit verbal formulations of characteristics of the target language (e.g. the rule for forming the passive in English).
   b. *Cues*, hints that draw the attention of the learner to features of the target language, but do not provide a rule or an explicit

explanation (e.g. the use of underlining in blackboard work
to draw attention to structural similarities or differences
between two sample sentences).

c. *Simple Knowledge of Results*, feedback that informs the learner
about success or failure, from which the learner may be able
to make inferences about the target language.

These three types of guidance are mutually exclusive by definition
but of course most often combined in practice. Guidance given
in the target language will simultaneously provide a sample or
samples of that language, as indicated above under 'samples'.
Guidance need not be provided in the target language, however,
nor even via language at all (note the 'underlining' example for
G2, above). Also, it must not be assumed that guidance comes
only from the teacher or the teaching materials.

3. *Management activities*, normally designed for the express purpose
of controlling the learners' exposure to the 'samples' of the target
language, and to the forms of 'guidance' thought most appropriate
by the teacher. It is normally the teacher, then, who is held
responsible for the management of the learners' learning activities.

'Samples' of the target language, and the second and third forms of
'guidance' (cues and simple KR), are held to constitute both the
necessary and the apparently sufficient characteristics of informal
language learning (i.e. out-of-class learning, including first-language
acquisition). It is thus the use of G1 (rules) and of 'management
activities' that distinguishes formal, or 'taught' learning, in classrooms,
from informal, or 'natural' learning.[5] Management activities, in particular, seem responsible for changing a learning situation from one of
incidental learning (slow but relatively permanent if first-language
acquisition is a guide, and perhaps not even so slow) to one of conscious-
ly directed learning (apparently faster but not always so long-lasting).
Management activities are activities *directed at* achieving, producing
learning, by ensuring, as suggested above, the occurrence of selected
'samples' of the target language and selected forms of 'guidance'.
Linguistic research has been used by applied linguists,[6] naturally
enough, as the basis for prescribing what samples of the target should
occur, and in what order, and also for prescribing the sorts of guidance
that should be provided (particularly the sorts of explanation, as a
direct reflection of linguistic theory, but also the use of cues to draw
attention to features of the language—note that psychological theory
has, of course, also been involved in decisions about guidance[7]). There
is considerable doubt, however, concerning the state of our knowledge
in all these areas,[8] and at least some feeling that informal language

learning (particularly of the first language) is remarkably more efficient than whatever goes on in classrooms when we set out to control the selection and sequencing of the target language samples and the types of guidance provided.[9] A minimal model of language teaching (to use Newmark's term[10]) might therefore demand of the teacher only that samples of the target language, and guidance (at least G2 and G3, cues and simple knowledge of results) as to the nature of the target language, should be made to occur, without pre-selection, and in any order. The strong form of such a minimal strategy could be defended on the grounds that any attempt at control would be most likely to interfere with learning, since, given the state of our knowledge in such matters, it could only be appropriate by chance.[11]

The link between this somewhat perverse line of argument and communicative skills is remarkably simple. Self-evaluating activities directed at practising communicative skills can easily be arranged to necessitate the generation, by the learners, of 'samples' of the target language. The success or failure of successive attempts to communicate in such tasks provides, automatically, G2 and G3 ('cues' and 'simple KR') from which the learners can infer the characteristics of the target language, as they might in the informal language learning situation this closely parallels.

If this is so, then we may conclude that if the 'language teacher's' management activities are directed exclusively at involving the learners in solving communication problems in the target language, then language learning will take care of itself, and the teacher can be fairly sure of not being guilty of unwarranted interference in the process. (Notice that 'normal' language teaching has great potential for confusing learners about the nature of the target language, precisely because, it seems, of the difficulties that arise when a teacher attempts, as most do, to *systematise* the learners' exposure to the language.[12])

A case can be made, therefore, for reorienting 'language' teaching towards communication practice, not just because the eventual product aim is 'communication', but because communication practice can be expected to develop linguistic skills.[13]

There is an obvious objection to such a strategy, so obvious that it needs to be dealt with immediately. It seems patently clear that absolute beginners cannot be expected to solve communication problems in a language of which they are totally ignorant. An answer could be suggested in terms of the judicious management of small mixed ability learning groups, but its defence would take too much space. For the present, therefore, this objection is accepted, and Part Two will be devoted to a description of an attempt to apply this minimal language teaching strategy in what would usually be called a 'remedial' situation.

The minimal teaching strategy in action

The 'remedial' situation

For several years the Department of Language and Linguistics at the University of Essex has been providing remedial English classes, during term-time, for foreign students. More recently this service has been extended, so that we have been able to offer a sixty-hour, three-week pre-registration course in September each year.[14] Although Essex attracts a very high proportion of foreign students, the total numbers have been relatively small (given the small overall student population of the university), so that typically not more than about twenty foreign students have been involved each year. The small scale of the operation has encouraged an experimental approach but ruled out a strategy which has been favoured elsewhere—that of grouping students in classes according to their academic specialisation and of developing highly specific materials for each group. At Essex, by contrast, we have had to face the problem of a relatively small group of learners who are heterogeneous as to academic specialisation and also as to command of English.

At the same time, evidence has accumulated[15] suggesting that foreign students' problems are primarily problems of integration, of coping socially and financially, and only secondarily problems of linguistic competence. We had made some attempt to include what we have called 'orientation' work in our otherwise fairly standard 'remedial English' classes, but not really wholeheartedly, because it had never seemed to fit in very well with other sorts of work. The new evidence for the potential importance of 'orientation' work prompted the thought that communication problems could have, at least some of the time, an orientational content, thus killing the two birds with the one stone. The scene was therefore set, in September 1974, for a radically different pre-registration course, with its emphasis shifted entirely to communicative skills aimed at providing 'orientation' to the social and academic life of the university.

Two more factors made crucial contributions to the final decision to adopt a radically different strategy for the course. Firstly, there was a virtually total disenchantment with standard thinking about 'remedial' classes. It seemed to us that a 'brush up your English' approach, based on the idea that learners should receive a 'rapid review' of English grammar, is asking for trouble in two major ways.

To begin with, a 'rapid review' of English grammar, taken really seriously, is likely to take even longer in a remedial context, because so many misconceptions that have taken root ('fossilisations') will have to be dealt with. Then there is the severe risk of boring the learners since, by definition almost, they will have done it all before and presumably may also be expected to have bad memories of it from the first time around (given that they presumably failed to learn it satisfactorily, for whatever reason, at that time) or, conversely, they will be bored whenever the 'rapid review' reminds them of something they *have* already learned properly. This last consideration raises the interesting pedagogical problem that, in a heterogeneous class, with learners from a variety of linguistic backgrounds, the group as a whole will, collectively, know it all already,[16] so how do you select what to teach in your 'rapid review'? This last reflection raised the possibility of constructing a rational defence for a 'minimal strategy' that would leave guidance to chance, and to the learners, in a classroom situation that would prompt the learners to somehow pool their collective knowledge and learn from each other. This possibility then led to the idea that co-operative learning could be harnessed to facilitate the achievement of something too often neglected in the teaching of any subject—the development of learner independence (from the teacher, but mutual interdependence among the learners). Language learning puts the learner in an especially dependent position, usually, and this may well suit teachers who like the 'parent-child' relationship,[17] but learners, I suggest, need independence training. The failure of learners to use outside what they have apparently learned inside the classroom may perhaps be accounted for more appropriately in terms of a failure to develop psychological independence than in terms of a failure to teach to a sufficient degree of 'overlearning'.

The second major factor in the final decision was the example set by Paul Heinberg[18] and his colleagues in Hawaii, where they had used communication problem activities (some with an obvious orientational content) with considerable success, and with students in a similar university situation. This example was a source of one or two specific teaching ideas but mainly of general encouragement.

The course itself

1. Preliminary decisions. To bring the minimal strategy to life some practical (but, we hoped, principled) decisions had to be taken. In retrospect it seems possible to see a rational thread through the thinking that preceded the change of strategy, but at the time we[19] felt we were taking quick decisions on little more than very strong feelings of distrust concerning past experience, and strong, almost euphoric, self-confidence and optimism concerning the possibilities offered by a radical break with the past. The following decisions were somehow taken, either shortly before, or in some cases very soon after, the students arrived in the middle of September 1974.

Negative:

1. Use no materials, published or unpublished, actually conceived or designed as materials for language teaching.
2. Avoid linguistic correction entirely (from the teacher of course).
3. Refuse to supply words, or in any other way to simply 'give' language items to the learners.
4. Never introduce linguistic content for its own sake, or make any pre-selection of materials on a linguistic basis.

Positive:

5. Be extremely supportive, but primarily of the learners' struggles towards independence from the teacher, and towards peer interdependence.
6. Allow time for learners to work at their own pace (except where, as with some small-scale communication problems, an artificial time constraint may be intrinsic to the task—see below).
7. Keep the learners busy, constantly engaged in 'productive' tasks.

2. The orientation content. The decisions listed above are concerned with process aims—what we wanted the learning process to be like. The more important aims of the course were naturally the product aims—what we wanted our learners to take away at the end. Detailed decisions had therefore to be taken about the orientation content. We decided, somewhat autocratically, that we wanted the learners, by the end of three weeks, first of all to be familiar with the general layout of the university, and with its various facilities for food, recreation, health care, etc., as well as for study. Secondly we wanted them to know how to use such facilities, particularly the University Library, and also to be familiar with the regulations governing their various schemes of study. It also seemed important that they should get to know the Assistant Dean for Overseas Students, and realise his potential usefulness to them, that they should know at least something of the previous year's unrest in the university; and, perhaps above all, that they should know as much as possible about the particular course of study they intended to follow, especially in terms of the demands it was going to make upon them.

For many of these various purposes official documentation was readily available for exploitation in class, but, in line with the decision to emphasise the 'independence training' aspect, we decided to base exploitation on information retrieval problems to which such documentation would be relevant rather than on simple dissemination of the information. We also arranged such practical and familiar activities as an immediate guided tour of the whole university, and a guided visit to the Library, both followed up by associated information retrieval problems in conjunction with such documents as the Student Handbook and the official Guide to the Library. This approach dominated most of the orientation work: the emphasis was on making information available, but organising class activities so that students would have to dig for the relevant information, in the hope that by so doing they would learn about how to get all sorts of information, as well as learn the particular information needed to solve a retrieval problem. They would, at least, learn to 'find their way round' the various documents we were able to put in front of them.

For what seemed likely to be the most important of the purposes outlined above, that of ensuring that students would know as much as possible about the particular courses of study they intended to follow, a different approach was needed because the relevant documentation was not all readily available. A project approach was devised, calling upon the students first to collectively prepare the questions they would need to ask in order to find out all they wished to know about their intended courses of study, and then to go out to their various departments to seek the answers before returning to class to share the results.

A further approach adopted for the exploitation of orientation material was to draw attention to key passages in important documents (for example, the 'Annan Report' on the University's severe problems of the previous year, and the students' reply to that Report) by presenting the passages in a modified 'cloze' test form (i.e. with a number of words omitted, but not necessarily every nth word). With this sort of exploitation the co-operative element was introduced by what might be called 'progressively inclusive' group work. One form of this involved the students in first attempting to complete the gapped passage individually. The next step was for the students to form pairs and for each pair to attempt to reach consensus before joining another pair to attempt to reach a consensus again as a foursome. Then each four (in a class of sixteen) would join another group to reach consensus as a group of eight. Finally the two eights would compare and discuss their solutions to the 'cloze' problem, and attempt to reach a final consensus that could then be compared to the original document. This approach ensured very considerable discussion of the content of the documents of course, and thus provided important orientation work as well as reading comprehension practice (among several other things). At all stages the teacher would concentrate on 'management activities',[20] avoiding involvement in linguistic discussions, but prepared to help the learners in the content discussion so necessary to their successful filling of the gaps in the text. Even in the area of the content discussion a 'low profile' was adopted, with the teacher trying to ask 'attention-directing' questions rather than supplying relevant information.

A final approach to the exploitation of orientation materials was adopted for a particularly difficult problem, that of interpreting official regulations. Again, rather than involve the teacher in attempting to 'explain' (a teaching strategy that could be labelled 'telling', with all the inefficiency the term can suggest), a learner-centred approach was tried, calling upon the students, again in groups, to take a different regulation per group and attempt to paraphrase it in a way that would render it comprehensible to the others. This proved a productive exercise that very effectively drew attention to key disciplinary regulations, and of course to real problems (not just for non-native speakers of English) in their interpretation.

Of the four approaches outlined above the first two (the 'information retrieval' and the 'project' approaches) were fairly obviously non-language-centred, whereas the last two ('cloze' and 'paraphrase') were equally clearly calling for very special attention to be paid to language. In this way they came nearest to 'standard' language teaching practices, but it should not be forgotten that the content in each case was chosen solely for its orientation value, and the exploitation was designed to draw attention to the content via the language problems posed by the 'cloze' and 'paraphrase' tasks. Orientation was the 'product'; attention to language was an essential part of the 'process'. The teacher's role was therefore importantly different from that of the language teacher. It was not easy for the teachers[21] to avoid 'language teaching' (and we sometimes caught ourselves in the act), but it did seem right to try, because by strictly avoiding turning content discussions into linguistic discussions we seemed to be succeeding in building up our students' confidence in their ability to cope, in English, with a whole variety of problems. This confidence-building aspect became crucial to our whole approach. It felt somewhat perverse, even to us, to avoid linguistic correction as strenuously as we did, but it seemed to work. Our students kept themselves extremely busy, talking in English and often discussing English, without the inhibitions often created by the standard language-teaching strategy that naturally focuses on linguistic accuracy rather than on communicative effectiveness. (This focus on linguistic accuracy is very persistent among language teachers, for obvious reasons, but it can easily be counterproductive, of course, tending to produce learners afraid to risk using the target language for fear of making some linguistic mistake that may well be almost totally irrelevant to effective communication. The problem of the language teacher's natural focus on linguistic accuracy prompts the suggestion that study skills courses, for instance, ought to be taught by study skills experts sensitive to

language rather than by language teachers sensitive to study problems.)
This consideration leads easily on to the other aspect of course-content
—communicative skills development.

3. Communicative skills development. All the forms of exploitation of
orientation content involved a variety of forms of communication, and
this posed a variety of communication problems. It seemed worthwhile,
however, to draw attention to communicative skills themselves by
providing a number of communication problems, some very simple and
some very elaborate, that would provide light relief from the orientation
work in terms of content, but would nevertheless be of sufficient
intrinsic interest to ensure active productive student participation.

At the simplest level was the following communication game. Two
players are involved, seated at a table with a screen between them. In
front of each player is a set of five small objects (we used coloured
counters and dice). The players have identical sets. A third student
makes a pattern with the objects in front of one of the players. That
player must then attempt, in thirty seconds only, to give verbal instructions to the other player, to enable him to put his set of objects into
the same pattern. At the end of thirty seconds the screen is lifted so
that an immediate check can be made on the effectiveness of the
communication. The third student then makes a pattern for the second
player to describe. After each player has had three attempts, one of them
takes over the role of problem-setter and timekeeper from the third
student.

The thirty-second constraint guarantees failure most of the time, but
not all of the time. It has the great advantage of being obviously
monstrous, which in effect means that no one need feel ashamed of
failure. A more 'reasonable' time limit is disastrous psychologically, in
our experience (Heinberg's work in Hawaii was our model in this
respect).

This sort of 'instant', trivial, silly communication problem proved
extremely useful in itself, because it drew attention very successfully
to two key points. Firstly, it necessitated the precise use of language,
and equal precision in listening. Secondly, and perhaps more importantly, it demonstrated that good communication with a poor command
of English may be better able to cope with communication problems
in English than much more fluent speakers who are poor communi-
cators. It was one of the 'weakest' students (on the ELBA[22] test) who
was the first to succeed in communicating a pattern in thirty seconds,
while much more fluent speakers (including myself!) struggled in vain
to reach the same degree of concise precision.

These 'simple' communication games also proved extremely useful
for a quite different reason. Given the intention to allow students to

work at their own pace as much as possible, it was natural that groups doing orientation work would finish at different times and necessary that no embarrassment or time-wasting should be allowed to ensue. It was very simple to divert the early finishers towards simple communication games that could be started very quickly and interrupted without difficulty when necessary. The classroom was so arranged that such games were left available at all times, ready for any students who might otherwise have time on their hands.

At the other extreme, the most elaborate of communication games took up to four class-hours to play, preferably with an overnight gap between two two-hour sessions. For this game the class was divided into two pairs of groups with four students in each group. Each group was in competition with the other in its pair, but could ignore the other pairs of groups. Each group was given a set of Lego bits (child's plastic construction kit) sufficient for the construction of a different model (in our game always a vehicle). With each set of bits was a set of purely visual instructions[23]. The first task was to build the model in accordance with the visual instructions, and then to write verbal instructions that would entirely replace the visual ones. This process would take the first two hours, often leaving the verbal instructions still incomplete. Hence the advantage of an overnight break for the students to continue with the task out of class. On the second day the groups would re-form and finalise their verbal instructions before exchanging them with the other group in the pair. The bits would also be exchanged, of course, but not the visual instructions. For the final phase of the game the groups attempted to build the models, following the written instructions to the letter, giving no benefit to the doubt and returning the instructions for refinement if they proved uninterpretable. The winning group was the group whose instructions led the more speedily to the correct construction of the model (by the rival group).

The competitive element proved quite unimportant in practice, because the tasks themselves proved extremely interesting and productive, particularly in terms of vocabulary expansion. Once again the teacher had to refrain from 'interfering' in any way, even when asked, as it seemed ultimately much more fruitful for the teacher to concentrate almost entirely on 'management activities'. Students frequently asked for help, of course, particularly for the words they lacked to describe the pieces of plastic themselves, but we tried very hard to refuse, and thus to force them to struggle until they found something adequate themselves, presumably by dredging their memories (and/or consulting dictionaries, of course, since the ability and willingness to consult a dictonary is crucial to 'independence training'). The wisdom of this refusal on the part of the teacher to act as a supplier of words was supported, long after the course itself was finished, when I played the

Lego game with some non-native teachers of English. I unthinkingly supplied a word to one of the groups, on request, only to hear them argue, shortly afterwards, that they could not in fact use the word I had supplied, because if they had previously lacked it, then it was most likely that their rival group also lacked it, and thus its use would be a barrier to effective communication. The point was neatly made that effective communication depends on a sensitivity to the receiver. To be effective messages do not need to be 'correct' in any absolute (linguistic?) sense. But they do have to be 'correct' in a relative sense, 'correct', that is, relative to the decoding abilities of the intended receiver.

The objection can be made here, and has often been made, that in the circumstances of the course under discussion the pressures for effective communication rather than linguistic accuracy must surely lead to the adoption of a classroom pidgin English, effective only between non-native speakers, and perhaps even peculiar to the particular group of students involved. This is a serious objection that deserves discussion. The danger involved would certainly be considerable if the group were homogeneous with regard to their mother tongue. That was not the case for the course under discussion, but the point remains and special measures would have to be devised to help homogeneous groups (perhaps by the introduction of native speakers as full partici-pants for at least some activities). With heterogeneous multilingual groups the problem is less severe, since what is understandable to a great variety of non-native speakers is likely to work at least with a reasonably tolerant native speaker. It may also be worth accepting the danger, because it can be argued that it is more important that the foreign students develop confidence in their ability to rely on each other. If they are pushed into trying to meet external standards of acceptability, they may become inhibited and not even have the confidence to use their English to develop relationships with other foreign students. Anecdotal evidence supports this view since one of our students did express his gratitude for our course precisely by pointing out that it had enabled him to make proper contact with some fellow-students, whereas he had spent the previous year (also at Essex) able to cope with 'official' demands on his English, but too inhibited in everyday exchanges to profit from the company of fellow-students. A further, and very important, point to be considered is that the development of communicative self-confidence in such learners is perhaps crucial to their further *linguistic* development. While it is undoubtedly true that some learners will respond well to strictly 'language' courses in circumstances where they also have pressing communication needs, it seems intuitively reasonable to suggest that the strain on most learners will be considerable, if they are faced with the twin problems of developing linguistic accuracy and achieving communicative self-confidence, but only receiving help with the first of the two. It would seem more helpful to concentrate on developing their communicative ease first, to facilitate their integration into academic and social life, and thus to clear the way for a subsequent development of such linguistic accuracy as they may desire,[24] free from any additional problem of communicative insecurity.

Concluding comments

The above description of the September 1974 course is necessarily partial, intended primarily to give the 'flavour' of the thinking and the various activities involved rather than an exhaustive account of the whole course. So far, however, nothing has been said about the success, or otherwise, of the minimal strategy as we first put it into practice. It is too easy to say to be convincing, perhaps, but the first comment to make under such a heading is that it is of course virtually impossible to evaluate such a course in anything other than a trivial way. We certainly attempted no systematic post-testing (being generally as disenchanted with tests as we were with standard teaching materials) and relied instead on a 'process' rather than a 'product' evaluation. In practice this meant trying to evaluate the extent to which the course fostered what appeared to be 'productive' learning processes. From this point of view most of the activities were highly successful (from our point of view as no doubt biased observers) in that they seemed remarkably productive in linguistic terms. The students were far busier, linguistically (using the language and grappling with the language), and attendance was far better, than on our previous standard remedial courses. The students were almost constantly involved in a linguistic struggle, but a well-motivated one. The course seemed to be providing what so many courses clearly fail to provide—*reasons for communicating* rather than 'items for use should a reason for communicating ever present itself'. By taking the focus completely off the language as content and putting it onto orientation problems or otherwise trivial but intriguing communication games, we paradoxically succeeded in drawing attention to the language and motivating intense concentration on its complexities.

We cannot know whether or not we were providing the best possible sort of course for our learners, but we do know we were far happier with what we were doing than we had ever been with more orthodox strategies. It made sense to us, and felt right.

Postscript, November 1976

The rationale presented in Part One was developed after the event as a major part of our attempt to understand what we had done, and why.

Since then I have had the opportunity to test out the essential ideas in a variety of situations with different 'content aims'. What has emerged most strongly as a problem is the question of how to 'sell' such a course to learners who expect (and of course may strongly believe they most need) a perfectly standard language course. If the teacher is convinced (as we were at the time) that the teacher is within his or her rights to impose a given strategy in what seem to be the best interests of the learners, then a 'cheerful steamroller' technique seems warranted, but only if the teacher is able to spend time, out of class probably, trying to convince those who are unhappy with such a radical departure from the norm. Teachers who are not themselves fully convinced about the likely usefulness of the strategy in their situation, but who are prepared to give it a fair trial, should be warned that a tentative approach to implementing the strategy is most likely to be doomed from the start (just as it is with any strategy, perhaps, but probably even more so in the case of the sort of 'bizarre' strategy under discussion). The teacher will therefore need to teach *as if* thoroughly convinced, while remaining inwardly sceptical.

To end on a wholly positive note, the most encouraging outcome of further use of the strategy is that it continues to 'feel right' both in day-to-day work with learners, and on reflection, in the light of the response of many learners, who value being prompted, and trusted, to make a more substantial contribution to their own learning.

Notes

Published in ELT Documents 76, 3: 2–14, The British Council, 1977.

1. I have in mind principally the whole ESP 'movement'. It uses a different terminology but reflects a serious concern with enabling learners to 'do things with words' rather than simply to 'know the language'.
2. Sandra Savignon's work is well-known in this respect. For an excellent report of her research see her 'Teaching for Communicative Competence' in *AVLA Journal*, Vol. 3, Winter 1972; pp. 153–162.
3. The relative size of the two circles is a matter of unquantifiable conjecture, however reasonable or unreasonable it looks.
4. Allwright, R. L. (1976).
5. For important related discussion see Krashen, S. D. and Seliger, H. (1975).
6. For example see Politzer, R. L. (1961).
7. But J. B. Carroll, in 1966, drew attention to the poor use being made of psychological theory in language teaching. See Carroll,

J. B.: 'Psychology, Research, and Language Teaching' in Valdman, A. (ed., 1966): *Trends in Language Teaching*, McGraw-Hill, p. 104.

8. Chomsky made the point rather memorably in 1966, at the North-East Conference on the Teaching of Modern Languages, and things do not seem to have improved since then.

9. But see Krashen, S. D. (1976).

10. See his contribution to the Second AILA Congress, Cambridge, 1969, printed in *The Psychology of Second Language Learning*, Pimsleur, P. and Quinn, T. (eds), CUP, 1971, entitled 'A Minimal Language-Teaching Program', pp. 11–18.

11. This argument rests on a denial of the validity of experience un-supported by research and theory. Humans do find it extraordinarily hard to learn by experience, in such matters, however, and the 'common sense' they do thus acquire is notoriously suspect, of course.

12. See Allwright, R. L. (1975). See also: McTear, M. (1975).

13. Accuracy, it may be objected, must surely suffer. Any loss, however, might well be more than compensated for by a corresponding gain in communicative skill. Also, it is arguable that communicative ease is necessary, though insufficient, for the development of accuracy. (Recent research by David Richards at the University of Essex, under the title 'The development of communicative efficiency in second language learning—a case study of two adult French learners of English', is relevant to this argument, though not conclusive.) My own experience suggests that accuracy can be developed, in the classroom, and within the principles of the minimal teaching strategy, after communication has been achieved.

14. Even more recently two full-time members of staff have been appointed to an EFL Unit to take over responsibility for all such service English courses.

15. See Sen, A. (1970). For a brief summary of Sen's survey see Yates, A. (ed.), (1971). For a very recent discussion on the same topic, see Davies, (1975).

16. An oversimplification, perhaps, but a useful one to take seriously.

17. See Stevick, E. Q. (1976). See especially Chapter 5: 'The Meaning of Drills and Exercises', pp. 65–84.

18. Personal communication. There appears to be nothing published of direct relevance. Dr. Heinberg can be contacted at the Speech and Communication Department, University of Hawaii, Honolulu, Oahu, Hawaii.

19. Working with me at this stage was Julia Cleave, whose enthusiastic co-operation was extremely valuable to me personally as well as to the course.

20. This frequently involved leaving the room to get on with the

preparation of future class activities. These teacher absences were originally the product of simple necessity, but they proved to be another valuable 'weapon' in the war against dependence on the teachers.

21.Julia Cleave and myself, principally, joined later by Valerie Kay and Ann Hosking.

22.The Edinburgh Language Battery devised by Elizabeth Ingram.

23.Provided by the manufacturer in each box.

24.'Such linguistic accuracy as they may desire' is intended to imply that learners need to be allowed to make up their own minds as to the level of linguistic perfection they should aim at. For some the achievement of communicative ease will suffice, and we should respect that (although we may still spend time trying to persuade a student otherwise, of course). Others will see increased linguistic accuracy as relevant to their academic and/or social aims and will respond accordingly.

Acknowledgements

Very special thanks are due to Julia Cleave, who devised the September 1974 course with me, and to Valerie Kay and Ann Hosking, who also helped teach it. All have been very helpful since in discussing the ideas set down in this paper.

'Communicative' language teaching: an educational perspective
Christopher Brumfit

In a recent paper,[1] I have suggested that the most lasting impact of the 'communicative' movement in language teaching may lie more in a reversal of traditional methodological emphases than in a reorganization of syllabus objectives. Particularly, I suggested that language courses have traditionally followed the pattern of procedure indicated in figure (i) below, but that a widespread post-communicative model may well be that outlined in figure (ii).

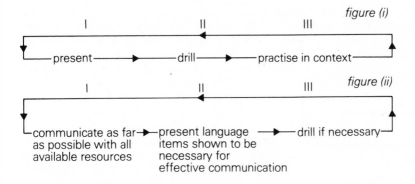

It is the purpose of this paper to explore some of the links between this trend and a number of general educational themes. Language teaching is only slowly beginning to respond to methodological changes which have for some time been influential in non-language-teaching circles. While it is true that the analogy with the teaching of other disciplines should not always be accepted automatically, it is also true that the view of language teaching as a purely technical operation, with no broader educational overtones, needs to be treated with suspicion.[2]

It is especially worth noting the increasingly held view that there is little difference in principle between acquiring a new functional dialect and acquiring a new language. Any interest in such a view should lead us to consider some of the discussion which has influenced mother tongue teaching in the last decade or so.

In *Notional Syllabuses*, David Wilkins distinguishes between two strategies for syllabus organization, calling these the synthetic and the analytic (Wilkins, 1976: 2). The latter strategy demands that the student be presented with data which has not been broken down analytically by the teacher. It is expected that the student will himself analyse this data, probably subconsciously, and convert it functionally to his use. This procedure resembles what the native speaker is held to do with his language as he acquires it.

There are a number of difficulties about Wilkins' formulation of the problem. The most important is that *any* process of presentation by the teacher (given that in the limited time available he cannot wait for foreign language to crop up accidentally) must involve him in judgements about selection, and these judgements will only be possible to evaluate if the teacher is aware of categories on which to base the identification of items to be selected. The teacher's analysis need not be grammatical, but there must be some analysis on the teacher's part, which will involve the learner in a synthetic process himself. Nonetheless, by emphasizing the learner's active role in the analytic procedure, Wilkins does force us to ask what kinds of classroom activity will most satisfactorily enable the learner himself to act as an unconscious analyser of the language data presented to him. Studies of language acquisition in natural circumstances, with either first or second languages, will help to shed light on this problem. In addition, discussion of mother tongue teaching methodology may be helpful, for teachers of English in Britain have, over the last fifty years, shifted from a synthetic to an analytic approach, a process which has been greatly accelerated since about 1960.

The move towards what has been characterized as a 'growth'[3] model of language work has engaged a number of authorities who do not fit easily together. Some (e.g. Holbrook, 1961, 1964) saw English teaching as a process enabling pupils to come to terms with the threats and traumas of growing up, through the development of the imagination. Others, particularly those associated with the work of Britton (Barnes, Britton, Rosen, 1969; Britton, 1970), were more concerned with the sociocultural dimensions of language use, demanding that pupils should be able to develop their linguistic, and often by implication cognitive, abilities without being forced to adopt a standard-

ized language which was associated with only one group of the population. Both schools emphasize the process rather than the product, and
both are concerned with the 'health' of society in a way which marks
them as continuing the Arnold–Leavis tradition, but the personal and
therapeutic claims at one extreme and the socio-political at the other
take us a long way from the mandarin view of earlier ideologues.

There are a number of ways in which contemporary foreign language
teaching is unlike any sort of growth model. Very often the reason
for the choice of a foreign language is far away from a student's own
perceived needs, and even in an adult ESP situation the teacher
usually sees himself as being in possession of relevant knowledge of
the target language which has to be organized for the benefit of the
learners. Nor, indeed, would it be desirable for teachers to emphasize
undirected growth as a major aim. The greatest risk of a position that
concentrates exclusively on the process with no reference at all to
the product is that of leaving teachers incapable of making any judgements at all. If it does not matter what sort of language we produce,
then there is little justification for going to school at all: we might as
well leave pupils at home to produce language there. If the school is
held to be able to facilitate certain processes, then there must be some
ways of recognizing these preferred processes in relation to the language
produced, so that we find ourselves looking again at the product as
well as the process. Such lack of direction could only be justified in
tandem with a totally relativistic position about alternative patterns of
behaviour—and a position such as this would make it difficult to justify
education at all.[4] However, as exact as possible a specification of the
desired final behaviour is necessary but such a specification should not
dictate in any simple way the total structure of the course, nor the
methodology. The growth model, at its best, recognizes both the
complexity of linguistic operations and the close relations between
language, personal needs and social situations. A linguistic model is
always external to the student, but growth takes place inside him. Too
much foreign language emphasis on linguistic models in foreign
language teaching, whether conceived in formal or functional terms,
will lead to a neglect of process which will be pedagogically disastrous.

When teachers, representing an educational system, seek to intervene
in learning, as they do by definition when they teach, they need to be
able to justify themselves on two main counts.[5] First, they need to be
able to show that what is being taught is desirable, directly or indirectly,
for the good of society at large,[6] and second they need to show that
the procedures being used relate explicitly to pupils as they actually
are, to the teaching situation as it actually is, and to the desired

objectives. While it is clearly true that neither of these questions can be answered simply, the obligation to produce as clear answers as possible must be insisted on. The alternative is to proceed irresponsibly by tradition or the whims of fashion.

In language teaching there has been a shift in recent years from an emphasis on intrinsic motivation to a concern with extrinsic factors. Only a small minority of writers will argue now that the process of learning a language is in itself intellectually beneficial, or that we learn languages to understand other cultures and thus define our own and ourselves.[7] Now it is far more likely that terminal behaviours of a strictly utilitarian kind will be specified.[8] But the trouble with such summaries of terminal behaviour is that they tend to treat the instrumental role of language as if it can be isolated from educational issues altogether. The teaching of language then does become a purely technical problem, without personal or ideological significance. This tempting view can only be justified, however, when the language being taught can only be used technically—that is, predictably. Very little language teaching is of this type, for as soon as the language becomes sufficiently complex for a generative system to be operating, the user's personal needs will determine its use, and these needs will never be purely technical. It is significant that many recent writers have found it necessary to repudiate an under-emphasis on the total involvement of any learner in the acquisition of a new language.[9] The point is that, however the teachers may choose to define the syllabus, the student receives a system with semantic potential. How he decides to use it will depend on his character and his opportunities, but the teacher cannot avoid offering something with a potential which goes beyond the specifics of a particular needs analysis. Not to allow the learner *some* freedom to use the newly developed skills in unpredictable directions will be to frustrate the very abilities which will be necessary for the most effective response to the predicted needs. Language uses which do not require improvization are really demanding language-like behaviour rather than true linguistic behaviour, for improvization is a characteristic of any human interaction. A needs profile can only be a guideline, a way of measuring a syllabus against the necessary demands of the real world; it is unclear in what way such an analysis can be a sufficient measure of the adequacy of a syllabus. Thus, there are difficulties, caused partly by our ignorance, and partly by social forces operating on language teaching, in reconciling a number of aspects of current discussion and practice in methodology. In particular, we have to recognize that there is a heavy consumer demand for language courses which teach a code to solve specific (allegedly limited) communication problems.[10] Whether or not such a demand reflects an over-simple view of language learning, it certainly constitutes a major economic pressure. But our understanding of the language learning process is still too unclear for us to be able to control it fully, or to be sure what the effects of our interventions are on the learner.

Paradoxically, then, one pressure leads us to restrict the scope of our courses to elements related to particular needs, while another causes us to increase emphasis on the indivisibility of language into separate aspects for code and personality. One of the biggest general challenges at the moment is to devise a methodology which is economical enough for the restricted course, and honest enough still to be concerned with language. Such a methodology, though not usually discussed in quite these terms, has been the preoccupation of many teachers for several years. There has been a widespread assumption that communicative teaching should not simply be a matter of the specification of the elements in a course, but that it should involve a profound change in the methodology.[11] Yet it is noteworthy that most discussion has been based on long-standing procedures, such as use of group and pair work, simulation and role-play exercises, and other techniques which have been used, though possibly more in the second than the foreign language situation, for many years.

One of the emphases in mother tongue teaching discussion has concerned the role of fluent talk, or at least talk as fluent as the participants wish and are able to make it. The primacy of speech is no stranger to the foreign language methodologist, but an emphasis on fluency is.[12] Traditional syllabuses have always had a basis in the accurate construction of the target language, rather as if it were a building being built to a blueprint. It might be worth considering, however, what would be the implications if we used *fluency* as the basis for a language curriculum, rather than accuracy.

The reasons for being uncertain about the wholly desirable effects of the accuracy basis can be stated fairly briefly. First of all, 'accuracy' is a relative term, based on a social judgement of the language used by a speech community. When, for the teacher, an idealized accuracy is set up, it must be based on a model (which may or may not have a strong empirical source) devised by a descriptive linguist. Such a model is most frequently based on literary sources, though it need not be, and it always involves a strong degree of idealization. Pedagogically, it can be justified only as a short cut, as a way of enshrining the central truths of the target language, so that subsequent modification can take place as experience is gained of a wider and wider variety of situations. To insist on a model of accuracy, whether conceived in grammatical or functional terms, entails taking a number of risks: that inflexibility will be trained through too close a reference to a descriptive model, that adaptability and the ability to improvise will be neglected, that written forms will tend to dominate spoken forms, and so on. Such disadvantages can be overcome, especially in second language situations where the language exposure outside class, since it involves language which is functionally active, will compensate for the unrealities of the classroom. In the foreign language situation, however, such disadvantages become much more significant.

It is also possible—though we should not minimize the socializing effect of school in leading learners to want accuracy-based teaching—that learners may be more responsive to an emphasis on fluency. The reasons will be similar to those which Wilkins outlines in support of notionally organized syllabuses (Wilkins, 1972b, p. 82 in this volume). Certainly, insofar as the naive language learner's instincts recognize intuitively the flexibility of the language system and the close relationship between form, function and paralinguistic features, they are surely to be encouraged. To this extent, the question posed by Allwright (1977a and this volume) about the ways in which teachers interfere with learning cannot be ignored. The question is not *whether* to accept learners' resistance to an idealized model for accuracy, but *how* to.

Fluency as a basis, then, may be closer to the apparent learner syllabus of the natural learner in a total immersion situation, in that the naive learner operates more on an oral basis of fluent and inaccurate language than on a careful building up analytically of accurate items according to a descriptive model. Such a basis will also lead us to focus on how what is known is used, rather than on the form of what is known. It would also lead us to look more carefully at the role of methodology, of the relationship between teacher and pupil, and the content of language used, rather than simply the syllabus specifications. Methodologically, also, it would make a student-centred curriculum far more attainable. An accuracy-based curriculum is by definition a deficit curriculum for students, because it does not start from what the student does. Since its starting point is the descriptive linguist's model (for reasons which have been outlined above), and since all learners can learn language but not necessarily, without training, describe it, there is a permanent mismatch between what the teacher offers and what learners can most easily do.[13] A course which was based on what the student could do himself most naturally would simultaneously indicate to the teacher what his next moves should be, and to the student where he needed to adjust his intuitions and where, therefore, he required help most. At the same time the student will be expected to grope and paraphrase, and thus to learn the strategies for communication which all language users possess in their mother tongues, and which all need to develop in foreign languages. The emphasis is thus on the use, not the possession of the target language.[14]

A communicative methodology, then, would start from communication, with exercises which constituted communication challenges for students.[15] As they attempted the exercises, students would have to stretch their linguistic capabilities to perform the given tasks, and would be given subsequent teaching, which could be of a traditional form, where they clearly perceived themselves to need to improve to establish communication adequately in relation to the task. Such a procedure is not simply an answer to a motivation problem; even more it is a matter of learning principle, for the complexity of the linguistic and communicative systems being operated require that new learning must be closely assimilated with what is already known, and if language is being learnt for use, then new learning must be directly associated with use. And use implies more than simply more or less meaningful language functions in the classroom: ideally the language used should have a specifiable cognitive and affective relationship with the learner-users. The old question of what learners use the language for, what subject matter is appropriate, takes on a new urgency.[16]

It may appear that a fluency-based syllabus would be harder to specify than an accuracy-based one. In fact, though it may be true that the syllabus specification is less apparent on the surface, the discussions of syllabus which have occupied many applied linguists in recent years will be particularly important in establishing the appropriate content for fluency work. Analysis of spoken discourse will necessarily enable us to make predictions about the kind of interaction likely to develop in a classroom based on oral fluency, but such analyses will need to be coupled with analyses of foreign language learners and their difficulties in spoken discourse, both in natural and classroom settings.[17] The relationship between such research, syllabus design, materials development, and methodology, is primarily an empirical question. Matching exercises to stages in learner progress needs to be achieved partly by a process of trial and error, but the attempt seems to be well worth making.

In one sense, it will be appreciated, the contrast between accuracy and fluency is largely metaphorical. Classrooms are always concerned with both. But the shift in emphasis outlined above does lead us to consider a number of old questions in new terms, and to give discussion of communicative teaching a very simple contrast to use in examining methodology. In spite of difficulties in defining accuracy and fluency, the distinction between them has a value in centring methodological discussion on a number of crucial, and as yet unsolved, problems.[18]

It has been suggested in this paper, then, that language teaching needs to concentrate far more on the concept of 'fluency' in order to restore a genuine educational perspective to its aims. To some extent, this is already happening, for as we come to understand learning processes more fully we become aware of the limitations of considering language in isolation from the cognitive and cultural processes in which it is embedded. These processes operate deep within the personality of the learner, and the language teacher's purpose is to link the integrated and internal needs of the learner to external demands of society. Because the analysis of the demands of society is dis-integrated so that it can be described and understood, the process of re-integrating it requires sensitivity and a response to learners as whole people. If 'communication' involves simply the substitution of one mechanical metaphor for another, it has nothing to offer. But it could mean that the machine is dead: language teaching is not packaged *for* learners, it is made *by* them. Language is whole people.

Notes

Specially written for this volume.

1. 'Communicative' language teaching: an assessment, in Strevens (ed.), 1978.
2. This point particularly relates to many English for Specific Purposes courses. See, for example, several contributors to Holden (ed.), 1977.
3. See especially Dixon, 1975.
4. Though some writers, e.g. in Young (ed.), 1971, do get very close to this position.
5. Dick Allwright (1977b) distinguishes between the language teacher's 'intervention' and 'interference'—a useful distinction to make, but the basic point is still worth making.
6. Of course this fundamental question has been grossly over-simplified here—but there must be *some* relation between what is taught and a view of what society should be like.
7. Among modern language teachers in Britain this view is still encountered, but some desperation may be detected.
8. See, for example, the very detailed analysis in Munby (1978).
9. See, among others, Stevick, 1976; Curran, 1976; Finocchiaro, 1974.
10. See, for example, discussion of such courses in Mackay & Mountford (eds), 1978; Holden (ed.), 1977, Journal of the Midland Association for Linguistic Studies, Summer 1978.
11. As in several papers contributed to the British Association for Applied Linguistics seminar on communicative methodology, held at Bath, April 1977, organized by W. T. Littlewood, Swansea University, or in Johnson & Morrow (eds), 1978.
12. It has usually been discussed, if at all, with specific reference to advanced language work.
13. Cf. Krashen, 1977.
14. See Barnes, 1976, for a discussion of similar problems in the mother tongue context.

15. For one set of ideas, see Allwright, 1977a, but for discussion of general problems and principles at an earlier stage of learning see the other papers in the same issue of ELT Docs.
16. Indeed, it may be conceivable, in view of the difficulties of relating English teaching to other subjects, that literature may be able to justify a return to language teaching, in order to provide a subject for study in English which does not depart too far from conventional views of what 'English' should be.
17. Many of these considerations are discussed more fully in Widdowson, 1978.
18. For further development of this theme, see Brumfit, 1979a.

Communicative approaches and communicative processes

Keith Johnson

This paper has two, largely unrelated, parts. The first explores the relationship between the concepts of 'analytic' and 'synthetic' on the one hand, and particular ways of specifying teaching content on the other. The second part, starting from the assumption that any methodology (analytic or synthetic) must base itself on a view of what is entailed in ability to use a language, looks at some of the processes involved in fluent conversational interaction, and draws conclusions relevant to the teaching (and testing) of spoken language.

Part 1

Much of the very considerable momentum of present day language teaching may be seen as a response to a problem which teachers have been aware of for a long time. It is the problem of the student who may be structurally competent, but who cannot communicate appropriately. As Newmark (this volume, p. 161) expresses it, this student may know 'the structures that the linguist teaches, [yet] cannot know that the way to get his cigarette lit by a stranger when he has no matches is to walk up to him and say one of the utterances "Do you have a light?" or "Got a match?" (not one of the equally well-formed questions "Do you have a fire?" or "Do you have illumination?" or "Are you a match's owner?").'

Newmark's insight that 'being appropriate' is something different from 'being structurally correct' finds its place within a mode of thinking predominant in linguistics today, the pedigree of which is traced in Part I of this volume.[1] As a result of this mode of thinking we are now prepared to accept that 'there are rules of use without which the rules of grammar would be useless' (this volume, p. 15) and have consequently reformulated our aims in terms of Hymes' 'communicative' (rather than a Chomskian 'grammatical') competence.

Language teaching's most concerted response to the problem of communicative incompetence, to the mode of thinking which so neatly formulates this problem, to the reformulation of aims we now embrace, has been on the level of syllabus design. If we formerly regarded language learning as principally a question of acquiring structures, then it is natural that the items appearing on our syllabus inventory should have been structures. If we then reformulate our aims to include the 'teaching of use', then it would seem equally natural that our inventories should have to include items of use. Wilkins' 'semantico-grammatical categories' and his 'categories of communicative function' represent one attempt to itemize use for the purpose of syllabus design.

Once we admit this change to our syllabus inventories, other changes follow. The grammar of a language represents a finite set of structures, and if our aim is to teach those structures, we may simply 'work through' them. The scope of the operation is clear; we have a specific number of items to cover, and our motivation for covering them is that they exist. The situation is markedly different when we deal in items of use. We cannot 'work through' all possible uses in the same way. We have to develop some criterion of selection, and this we attempt to do by looking at students' predicted communicative needs. Inventories itemizing use, for general as well as ESP students, thus lead to needs-based teaching, and include items not because they exist but because they are deemed useful.

This, in outline, has been one widespread response to the problem of communicative incompetence and the work of writers like Hymes. So much so that when we speak of 'communicative language teaching' it is usually to these attributes which we are referring. It is (in this common usage) language teaching which, recognizing the necessity for teaching use (formulating, that is, its aims in terms of 'communicative competence'), bases itself on inventories specifying semantic and pragmatic categories which are arrived at by considering presumed communicative needs. The approach proposes what might be called a 'teaching content' solution to the problem of communicative in-competence. Applied to the particular instance Newmark cites, it is a solution which might account for the student's ignorance of how to ask for a light by the delightfully simple fact that items like 'asking for a light' have not formed part of our teaching content. Once we conceive our teaching in terms which embrace categories of use (including the general 'requesting services' and the particular 'asking for a light') then—this type of solution seems to be proposing—the major step to solving the problem has been taken. Of course it is recognized that the decision to teach language in relation to categories of use is likely to have methodological implications; but they are implications which follow and are contingent upon our prior decision, made at the syllabus planning level, to specify teaching content in a particular 'notional' way.

Given the predominance of the 'teaching content' solution in recent teaching, it is all the more interesting to note that it is not at all obviously the solution that Newmark himself proposes. Newmark does have things to say about the specification of teaching content (and some of these will be discussed later), but both his diagnosis and his treatment have a methodological base. According to him, the illness exists because we have failed to realize that (p. 161, this volume) 'acquisition cannot be simply additive; complex bits of language are learned a whole chunk at a time'. Consequently his recommended treatment is to exploit the 'exponential power available in learning in natural chunks'. This 'methodologically-based' solution is one which appeals because it seems potentially to offer an alternative to aspects of traditional methodology which have long caused widespread discontent and which, in the eyes of many, are responsible for communicative incompetence—aspects like painfully slow incremental teaching, the drilling of language items in isolation, and so on. It is also a type of solution which is gaining support today, and we find in the work of Brumfit (this volume), Allwright (1977a and this volume) and others, approaches to communicative language teaching which share in common a greater concern with issues of methodology than with the specification of syllabus content, and within which the traditional sequence of atomistic→ holistic language practice is usually reversed.

We have, then, a situation in which there are effectively two ways of accounting for communicative incompetence, two types of proposed solution to the problem. Are there then two types of communicative language teaching? There certainly seem to be in practice two broad approaches. One is characterized by the rigorous specification of communicative needs typical of much ESP work, but often coupled with a methodology which is not significantly unlike traditional methodology. The other proposes methodological procedures that are quite often revolutionary, but equally often remain uncommitted on questions of syllabus design. It is a situation that certainly prompts us to ask what the relationship between the two approaches is, what the methodological implications of the 'teaching content' solution are, and what the methodologically-based solutions imply in terms of syllabus design.

Attempts have certainly been made to link the two approaches together. Indeed, at times Newmark (with his 'methodological approach') makes statements which suggest that he would look with favour on the kind of precise notional terms in which most teaching content solutions express themselves. This is particularly true when he laments the lack of precision in the specification of categories of use, and notes (p. 162, this volume) that 'the kinds of linguistic rules that have been characterized so far . . . bear on questions of well-formedness of sentences, not on questions of appropriateness of utterances'. We need more rules, he seems to be saying, but of a different type. Rules, perhaps, that can eventually be incorporated into syllabuses? Wilkins' attempt to link the two types of approach (1976) is more explicit. He draws a distinction between 'synthetic' and 'analytic' teaching strategies, a distinction which has much in common with the one Newmark is making, and the one between traditional methodologies on the one hand and the kind of 'methodological solution' we have been considering here on the other. In a synthetic approach the teacher isolates and orders the forms of the linguistic system, systematically presents them to the student one by one and thus incrementally builds up language competence. In analytic teaching it is the student who does the analysis from data presented to him in the form of 'natural chunks'. Wilkins associates the synthetic approach with structural syllabuses, and the analytic with notional specifications.

One—if not the—central feature of Newmark's standpoint is that (p. 161, this volume) 'consideration of the details supplied by . . . analysis has taken away from the exponential power available in learning in natural chunks'; that, in other words, the whole machinery of linguistic paraphernalia which we employ in teaching (particularly, one might think, in the specification of teaching content) constitutes an interference with the language learning process. At many points in Wilkins' discussion he seems to be leading towards a similar conclusion—that what is wrong with the synthetic approach is teacher preselection and isolation of items, and that this in some way does not happen with the analytic approach. It is with the distinction made in this way that we are able to make a clear-cut methodological differentiation between the strategies, and are able to give the kind of coherent psycholinguistic justification for the analytic that Newmark hints at, making reference to the process of first language acquisition. One might indeed argue that it is only with the distinction made thus that we can meaningfully claim to be 'basing our approach on the learner's analytic capacities' (Wilkins, p. 14), something which seems to necessitate the degree of student control over teaching content that solutions like Brumfit's (with its 'initial communication with available resources') appears to imply. It is certainly difficult to see how an approach which condones and actively attempts to practise teacher preselection/isolation, and whose claim to 'analycity' rests only in that it presents the preselected and isolated items in 'natural chunks' can rely in any sense on the student's analytic capacities, or distinguish itself sufficiently from most so-called synthetic teaching to be worthy of another name.

We can argue, then, quite strongly, that a truly analytic approach should entail lack of teacher preselection and isolation of items. But what does this imply in terms of syllabus design? Is the implication that syllabuses, as the explicit formulation and preselection by the teacher of teaching content, should not be drawn up at all? Certainly Newmark's observations concerning the interference caused by 'the details supplied by . . . analysis' (together with the types of methodological solution being proposed nowadays) appear to entail at the very least a de-emphasis of the importance of syllabus design. But if de-emphasis (rather than abolition), then how does this manifest itself? What does a 'de-emphasized syllabus' look like? These general questions lead to specific ones, such as how we decide on (i.e. preselect) what the 'initial communication with available resources' in Brumfit's solution is to be communication about?[2]

Wilkins' answer is neither the abolition nor the de-emphasis of the syllabus. It is rather to draw a qualitative distinction between the formulation of teaching content in structural and in notional terms. His claim is that notional specification, because it is 'behavioural' rather than 'linguistic' is essentially part of an analytic strategy. But it is difficult to see how, once we are prepared to commit ourselves to entering into the process of specification (in whatever terms) we can fail to arrive at a syllabus content which is either explicitly linguistic or will implicitly shape the linguistic content of our teaching. As Wilkins (p. 13) admits: 'since it is language behaviour we are concerned with, it is possible, indeed desirable, that the linguistic content of any unit [in notional teaching materials] should also be stated', implying that the difference between notional and structural syllabuses is merely that the former has a behavioural underpinning that the latter lacks. The difference is in starting point, less clearly in final result. Certainly the amount of attention that has been paid to questions of notional syllabus design in the past few years, and the development of tools such as Munby's (1978) intended to make our specifications as 'scientific', precise and detailed as possible seem to violate the very spirit of Newmark's 'minimal strategy', and the belief that analysis interferes with acquisition. Certainly also many of the materials which have been produced following notional syllabuses indicate that this type of specification *can* lead to synthetic teaching. Indeed, if one argues that any detailed specification of teaching content (albeit made in semantic and pragmatic rather than, initially, structural terms) is synthetic, then one is forced to the conclusion that notional syllabuses are *a priori* synthetic constructs which not only admit, but also invite or even impose a synthetic strategy.

By way of conclusion: the kind of difficulties discussed here reflect a basic and perhaps unresolvable conflict between teacher and student control. In the reading of the present situation given above, some form of 'student control' is taken as central to the concept of analycity. In these terms, the 'methodological solutions' can lay more claim to analycity, though it does remain unclear whether (and if so, to what degree and in what form) they condone teacher control by preselection of content. But exactly because they are sufficiently recognizable as analytic, they give rise to a further question: the extent to which they can convince as general strategies for language teaching rather than merely as language àctivation procedures for advanced students. If, in other words, we accept them as analytic, we have still to determine whether analycity works.

There are two ways of viewing the notional 'teaching content' solution. One is an attempt to be analytic that failed. The other is to regard its main mistake as the attempt to associate itself with analycity at all. A standpoint which seems both more consistent with the way the notional syllabus has been applied, and quite capable of coherent justification, is for it unashamedly to fly synthetic colours. It would then rally those who believe in synthetic methodology, who believe that synthetic teaching has created structurally competent students and who might predict that it can produce appropriate ones as well, as soon as we specify our teaching content in terms of categories of use. Certainly for many the solution to Newmark's problem which claims that the major step towards teaching 'asking for a light' is taken when we accept 'asking for a light' as an item we wish to teach cannot be dismissed out of hand. If notional syllabuses do fly such colours, then we can recognize unequivocably what seems anyway to be the case, that there are indeed two general approaches to communicative language teaching which diverge—not because one is concerned with syllabus design and the other with methodology—but because each seems to carry different implications in terms of both syllabus design and methodology.

There is one sort of person for whom the conclusion that notional syllabuses do not preclude a synthetic methodology is particularly important. It is the teacher who, disillusioned with the results of synthetic teaching, seeks salvation in the notional syllabus. This sets him on a fresh analysis of language teaching content, this time made (initially) in notional rather than structural terms. His discovery that the syllabus he eventually produces can (or has to?) be taught synthetically, will lead to further inevitable disillusionment.

Part 2

The point has already been made that the 'teaching content' approach to communicative language teaching bases itself on a linguistic insight regarding what is entailed in knowing a language, and that now, following Hymes, a revised view of language competence is generally accepted. Use of the word 'knowing' in this context conjures up the spectre of a well-aired issue in applied linguistics—that 'knowledge of a language' is not the same thing as 'ability to use the language'. It was often said of the grammar-translation method that it provided knowledge without skill, and a similar criticism can be levelled at our early attempts at communicative language teaching. If this is—as it surely is—

a just criticism to level at any language teaching, then the implication is that methodologies should be based not only on *linguistic* insights as to the nature of 'knowledge of a language', but also on *psycholinguistic* insights as to the processes involved in its use. It is not a criticism that argues in favour of an analytic rather than a synthetic methodology (though it may be one that applies most obviously to what were called above the 'teaching content' solutions); after all, the highly synthetic audio-lingual methodology certainly had a psycholinguistic base (even if it is one that we may now discredit). What it does argue in favour of is, simply, a methodology; of, in the present situation, turning our attention to what communication scientists, skills psychologists and others can reveal about communicative processes.

To the extent that Part 2 of this paper follows a thesis, it is that these sources—the communication scientist and the skills psychologist—can contribute considerably (and in a way as yet only partially exploited) to the development of a communicative methodology. Specifically, we here consider some processes relevant to the teaching (and testing) of speaking. To provide a basis for discussion, consider the following set of possible simple interactions:

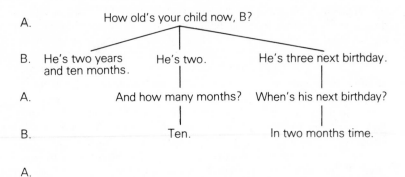

In this situation A's aim is to find out B's child's age in years and months. In order to do this he asks the question 'how old's your child now, B?' A number of possible interactional sequences might follow. In one, B replies 'he's 2 years and 10 months'. A compares this piece of information with the information he requires. He finds the two match, and the interaction therefore ends. In a second possible interaction, B replies 'he's 2'. When A compares this information with the required information, he finds a discrepancy. He now knows the child's age in

years, but not in months. His next question—'and how many months?'
—is calculated to eliminate this discrepancy. He is given the reply
'10', and the interaction ends. In a third possible interaction, B replies
'he's 3 next birthday'. After comparing given information with required
information, A formulates the question 'when's his birthday?' B's reply
eliminates the mismatch between given and required, and the third
interaction closes.

There are at least three processes which A must undertake if he is
to fulfil his role as interactant. Firstly, he must 'scan' B's utterance to
extract what Cherry (1957) calls its 'pragmatic information'. Pragmatic
information is not equivalent to semantic information; it is that part
of the total information conveyed which contributes to the information
required by the speaker. It is, in short, information which the listener
wants to receive. In order to receive this information the listener must
maintain a state of readiness. He approaches the task of listening
comprehension prepared to search for certain pieces of information
in his interactant's words. Once this information comes, it has to be
assessed according to the speaker's aim, and this is the second process
which A must undertake. The process is, in MacKay's (1972) words,
one of 'evaluation whereby some indication of the current outcome
is compared against some internal "target criterion" [what we have
called "speaker aim"] so that certain kinds of discrepancy or "mismatch"
would evoke activity calculated to reduce that discrepancy'. A compares,
then, what he is told with what he wants to know, identifies any
mismatch and then—as a third process—formulates his next utterance.
This he does by selecting from what Halliday (1970a: 142) calls the
'large number of interrelated options' embodied in the 'meaning
potential'. The three interactions considered earlier in the 'asking how
old the child is' situation constitute only a small part of the total
possible number which the interactants could have followed; just
as Halliday's ways of scolding a child (this volume) represent only a
small number of the possible ways of expounding that function.

If interactions are to continue in a natural way, the formulation of
utterances and the processes of scanning and evaluation which precede
it must of course be made extremely quickly—within 'real time'. The
ability to do this is what we generally mean by fluency in a language.

The first, most central, and by now most generally accepted
implication of the nature of these processes is that they can only
really be practised in a language teaching which is 'task-orientated'.
We are now accustomed to the view of language as a tool developed
to serve us in Halliday's social contexts and behavioural settings, and
it is such a view which led us in Part I of this volume to speak of the
'instrumentality of language teaching'. We also now recognize that
past language teaching often failed to practise language to some purpose

—somewhat akin to practising the use of an axe without providing any trees to cut down. It focused attention on 'how' without providing a 'why', asking students to produce sentences like 'the cat sat on the mat', not because anyone wished to know where the cat was (nor what was on the mat) but as a way of practising prepositional phrases using 'on'. One way in which 'non-instrumental language teaching' (which divorces language from the contexts and settings it should serve) fails is that it does not develop fluency in the processes involved in language use. We cannot expect listeners to approach interactions in a state of readiness, to learn how to scan for pragmatic information, unless we provide them with a reason for scanning; nor can we expect them to evaluate incoming information against a speaker aim, unless we provide them with a speaker aim (a communicative intent). Finally we cannot expect them to make appropriate selection from meaning potential unless they have an intention from which to derive meaning. This point is well exemplified by an anecdote from Savignon (1972b) who uses role play techniques to practise greetings in French with a group of students. The first volunteer walks up to the female experimenter and says 'Bonjour, monsieur'. Everyone realizes, in Savignon's words, 'how much they needed practice in linking expression to actual meaning'. There is indeed a crucial difference between practice involving the linking of expression to actual meaning, where expression is made to serve actual meaning—and practice in which the student's attention is focused on achieving correctness of expression. The difference doubtless partially accounts for Krashen's (1976) two systems for second language performance.[3]

It is for reasons such as this that fluency in communicative process can only develop within a 'task-orientated teaching'—one which provides 'actual meaning' by focusing on tasks to be mediated through language, and where success or failure is seen to be judged in terms of whether or not these tasks are performed.

A second implication relating to these processes concerns the concept of information. 'Conveying information' and 'communicating' are similar, though not identical notions. In a large number of conversational interactions the purpose of communicating is to convey information—factual information, information concerning feelings, information about what we wish to be done. The concept of conveying information involves, as many linguists have testified, a notion of doubt. We can only be said to be conveying a piece of information to someone if they do not already know it. As Lyons (1968: 413) says: 'if the hearer knows in advance that the speaker will inevitably produce a particular utterance in a particular context, then it is obvious that the utterance will give him no information when it occurs; no "communication" will take place'. 'Information', in Cherry's (1957: 168) words this time, 'can be received only when there is doubt.'

It is the absence of this element of doubt in much language teaching which makes it non-communicative. The conventional techniques of 'commentary' (telling a story from pictures, retelling it after the teacher, describing actions taking place in the classroom) provide useful structural practice but do not involve communication. Such practice fails in two ways. Firstly it does not generally capture student interest, and this may well be a significant factor contributing to the unpopularity of foreign languages in school curricula—one recipe for boredom being the repetition of the known to the knowers. But equally importantly it fails to involve the processes by which interaction takes place. These processes depend crucially on the existence of an information gap. If the listener already knows the pragmatic information content of what his interactant will say, then no scanning for such content will take place; nor will responses be formulated within real time based on information just received. In this sense the existence of doubt is an important prerequisite to fluency practice.

The attempt to create information gaps in the classroom, thereby producing communication viewed as the bridging of the information gap, has characterized much recent communicative methodology. These attempts take many forms: Wright (1976) achieves it by showing out-of-focus slides which the students attempt to identify; Byrne (1978) provides incomplete plans and diagrams which students have to complete by asking for information; Allwright (this volume) places a screen between students and gets one to place objects in a certain pattern. This pattern is then communicated to the student behind the screen. Geddes & Sturtridge (1979) develop 'jig-saw' listening in which students listen to different taped materials and then communicate their contents to others in the class. Most of these techniques operate by providing information to some and withholding it from others. Often it is the students who give information to each other, but sometimes—particularly when the language is to be learned receptively rather than productively—it is more appropriate for the teacher to play this role. Morrow & Johnson (1979) for example ask students to follow street directions given by the teacher and to mark given locations on a map. In this exercise, it is the receptive understanding of directions rather than the production of them which is being practised.

Providing information to some and withholding it from others is one of several ways to create an information gap. Another, which constitutes the final aspect of communication to be considered here, is simply to permit the student some choice in what he says.

The concepts of selection and doubt are closely linked. To continue the earlier quotation from Cherry: 'information can be received only when there is doubt; and doubt implies the existence of alternatives—where choice, selection or discrimination is called for'. If Speaker A can select what he says, then Listener B will be in doubt as to what will be said to him; speaker selection implies listener doubt. Thus if we create classroom situations in which the students are free to choose what to say, the essential information gap will have been created.

But the importance of selection goes far beyond its utility in the creation of information gaps. Central to Halliday's view of language (exemplified in this volume) is that it constitutes sets of options at various levels. The *concept* of selection, as choice from various sets of options, is thus basic to the concept of communication; and the *process* of selection in real time from various sets of options is basic to the process of fluent communication. From this point of view a communicative language teaching may be seen as the provision to students of sets of options from which selection can be made. It must also provide practice in the process of selecting from these options within real time.

One of the major advantages—if not indeed *the* major advantage—of teaching materials that are organized functionally or according to some other non-structural principle, is that they provide the opportunity to present language in semantically-homogeneous units. This makes it possible to practise interactions which (like 'real' interactions) centre upon related semantic areas; also, to practise the process of selection from a semantic network in real time. Thus when we teach 'invitations' for example, we can deal not only with inviting, but with accepting and declining invitations as well, giving a number of alternative exponents for each. What we are providing is a set of semantic options for the network of invitations. Once this is provided, we can practise selection from it in real time: Student A can invite (selecting from the various exponents provided), and Student B can select whether to accept or decline (again choosing from various exponents, at the same time making sure that his exponent is textually appropriate to the exponent of invitation he hears). It will be the materials producer's task to provide techniques by which this process of selection can be meaningfully made (i.e. in relation to a created context)[4].

As the students work through the materials, and as long as the syllabus has been constructed to deal with interactionally-related semantic areas in sequence, the selections which we can expect the student to make will increase exponentially. Consider for example a possible situation in which we follow our 'invitations' unit with one on 'making arrangements'. The number of interaction sequences involving selection might be as follows:

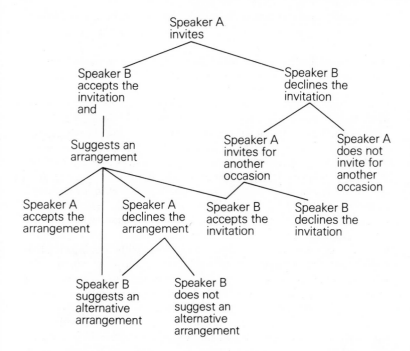

In a structural syllabus the situation is different. Language is presented in structurally-homogeneous but semantically-heterogeneous units, the result being that semantically-related but structurally-unrelated sequences (for example 'invitation—acceptance' where the exponents used are structurally unrelated) will tend not to occur. This is partly because in their desire to focus on structural concerns the materials will actively seek structurally-homogeneous interactions, and partly because the structural grading will at any given point restrict the number of semantically-related interactions the student can handle. Consequently most of the communicative practice in which the students will have to develop interactions involving the selection of realistic options from a semantic network will tend to occur towards the end of a structural course, when the students' structural knowledge is developed. Certainly such practice, important to the development of fluency, will not occur regularly throughout the course.

   Part 2 of this paper has considered ways in which classroom teaching procedures can be made to reflect a coherent model of communicative skill. Similar remarks may be made about testing procedures. It is certainly the case that testing (as teaching) must be concerned not only with 'knowledge of a language' but also with 'ability to use it'. We must do more, that is, than ask the student whether he *knows* that Exponent X is appropriate to Intent Y in Context Z; we must find out whether he *is able to produce* Exponent X when he intends Y in context Z.

It may be that a valuable and insufficiently tapped source of inspiration for the testing of fluency of communicative process lies in the area of skills psychology. Reed (1968), for example, lists a number of ways in which skilled performance differs from non-skilled performance, and his observations on the variable of speed are particularly interesting. 'In many skilled activities', he says, 'improvement is assessed in terms of speed and it is commonly assumed that the overall time taken to complete any activity reflects the level of skill. But in absolute terms this is not necessarily so. . . . As Woodworth (1938) pointed out, expert performance is not merely that of the beginner executed more quickly.' Other important indicators of skilled performance are: the 'suppression of flourishes'; the ability to carry out a task with less information; confidence; the ability to check mistakes; anticipation; automation; reliability. The extent to which these various measures can be related to language teaching through formal testing procedures is of course doubtful, but at least some (the ability to carry out a task with less information; the ability to check mistakes; anticipation) might be explored. It is particularly interesting to note that the ability to recognize and check one's own mistakes is, according to Bartlett (1947) 'the best single measure of mental skill'.[5]

Notes

Specially written for this volume.

1. One might be forgiven for suggesting that the concerted response within language teaching to solve this problem springs as much from the fact that linguistic studies provide such a neat way of posing it, as from a conviction of the problem's gravity.
2. One interesting suggestion for the nature of the syllabus in analytic teaching concerns not the types of category (notional or structural) it specifies, but the role it plays. The syllabus might function, it is suggested, as a 'checklist' with the help of which (after the teaching event) we monitor teaching content. In this role the syllabus must be seen as a list of desirable—rather than rigidly prescribed—items to teach. There are of course problems: should the teacher attempt to guide students' attention away from detailed consideration of items which occur in the classroom (and to which the student turns

his analytic powers), yet which are not on the 'checklist'? What does the teacher do when he finds an item on the checklist has not been covered? To the extent that the teacher follows the checklist it differs only terminologically from the syllabus as prescription of teaching content; to the extent he ignores it it becomes a valueless document.

3. The concept of 'meaningful language practice' (e.g. in Dakin, 1973) as practice involving relating language to a situation is of course generally accepted. What is intended here is something more, in which the language is not merely related to a situation but 'made subservient' to it.

4. This may be done, for example, by providing realia, such as a diary in which the student fills in appointments. He then accepts invitations at times when he is free and declines them when he is not. This is the technique used in Johnson & Morrow (1979) and in other materials.

5. Cloze procedures do of course test anticipation.

Conclusion

The early papers in this book have all been influential in the development of a 'communicative' approach to the teaching of languages. Nonetheless, it will be clear from the papers in the final section that there is no direct transfer from the theoretical issues raised to teaching methodology. Methodology is of course an attempt to solve specific practical problems, and insofar as it relates to the complexities of real people and real institutions it must embody attitudes drawn from a number of different theoretical disciplines. There is a particularly difficult epistemological problem here, for the status of the various insights drawn from different disciplines, with different aims and investigatory procedures, is difficult to establish when such insights have to be interpreted in relation to each other: a psychologist's view of language does not confront directly the views of a linguist or a sociologist. But methodologists can neither afford to ignore the contributions of different disciplines nor establish their own procedures on a principled basis independently, for the concern of methodology is not knowledge but effective performance. So it will be apparent that there is some discontinuity between the first three sections and the fourth. In many ways all the papers in the fourth section produce answers to questions of teaching practice which are informed by, rather than arise directly from, the arguments and exemplifications of the previous sections. Furthermore, teachers, concerned as they are with student responses, must convert linguistic discussion into learning practice, and they cannot ignore either learning theories or successful classroom experience. Designers of syllabuses and teaching materials have often been able to reflect the assumptions of linguists fairly closely, but teachers have had to mediate between syllabus, textbook and students by calling into operation all the possible resources of human contact. Applying ideas to the classroom is a conceptual activity, and is not the same as teaching, which is an interactive negotiation. The papers in this book indicate both the strengths and limitations of pedagogical theory. All language teachers will find themselves, over the next few years, recreating such ideas in the context of their own classrooms.

Appendix Examples of teaching materials.

This appendix contains extracts from materials which can be said to make a claim, either explicitly or implicitly, to follow the kind of principles discussed in this volume. Readers may like to examine them in this light.
Note: These materials have been photographically reproduced and do not reflect the quality of the originals.

Extract 1

From 'Kaleidoscope: English for Juniors, Stage I', University of York/Macmillan Education, 1976.
These materials are for junior learners at the beginner level.

From Pupil's Book (p. 41)

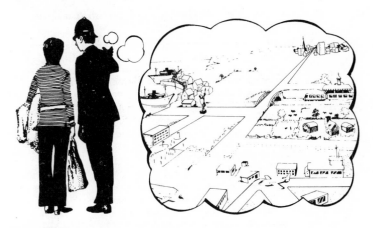

From Teacher's Guide (pp. 214-6)

UNIT 5 STEP 7	GIVING DIRECTIONS

Introduction	Pupils learn to give directions using maps; one imaginary and one of the area around the school. Further directions are learnt, and the revision of vocabulary items denoting places, for understanding only.

Language introduced in this Step	*For Understanding Only*	*For Speaking*
	Can you tell me the way to your house?	Start walking.
		Turn round.
	Airport, farm, railway station, school, town.	Go straight on.
		Again.
	(and see Tapescript)	
Language which has occurred earlier, re-used in this Step	Point to the (harbour).	Here.
	Where's the (harbour)?	Stop.
	This is the (harbour).	Turn left/right.
	Turn to your left/right.	(Come) this way.
	(John)'s left is your right.	
	Harbour, statue.	

Tape	Tape to be played in class: 5.7b.
	Tape for the teacher only: 5.7c, 5.7e.

5.7a

Discussion in L1: Usefulness of English as a lingua franca

Materials	Pupil's Book, page 5.

Discuss with the pupils where and when English might prove useful as a *lingua franca*. Tell them to look at the picture of a tourist using English to ask the way (Picture 7), on page 5 of the Pupil's Book.

5.7b

Listening for understanding: At the airport

Materials	Pupil's Tape to be played in class: 'Excuse me!'
	Pupil's Book, page 41: 'Excuse me!'

Tapescript: 'Excuse me!'	*Tourist 1*	Excuse me. Can you tell me the way to town?
	Policeman	Yes, sir. Go out of the airport, go straight on over the bridge, and you're there. It's not far.
	Tourist 1	Thank you very much.
	Policeman	Can I help you, madam?
	Tourist 2	Yes. Can you tell me the way to Macdonald's Farm, please?
	Policeman	Yes. Go out of the airport, then turn right. It's not far.
	Tourist 2	Thank you.
	Tourist 3	Excuse me. Can you tell me the way to the harbour?
	Policeman	Yes, sir. Go out of the airport, then turn left.
	Tourist 3	Thank you very much.

Policeman	Can I help you, sir?
Tourist 4	Can you tell me the way to the school, please?
Policeman	Go out of the airport, turn left, then turn left again at the statue.
Tourist 4	Thanks.
Tourist 5	Excuse me. Can you tell me the way to the railway station, please?
Policeman	Yes, madam. Go out of the airport, go straight on over the bridge, and then turn right.
Tourist 5	Thank you very much.

5.7c

Listening and doing: Map work

Materials

> Pupil's Book, page 41: 'Excuse me!'
> Teacher's Tape, tapescript page 36: (Lesson model).

Tell the pupils to study the map on page 41 of the Pupil's Book, and to point to the places that you name.

Teacher	Point to the harbour (on the map).
	Point to the school (on the map).
	Point to the airport (on the map).

Name some of the places in a question:

Teacher	Where's the town?
	Where's the railway station?
	Where's the farm?

Go round the class and help any pupils who cannot find a particular place on the map. Point and say:

Teacher	This is the (harbour) . . . here.

5.7d

Listening for understanding: 'Excuse me!'

Materials

> Pupil's Book, page 41: 'Excuse me!'
> Pupil's Tape to be played in class: 'Excuse me!'

Play the tape 'Excuse me!' again, as the pupils continue to look at the picture map on page 41 of the Pupil's Book.

5.7e

Listening and doing: Directions in the classroom

Materials

> Teacher's Tape, tapescript page 37: (Pronunciation model).

Make sure that all the pupils in the class are sitting facing in the same direction. Go and stand at the back of the class, so that you also are facing in the same direction. Tell a pupil to stand up. Explain that he/she must start walking slowly, and must change direction in accordance with your commands.

Choose those commands that will serve to steer the pupil round the classroom and back to his/her place.

Teacher   Start walking.

Go straight on.

Turn left.

Turn left again.

Turn right.

Stop.

Start walking again.

Turn round.

Come this way.

Turn right.

Stop. You're there.

When the pupil who is responding to the commands has turned several times and is momentarily facing in the opposite direction to the rest of the class, make sure that the left/right difference is clear by saying:

Teacher   Turn to *your* left/right, (John).

and addressing the class say:

Teacher   (John's) left is your right.

5.7f   Repetition

Let several pupils take over the giving of commands, as given by you in Step 7e.

Pupil   Start walking.

Go straight on.

Turn left. (etc.)

If any confusion arises attach labels with *left* and *right*, written on them, to the pupil's wrists.

5.7g   Practical work: Drawing maps

Materials

> Paper and pencil for each pupil.
> A street plan, showing the neighbourhood of the school (optional).

Tell every pupil to draw a rough map, showing the route from school to his/her home. It is not essential that a complete map be drawn. All that is required is an indication of the principal turnings taken by each pupil. Help the pupils by drawing a map on the blackboard, showing the school and the principal streets leading to and from it. Refer to a street plan if need be.

From Teacher's Tapescript (pp. 36-7)

5.7c   **Listening and doing. Mapwork.**

(Lesson Model)

Teacher	Point to the harbour on the map.
	Point to the school.
	Point to the airport.
	Anne, where's the town?
Pupil 1	Here.
Teacher	Yes.
	Billy, where's the railway station?
Pupil 2	Here.
Teacher	Yes. And where's the farm, Tom?
Pupil 3	. . . er . . . Here, sir.
Teacher	Yes.
	Everyone, where's the harbour?
	The harbour.
	Look. This is the harbour.
	And this is the school.
	Where's the airport?
	Yes. That's right.

5.7e   **Repetition.**

(Pronunciation Model)

Pupil 1	Can you tell me the way to your house?
Pupil 2	Start walking.
	Go straight on.
	Turn left.
	Turn left again.
	Turn right.
	Stop.
	Start walking again.
	Turn round.
	Come this way.
	Turn right.
	Stop. You're there.

Extract 2

From 'Crescent English Course: Book I', T. O'Neill & P. Snow, English Language Teaching for the Arab World, Oxford University Press, 1976. These materials have been especially designed for the Arab World. Book I is for beginners, and the materials are intended for the young learner. The original is in full colour.

From the Pupil's Book (pp. 76-8)

Ask each other the way.

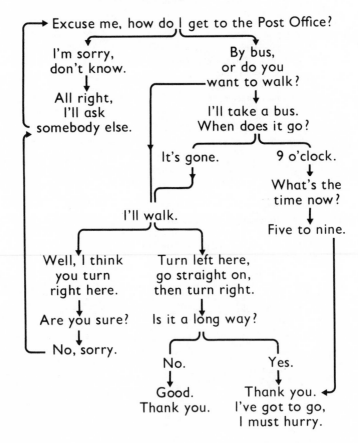

Find out ...

How many people are there
in your school?

How many fingers are there
in your class?

How long is your classroom?

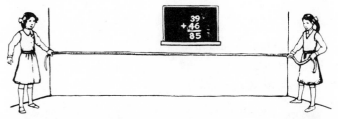

What did your friend eat yesterday?

How many windows are there
in your classroom?

What do wolves eat?

When was your grandfather born?

Find out ...

Where's your friend's house?

How many people live in it?

How far is it from here?

Find out ...

What does this mean?

GRQW	WHOO	SHRSOH	BRX
FDQ	VHH	D	ZROl
ZKHQ	BRX	FDQW	

It is written in a secret language.
Can you understand it?
This will help you.

D=A	I=F	N=K	S=P	X=U	A=X
E=B	J=G	O=L	T=Q	Y=V	B=Y
F=C	K=H	P=M	U=R	Z=W	C=Z
G=D	L=I	Q=N	V=S		
H=E	M=J	R=O	W=T		

Extract 3

From 'Say what you mean in English', J. Andrews, Nelson, 1975.
This book is for elementary students.

From Teacher's Book (pp. 88-91)

Unit 21

Can I help you?

a tube of toothpaste with stripes

a writing-pad

a shoe with laces

a slip-on shoe

Listen to this:

Shop Assistant: Can I help you?
Customer: Yes, I need a tube of toothpaste.
Shop Assistant: Any special sort?
Customer: Well . . . no, not really.
Shop Assistant: How about this one?
Customer: Is there a smaller size?
Shop Assistant: Yes, here you are.
Customer: Has this got red stripes in it?
Shop Assistant: Yes, it has.
Customer: Oh . . . haven't you got a plain sort?
Shop Assistant: Here's one.
Customer: Good. I'll take that one.
                How much is it?
Shop Assistant: Fourteen, please.
Customer: Thank you!

Now say this (listen and repeat):

He needs a tube of toothpaste.
He doesn't want any special sort.
He wants a small size.
He doesn't want toothpaste with red stripes in it.
He wants a plain sort.

Listen to this:

Shop assistant: Yes, please?
Customer: I'd like a writing-pad.
Shop assistant: Any special make?
Customer: Not really . . . anything will do.
Shop assistant: How about this one?
Customer: Is there a cheaper one?
Shop assistant: Yes, here you are.   . . . .
Customer: This is blue, isn't it?
Shop assistant: Yes . . .
Customer: Oh . . . haven't you got white?
Shop assistant: Here's one.
Customer: Good, I'll take that one. How much is it?
Shop assistant: Seventeen, please.
Customer: Thank you.

Now say this (listen and repeat):

He wants a writing pad.
He doesn't want any special make.
He wants a cheap one.
He doesn't want blue, he wants white.

Look at this:

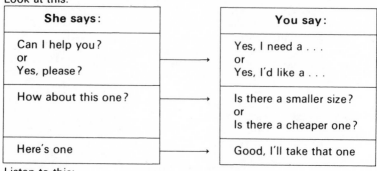

She says:	You say:
Can I help you? or Yes, please?	Yes, I need a . . . or Yes, I'd like a . . .
How about this one?	Is there a smaller size? or Is there a cheaper one?
Here's one	Good, I'll take that one

Listen to this:

Shop assistant: Can I help you?
Customer: Yes, I want some brown shoes.
Shop assistant: With laces, or slip-on?
Customer: With laces, please.
Shop assistant: What size?
Customer: Nine, I think, but would you measure my foot?
Shop assistant: Certainly! Yes, nine it is.
Now . . . how about these?
Customer: Well, they feel a bit tight here. Can I try the next size?
Shop assistant: Of course. Try these.
Customer: They're a better fit, but I don't like the colour.
Have you got them in a darker brown?
Shop assistant: I'm afraid not. These are all we have.
Customer: Oh well, I think I'll leave it, then.
Thank you very much!

Now say this (listen and repeat):

He wants some brown shoes with laces, size nine.
The first pair are a bit tight, so he asks for the next size.
The second pair are a better fit, but he doesn't like the colour.
He decides not to buy them.

Now, imagine you want to buy some toothpaste. Can you say the right things? Try.

Shop assistant: Can I help you?
Customer: . . . .
Shop assistant: Any special sort?
Customer: . . . .
Shop assistant: How about this one?
Customer: . . . .
Shop assistant: Yes, here you are.
Customer: . . . .
. . . .
Shop assistant: Fourteen, please.
Customer: . . . .

Now act the part of the shop assistant, and get your neighbour to be the customer. Do this without looking at the book.

Extract 4

From 'Strategies', B. Abbs, A. Ayton, I. Freebairn, Longman, 1975.
The materials are at a pre-intermediate level.

From Student's Book (pp. 91-3)

unit 10 **CREATIVE SPEAKING AND WRITING**

Degrees of certainty about the future

Exercise 1. Discussing future possibilities

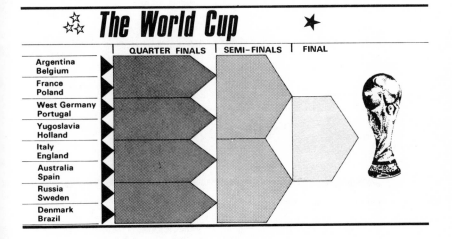

INFORMATION CHART				
Country	Last 20 matches			Other information
	Won	Lost	Drawn	
Argentina	6	5	9	New goalkeeper
Belgium	5	7	8	New captain
France	11	5	4	Lost against Italy last year
Poland	10	3	7	Weak defence
West Germany	13	3	4	New manager
Portugal	9	7	4	Beat Russia last year
Yugoslavia	14	4	2	Three players ill
Holland	9	6	5	Won Cup two years ago
Italy	8	5	7	Three new players
England	7	4	9	Weak attack
Australia	8	8	4	Weak goalkeeper
Spain	8	8	4	Weak defence but good goalkeeper
Russia	10	5	5	Brilliant centre forward
Sweden	11	4	5	Strong defence
Denmark	8	7	5	In cup final four years ago
Brazil	12	5	3	Won last World Cup

unit 10

The World Cup Discussion. Group or pair work: Discuss the chances of different countries playing in the next World Cup. Use the information chart to help you make your decisions to find out who you think might win the cup. You first decide about all the teams in the quarter finals, then who will reach the semi-finals and finally who will reach the finals. Your discussion might go something like this:

A: *Well, Argentina might beat Belgium, but I doubt it.*
B: *Why do you think that?*
A: *They've won more matches than Belgium, but they've got a new goalkeeper. And Belgium's new captain is very good.*
B: *I don't agree with you. No, I'm certain now that Argentina will beat Belgium.*

Now discuss the chances of all the other teams in the same way. Write the names of the teams in the chart when you have made your decisions.

Exercise 2. Writing about future possibilities

Give a written account of what you think may happen in the next World Cup.

Exercise 3. Asking about plans

A reporter from a London newspaper is interviewing Neville about the future plans of the Leave London Alone Action Group. Some of the plans are certain, some of the plans are not so certain. Read this conversation with a partner. You are the reporter. Notice how he stresses the certainties and uncertainties of the situation in his first two exchanges with Neville, and carry on in the same way.

Reporter: What plans have you got for your campaign? I'd like to write an article about the group for my paper.
Neville: Well, our plans at the moment haven't been finally decided, but one thing is certain and that is, that we intend to fight on.
Reporter: Oh, so you will fight on?
Neville: Oh yes, most definitely. However, its not going to be easy. We could have problems . . .
Reporter: Oh, so you may have problems?
Neville: Minor ones, I hope. You know that we've decided to open the cam-paign next month.
Reporter: ....
Neville: Yes, that's the idea. Some of the members would like to have a mass meeting in Trafalgar Square, but we're not sure about that.
Reporter: ....
Neville: Possible, but as I said, it's not certain. One thing that is certain is that we've booked a small hall in the Covent Garden area so that we can hold a meeting for the local people.
Reporter: ....
Neville: Yes, that's fixed. And another thing that's being organised now is a petition which we want to take to the Prime Minister.
Reporter: ....
Neville: Right. Also, some of the members want to march on the House of Commons, but we haven't finally decided on that.
Reporter: ....
Neville: Well, I want to, for one. But some of the others don't think it's a good idea. However, the thing that we are all agreed on is that we must fight the plan until we win.
Reporter: ....
Neville: And you can help by writing us a good article.

The equity in

Obligation and necessity (present and future) (1) unit 10

Set 2

5. Confirming procedures.

Maggie's nearly ready to take her driving test. She's telling herself what to do and the driving instructor's checking what she says.

1. MAGGIE: Check . . . gears.
   INSTRUCTOR: *Yes, you must check the gears.*

2. MAGGIE: Check . . . handbrake.
   INSTRUCTOR: *Yes, you must check the handbrake.*

6. Confirming obligations.

Stephen's helping Maggie to prepare for her driving test oral examination. This means that she has to answer certain questions based on the Highway Code.

1. STEPHEN: What about driving without lights at night?
   MAGGIE: *You must never drive without lights at night.*

2. STEPHEN: That's right. And stopping on the motor-way?
   MAGGIE: *You must never stop on the motorway.*

7. Recognising obligations (1)

Things you have to have and pay for:
Life isn't easy and life isn't free. For example, in Britain, if you have a car, you also have to have a licence, insurance, and you have to pay road tax. If you have a television set you have to have a licence and so on.

1. OFFICIAL: Now you've got your lovely new car, Mr Smith, you must pay road tax.
   MR SMITH: *I know I have to pay road tax.*

2. OFFICIAL: And insurance Mr Smith, don't forget.
   MR SMITH: *I know I have to pay insurance.*

3. OFFICIAL: And you must have a driving licence.
   MR SMITH: *I know I have to have a driving licence.*

8. Recognising obligations (2)

We can also say *have got to* instead of *have to*.
MR SMITH: *I know I've got to pay road tax and I know I've got to pay insurance.*

9. Questioning obligations.

A little boy is going to visit the zoo with his grandmother. His mother wants him to get ready.

1. MOTHER: Right! You must wash your hands.
   BOY: *Do I have to wash them?*

2. MOTHER: Yes, you do. And you must comb your hair too.
   BOY: *Do I have to comb it?*

10. Releasing people from obligations (1)

The boy doesn't want to do what his mother tells him to do. So he asks his grandmother if he really has to.

1. BOY: Gran, must I really wash my hands?
   GRANDMOTHER: *No, you needn't wash them if you don't want to.*

2. BOY: And must I really comb my hair?
   GRANDMOTHER: *No, you needn't comb it if you don't want to.*

11. Releasing people from obligations (2)

This time the grandmother is going to say the same thing but in a different way.

1. BOY: Gran, must I really wash my hands?
   GRANDMOTHER: *No, you don't have to wash them if you don't want to.*

2. BOY: And must I really comb my hair?
   GRANDMOTHER: *No, you don't have to comb it if you don't want to.*

Extract 5

From 'Approaches', K. Johnson & K. Morrow. Cambridge University Press, 1979.

These materials are intended for intermediate students, particularly those following short-term intensive courses in Britain.

From Student's Book (pp. 43-45)

Section A: Oral Practice

1   What would you say?

Lynne has lost her purse. She looks everywhere but can't find it so she goes to ask the school secretary, Mrs. West, for help.

She goes into Mrs. West's room. She is disturbing Mrs. West, but Mrs. West doesn't mind.

Lynne says she needs help. Mrs. West asks what she can do.

She explains the problem and Mrs. West agrees to help.

2 a) John's car has broken down, and he's late for a party. So he rings a friend. . .

Sally wants to open the window, but finds it's stuck. So she knocks on Paul's door. . .

What would *you* say in these situations:

i)   You want to look up a word in the dictionary, but find you've left yours at home. Your teacher has got one.

ii) You've got to take your suitcase upstairs, and it's very heavy. Perhaps your flatmate could help.

iii) You want to phone the doctor urgently, but the phone is in your landlady's room.

iv) You find you've forgotten to buy some eggs, and your friend Anita is about to go shopping.

v)   You find that your bicycle has a flat tyre, and you're late for lessons. Your landlady could help perhaps.

vi) You want to do your washing, but you're not sure how the machine in the launderette works. Maybe one of the other people there knows.

vii) You've just written a letter to your parents, and you know your flatmate is going past the post office.

viii) Your landlady has said you can watch her TV, but you don't know how it works.

b) Now practise again. This time say:

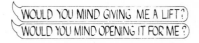

c) If someone asks for your help, what do you say? Do the exercise again. Sometimes you can help, sometimes you can't. Why not?

3 Helpless neighbours

You're sitting in your room listening to your favourite radio programme. You're tired, and you're going to bed soon. Then there's a knock at the door. It's George, the boy from the next flat. He asks you a favour. He's having a party tonight, and needs some help...

What help do you think he needs? Decide, then practise with your partner:

You	George
Say hello.	Say hello.
	Ask a favour. Explain what you want your friend to do.
Say you'll help.	
Ask if you can help in any other way.	
	Tell your friend if you need any more help.
Finish the conversation.	Finish the conversation.

4

Your neighbour on the other side, Pauline, is even worse than George! The next evening she knocks on your door. What does *she* want? How do you think she finishes her sentences?

I want to make a cup of coffee, and...
My watch has stopped, and...
The point is, my hoover's broken, and...
I've discovered that there's a spider...
I want to see what's on TV tonight, and...

How would you reply?

Extract 6

From 'Functions of English', L. Jones. Cambridge University Press, 1977.
The materials are for upper-intermediate and advanced students.

From Student's Book (pp. 41-3)

7.4   Presentation: asking permission

Sometimes we need to do more than just offer to do something – we may need to ask permission to make sure we are allowed to do it. The expression to use depends on:
a) The type of task you want to do and the degree of resistance you anticipate.
b) Who you are and who you are talking to – the role you are playing and your status.

Here are some useful ways of asking permission. They are graded in order of politeness:

★   I'm going to leave early.
I thought I might leave early.
I'd like to leave early.
Alright if I leave early?
Anyone mind if I leave early?
D'you mind if I leave early?
Is it alright if I leave early?
Would it be alright if I left early?
Would you mind if I left early?
I wonder if I could possibly leave early?
★★★★★   I hope you don't mind, but would it be at all possible for me to leave early?

We tend to give permission in just a short phrase, like:

Yes, go ahead.
Yes, I suppose so.
Oh well, alright.

And we refuse permission like this:

I'd rather you didn't, if you don't mind.
I'm sorry, but it's not possible.

Discuss with your teacher when you might use the expressions.

7.5   Practice

Make a list of five things you would like to do, but which would need your teacher's permission. Ask for permission to do them – but be warned, he may ask you why! Later he will change roles and play the role of the principal, so you may then need to change the way you ask.

7.6   Presentation: giving reasons

When you ask someone for permission, or refuse someone permission, he is likely to ask for reasons. Here are some useful ways of giving reasons:

Well, you see...
The reason is...
If I could explain...
...and that's why I'd like to...

Discuss with your teacher how you would give reasons using these phrases.

7.7 Practice

Build conversations following the pattern suggested in 7.4 and 7.6 using these prompts:

leave room	stay for tea
smoke my pipe	borrow umbrella
borrow car	use phone
day off	watch TV
open window	write in book

Here is an example:

A: Would it be alright if I left the room for a moment, you see I have to make a phone call.

B: I'd rather you didn't if you don't mind, you see this is a very important part of the lesson.

A: Oh, alright, I see.

7.8 Practice

Here are some things you want to do. Get together with another student and play the roles of boss and assistant. Keep changing roles after each scene. Remember to give good reasons for wanting to do these things:

Have the afternoon off – a day off – a week off.
Leave 5 minutes early – ½ hour early – 2 hours early.
Change your holiday – your desk – your secretary.
Get an assistant – your own phone – a company car.

7.9 Practice

Team up with two other students. Imagine one of you has just moved into a new flat and a lot of things need doing. One of you is very lazy, another very eager to do things, and the third normal. Decide together what needs doing (you will also need to cook a meal this evening) and who is going to do what.

Discuss these ideas with your teacher before you start writing.

a) Write a letter on behalf of your class requesting permission from the town council to hold a barbecue in a local park. Then 'deliver' it.

b) Write a letter to a friend who owns a country cottage, asking him if you can spend a weekend with some of your friends there. Then 'deliver' it.

c) Read the letter you have received and reply to it as you think fit.

Extract 7

From 'English in Physical Science', J. P. B. Allen & H. G. Widdowson. Oxford University Press, 1974.

These materials are for students entering higher education to follow specialist programmes of study. The emphasis in the course is on reading and writing.

From Student's Book (pp. 30-1)

30   *English in Physical Science*

II   PROBLEMS
INFORMATION TRANSFER

A. Draw the table below and arrange the following information in it.

1. *Regular bodies:* cube, cylinder, cone, sphere
2. *Shapes:*

(a)   (b)   (c)   (d)

3. *Volumes:* l(ength) $\times$ b(readth) $\times$ h(eight), $\frac{4}{3}\pi \times r^3$,

$$\pi r^2 \times h, \qquad \pi r^2 \times \frac{h}{3} \qquad (\pi = 3\cdot 14)$$

EXAMPLE

1 Body	2 Shape	3 Volume
cube		l x b x h

B. Make statements about the objects illustrated below by using the following terms:

cube	cubical
sphere	spherical
cone	conical
cylinder	cylindrical

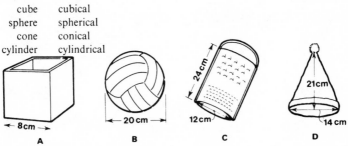

A   B   C   D

EXAMPLE
   Object A is a cube.
   Object A is in the shape of a cube. ⎫ Its volume is . . . cm³,
   Object A is cubical.   ⎬   or . . . m³.
   Object A is cubical in shape.   ⎭

C. Read this description of an experiment.
The measurement of the volume of irregular solids
Water is poured into the displacement vessel until it overflows through the pipe into the measuring jar. The level of the water surface in the measuring jar is read, and then the solid is lowered into the vessel until it is completely covered by the water. Water is displaced and flows down the pipe into the measuring jar, and the level of the water surface in the measuring jar is read again. The volume of water displaced is equal to the volume of the body.
(i) Draw the diagram below and label it. Then draw a second diagram to illustrate the measurement of the volume of irregular solids described above.

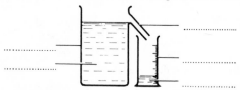

(ii) Change the description of measurement given above into a set of directions etc. for measuring the volume of irregular solids by using the following framework and by referring to the problems in Unit 1.
(1) DIRECTIONS
   Take a displacement vessel and a measuring jar.
   . . . .
   . . . .
   . . . .
(2) STATEMENT OF RESULT
   Water is displaced and flows down the pipe into the measuring jar.
(1) DIRECTIONS
   . . . .
(2) STATEMENT OF RESULT
   The volume of water displaced is equal to the volume of the body.

References

Note: This bibliography includes all references in the book, together with references to standard works by writers whose work is mentioned in passing.

Abbs, B., Ayton, A. and Freebairn, I. 1975, *Strategies*, Longman. Extract, this volume, p. 217.

Abrahams, R. D. 1967, *'Patterns of performance in the British West Indies'*, mimeographed working paper.

Albert, E. M. 1964, *'Rhetoric, logic and poetics in Burundi: culture patterning of speech behaviors'*, in Gumperz and Hymes (eds) 1964.

Allen, J. P. B. and Corder, S. P. 1974, *The Edinburgh Course in Applied Linguistics*, Vol. 3, Oxford University Press.

Allen, J. P. B. and Van Buren, P. 1971, *Chomsky: Selected Readings*, Oxford University Press.

Allen, J. P. B. and Widdowson, H. G. 1974, 'Teaching the communicative use of English', *International Review of Applied Linguistics*, 12, 1, 1–21 and this volume, p. 122.

Allen, J. P. B. and Widdowson, H. G. (eds) 1974 onwards, *English in Focus* (Physical Science, Basic Medical Science, Workshop Practice, etc.), Oxford University Press. Extract from *'English in Physical Science'*, this volume, p. 225.

Allwright, R. L. 1975, *'Problems in the study of the language teacher's treatment of learner error'*, in Burt and Dulay (eds) 1975.

Allwright R. L. 1976, Putting Cognitions on the Map, *UCLA TESL Working Papers*.

Allwright, R. L. 1977a, 'Language learning through communication practice', *ELT Docs* 76/3, 2–14, and this volume, p. 167.

Allwright, R. L. 1977b, *Interference and intervention in language learning'*, University of Essex, mimeo.

Andrews, J. 1975, *Say What You Mean in English*, Nelson. Extract, this volume, p. 214.

Austin, J. L. 1962, *How to Do Things with Words*, Oxford University Press.

Austin, J. L. 1963, *'Performative-constative'*, in Caton (ed.) 1963.

Bach, E. and Harms, R. T. 1968, *Universals in Linguistic Theory*, Holt Rinehart and Winston.

Bandura, A. and Walters, R. H. 1963, *Social Learning and Personality Development*, Holt Rinehart and Winston.

Bar Hillel, Y. 1971, 'Out of the pragmatic wastebasket', *Linguistic Enquiry*, II/3, 401–6.

Barnes, D. 1976, *From Communication to Curriculum*, Penguin Books.

Barnes, D., Britton, J. and Rosen, H. 1969, *Language, the Learner and the School*, Penguin Books.

Bartlett, F. C. 1947, 'The measurement of human skill', *British Medical Journal*, nos 4510, 1.

Bernstein, B. 1971, *Class, Codes and Control*, Vol. 1, Routledge and Kegan Paul.

Bernstein B. ed., 1973 *Class, Codes and Control*, Vol. II, Routledge and Kegan Paul.

Black, M. (ed.) 1965, *Philosophy in America*, Allen and Unwin.

Bloomfield, L. 1927, *'Literate and illiterate speech'*, American Speech, Vol. 2, 432–9.

Bloomfield, L. 1933, *Language*, Allen and Unwin.

Bolinger, D. 1971, 'Semantic overloading: a study of the verb "remind" ', *Language*, 47, 3, 522–47.

Bolinger, D. *et al.* 1960, *Modern Spanish*, Harcourt Brace and Co.

Bonhoffer, D. 1965, 'What is meant by "telling the truth"?', *Ethics*, 363–72.

Boyd, J. and Thorne, J. P. 1969, 'The semantics of modal verbs', *Journal of Linguistics*, 5, 57–74.

Bright, W. 1966, *Sociolinguistics*, Mouton.

Britton, J. 1970, *Language and learning*, Allen Lane, The Penguin Press.

Broughton, G. 1968, *Success with English*, Coursebook 1, Penguin Books.

Brumfit, C. J. 1978, ' *"Communicative" language teaching: an assessment'*, in Strevens (ed.) 1978.

Brumfit, C. J. 1979a, 'Accuracy and fluency as polarities in foreign language teaching materials and methodology', to be published in *Bulletin CILA*, April.

Brumfit C. J. 1979b, ' *"Communicative" language teaching: an educational perspective'*, this volume, p. 183.

Burke, K. 1966, *Towards a Better Life. Being a Series of Epistles, or Declarations.* University of California Press (first publication 1932).

Burt, M. K. and Dulay, H. C. (eds) 1975, *New Directions in Second Language Learning, Teaching and Bilingual Education*, TESOL.

Burt, M. K., Dulay, H. C. and Finocchiaro, M. (eds) 1977, *Viewpoints on English as a Second Language*, Regent.

Byrne, D. 1978, *Materials for Language Teaching: Interaction Packages*. Modern English Publications.

Campbell, R. and Wales, R. 1970, '*The study of language acquisition*', in Lyons (ed.) 1970.

Candlin, C. N. 1971, 'Sociolinguistics and communicative language teaching', *paper presented to IATEFL Conference*, London, mimeo.

Candlin, C. N. 1972, '*Acquiring communicative competence*', 32nd conference of philologists, Utrecht, not published.

Candlin, C. N. 1973, '*The status of pedagogical grammars*', in Corder and Roulet (eds) 1973, and this volume, p. 72.

Candlin, C. N. 1976, '*Communicative language teaching and the debt to pragmatics*', Georgetown Round Table 1976.

Candlin, C. N., Kirkwood, J. M. and Moore, H. M. 1971, '*Teaching study skills in English*, BAAL Conference, University of Essex, not published.

Carroll, B. J. 1977, *Specifications for a New English Langage Examination*, Royal Society of Arts, mimeo.

Carroll, B. J. 1978, *An English Language Testing Service: Specifications*, The British Council, mimeo.

Carroll, J. B. (ed.) 1956, B. L. Whorf, *Language, Thought and Reality*, M.I.T. Press.

Carroll, J. B. 1966, '*Psychology, research and language teaching*', in Valdman (ed.) 1966.

Carroll, J. B. 1968, '*The psychology of language testing*', in Davies (ed.) 1968.

Carswell, E. A. and Rommetweit, R. 1970, *Social Contexts of Messages*, Academic Press.

Catford, J. C. 1965, *A Linguistic Theory of Translation*, Oxford University Press.

Caton, C. E. 1963, *Philosophy and Ordinary Language*, University of Illinois Press.

Cazden, C. 1966, '*Subcultural differences in child language: an interdisciplinary review*', Merrill-Palmer Q., Vol. 12, 185–218.

Chafe, W. 1970, *Meaning and Structure of Language*, University of Chicago Press.

Cherry, C. 1957, *On Human Communication*, M.I.T. Press.

Chomsky, N. 1957, *Syntactic Structures*, Mouton.

Chomsky, N. 1965, *Aspects of the Theory of Syntax*, M.I.T. Press.

Chomsky, N. 1966, Northeast Conference on the Teaching of Foreign Languages, *Working Committee Reports*, ed. Robert C. Mead, jr., 43–9.

Chomsky, N. 1968, '*Deep structure, surface structure and semantic representation*', in Steinberg and Jakobovits (eds) 1971, and Chomsky 1972.

Chomsky, N. 1971, *Selected Readings*, ed. Allen, J. P. B. and Van Buren, P., Oxford University Press.

Chomsky, N. 1972, *Studies on Semantics in Generative Grammar*, Mouton.

Corder, S. P. 1967, 'The significance of learners' errors', *International Review of Applied Linguistics*, 5.

Corder, S. P. 1970, 'Error analysis', *German Applied Linguistics Association Conference*, Stuttgart, not published.

Corder, S. P. 1975, 'Error analysis, interlanguage and second language acquisition', *Language Teaching and Linguistics Abstracts*, 8, 4.

Corder, S. P. and Roulet, E. (eds) 1973, *Theoretical Linguistic Models in Applied Linguistics*, AIMAV/Didier.

Corder, S. P. and Roulet, E. (eds) 1974, *Linguistic Insights in Applied Linguistics*, AIMAV/Didier.

Coulthard, M. 1977, *An Introduction to Discourse Analysis*, Longman.

Crystal, D. and Davy, D. 1969, *Investigating English Style*, Longman.

Curran, C. 1976, *Counselling Learning in Second Language Learning*, Apple River Press.

Dakin, J. 1973, *The Language Laboratory and Language Learning*, Longman.

Dakin, J., Tiffen, B. and Widdowson, H. G. 1968, *Language in Education*, Oxford University Press.

Dance, F. (ed.) 1967, *Human Communication Theory*, Holt Rinehart and Winston.

Davies, A. (ed.) 1968, *Language Testing Symposium*, Oxford University Press.

Davies, A. 1975, *'Do foreign students have problems?'*, ELT/Docs 75/3.

Davies, A. 1978, 'Language testing', *Language Teaching and Linguistics Abstracts*, 11, 3/4.

Dixon, J. 1967, *Growth through English*, Oxford University Press.

Dykstra, G., Port, R. and Port, A. 1966, *A Course in Controlled Composition: Ananse Tales*, New York, Teachers College Press.

Estes, W. K. 1962, 'Learning theory', *Annual Review of Psychology*, 13, 110.

Ferguson, C. A. 1966, 'On sociolinguistically orientated surveys', *Linguistic Reporter*, Vol. 8, 4, 1–3.

Fillmore, C. 1968, *'The case for case'*, in Bach and Harms (eds) 1968.

Fillmore, C. 1969, *'Types of lexical information'*, in Kiefer (ed.) 1969.

Fillmore C. 1971, *'Verbs of judging: an exercise in semantic description'*, in Fillmore and Langendoen (eds) 1971.

Fillmore, C. and Langendoen, T. (eds) 1971, *Studies in Linguistic Semantics*, Holt Rinehart and Winston.

Finocchiaro, M. 1974, *English as a Second Language*, 2nd ed., Regent.

Fodor, J. A. and Katz, J. J. (eds) 1964, *The Structure of Language*, Prentice Hall.

Fodor, J. D. 1977, *Semantics: Theories of Meaning in Generative Grammar*, Harvester Press.

Garfinkel, H. 1970, '*Remarks on ethnomethodology*', in Gumperz and Hymes (eds) 1970.

Garvin, P. (ed.) 1957, *Report on the Seventh Annual Round Table Meeting on Languages and Linguistics*, Georgetown University Press.

Geddes, M. and Sturtridge, G. 1979, *Listening Links*, Heinemann.

Giglioli, P. P. (ed.) 1972, *Language and Social Context*, Penguin Books.

Goffman, E. 1956, 'The nature of deference and demeanor', *American Anthropologist*, Vol. 58, 473–502.

Goffman, E. 1959, *The Presentation of Self in Everyday Life*, Doubleday and Allen Lane, The Penguin Press.

Goffman, E. 1963, *Behavior in Public Places*, The Free Press.

Goffman, E. 1964, '*The neglected situation*', in Gumperz and Hymes (eds) 1964.

Goffman, E. 1967, *Interaction Ritual*, Doubleday.

Goodenough, W. H. 1957, '*Cultural anthropology and linguistics*', in Garvin (ed.) 1957.

Grice, H. P. 1957, 'Meaning', *Philosophical Review LXVI*, 377–88, reprinted in Steinberg and Jakobovits (eds) 1971.

Gumperz, J. J. 1964, '*Linguistic and social interaction in two communities*', in Gumperz and Hymes (eds) 1964.

Gumperz, J. J. and Hymes, D. (eds) 1964, The Ethnography of Communication, *American Anthropologist*, Vol. 66, 6, part 2.

Gumperz, J. J. and Hymes, D. (eds) 1970, *Directions in Sociolinguistics*, Holt Rinehart and Winston.

Gumperz, J. J. and Rumery, J. 1962, *Conversational Hindi–Urdu*, not published.

Halliday, M. A. K. 1967/8, 'Notes on transitivity and theme in English', *Journal of Linguistics*, 3, 37–81 and 199–244, 4, 179–215.

Halliday, M. A. K. 1969, 'Relevant models of language', *Educational Review*, 22, 1, 26–37.

Halliday, M. A. K. 1970a, 'Language structure and language function', in Lyons (ed.)

Halliday, M. A. K. 1970b, 'Functional diversity in language as seen from a consideration of modality and mood in English', *Foundations of Language*, 6, 322–61.

Halliday, M. A. K. 1973, 'Towards a sociological semantics', in *Explorations in the Functions of Language*, Edward Arnold. Extensive extracts in this volume, p. 27.

Halliday, M. A. K. 1978, *Language as Social Semiotic*, Edward Arnold.

Halliday, M. A. K., McIntosh, A. and Strevens, P. 1964, *The Linguistic Sciences and Language Teaching*, Longman.

Harris, Z. 1952, 'Discourse analysis', *Language 28*, reprinted in Fodor and Katz (eds) 1964.

Hasan, R. 1968, Grammatical Cohesion in Written and Spoken English, Longman, *Programme in Linguistics and Language Teaching*, Paper 7.

Helm, J. (ed.) 1968, *Proceedings of the 1967 Spring Meeting of the American Ethnological Society*, University of Washington Press.

Hinde, R. A. (ed.) 1972, *Non-verbal Communication*, Cambridge University Press.

Holbrook, D. 1961, *English for Maturity*, Cambridge University Press.

Holbrook, D. 1964, *English for the Rejected*, Cambridge University Press.

Holden, S. (ed.) 1977, *English for Specific Purposes*, Modern English Publications.

Huddleston, R. *et al.* 1968, *Sentence and Clause in Scientific English*, Communication Research Centre, University College, London, mimeo.

Hymes, D. 1964, '*Directions in (ethno-)linguistic theory*', in Romney and D'Andrade (eds) 1964.

Hymes, D. 1968a, '*Linguistic problems in defining the concept of the tribe*', in Helm (ed.) 1968.

Hymes, D. 1968b, 'Linguistics—the field', *International Encylopaedia of the Social Sciences*, Macmillan.

Hymes, D. 1970, '*On communicative competence*', in Gumperz and Hymes (eds) 1970. Extensive extracts in this volume, p. 5.

Jacobs, R. A. and Rosenbaum, P. S. (eds) 1970, *Readings in English Transformationl Grammar*, Ginn.

Jacobson, R. 1966, 'The role of deep structure in language teaching', *Language Learning 16*.

John, V. 1967, 'Communicative competence of low-income children: assumption and programs', *Report of Language Development Study Group*, Ford Foundation.

Johnson, K., 1979 '*Communicative approaches and communicative processes*', this volume, p. 192.

Johnson, K. and Morrow, K. (eds) 1978, *Functional Materials and the Classroom Teacher*, University of Reading.

Johnson, K. and Morrow, K. (eds) 1979, *Approaches*, Cambridge University Press. Extract, this volume, p. 220.

Jones, L. 1977, *Functions of English*, Cambridge University Press. Extract, this volume, p. 223.

Journal of the Midlands Association for Linguistic Studies 1978, English for Specific Purposes.

Jupp, T. C. and Milne, J. 1968, *Guided Course in English Composition*, Heinemann.

Kac, M. B. 1969, 'Should the passive transformation be obligatory?' *Journal of Linguistics*, 5.

Kaleidoscope: *English for Juniors, Stage 1*, 1976, University of York/ Macmillan Education. Extract, this volume, p. 207.

Karttunen, L. 1970, 'On the semantics of complement sentences', *Papers for the Sixth Regional Meeting, Chicago, Chicago Linguistic Society*.

Karttunen, L. 1971, '*Implicative verbs*', Language, 47, 340–58.

Katz, J. J. 1966, *The Philosophy of Language*, Harper and Row.

Katz, J. J. 1967, 'Recent issues in semantic theory', *Foundations of Language*, 3, 124–94.

Katz, J. J. and Postal, P. M. 1964, *An Integrated Theory of Linguistic Description*, M.I.T. Press.

Kiefer, F. (ed.) 1969, *Studies in Syntax and Semantics*, Dordrecht: Reidel.

Krashen, S. D. 1976, 'Formal and informal linguistic environments in language acquisition and language learning', *TESOL Quarterly*, 10, 2, 157–68.

Krashen, S. D. 1977, '*The monitor model for adult second language performance*', in Burt, Dulay and Finocchiaro (eds) 1977.

Krashen, S. D. and Seliger, H. 1975, 'The essential contributions of formal instruction in adult second language learning', *TESOL Quarterly*, 9, 179–83.

Labov, W. 1965, '*Stages in the acquisition of standard English*', in Shuy (ed.) 1965.

Labov, W. 1966, *The Social Stratification of English in New York City*, Center for Applied Linguistics.

Labov, W. 1969, *The Study of Non-standard English*, National Council for Teachers of English.

Labov, W. 1970, 'The study of language in its social context', *Studium Generale*, 23, 30–87, reprinted in Giglioli (ed.) 1972.

Lado, R. 1961, *Language Testing*, Longman.

Lakoff, R. 1969, 'Transformational-grammar and language teaching', *Language Learning*, 19.

Lakoff, R. 1970, 'Tense and its relation to participants', *Language*, 46, 838–49.

Lane, H. 1964, 'Programmed learning of a second language', *International Review of Applied Linguistics*, 2, 250.

Laver, J. and Hutcheson, S. (eds) 1972, *Communication in Face to Face Interaction*, Penguin Books.

Leech, G. 1969, *Towards a Semantic Description of English*, Longman.

Lester, M. (ed.) 1970, *Readings in Applied Transformational Grammar*, Holt Rinehart and Winston.

Lunzer, E. A. and Morris, J. F. 1968, *Developments in Human Learning*, Staples.

Lyons, J. 1968, *Introduction to Theoretical Linguistics*, Cambridge University Press.

Lyons, J. (ed.) 1970, *New Horizons in Linguistics*, Penguin Books.

Lyons, J. 1972, '*Human language*', in Hinde (ed.) 1972.

McCawley, J. D. 1968, '*The role of semantics in a grammar*', in Bach and Harms (eds) 1968.

Mackay, D. M. 1972, '*Formal analysis of communicative processes*', in Hinde (ed.) 1972.

Mackay, R. and Mountford, A. (eds) 1978, *English for Specific Purposes*, Longman.

Mackey, W. F. 1966, '*Applied linguistics: its meaning and use*', English Language Teaching 20.

McTear, M. 1975 'Potential sources of confusion in foreign language classrooms' *Paper delivered to AILA Congress*, Stuttgart, August 1975.

Marshall, J. C. and Wales, R. 1966, 'Which syntax: a consumer's guide' *Journal of Linguistics* 2.

Mitchell, T. F. 1957, 'The language of buying and selling in Cyrenaica: a situational statement', Hesperis. Reprinted in '*Principles of Firthian Linguistics*', Longman, 1975.

Moody, K. W. 1966, *Written English under Control*, Oxford University Press, Ibadan.

Morrow, K. 1977, *Techniques of Evaluation for a Notional Syllabus*, Royal Society of Arts, mimeo.

Morrow, K., 1979 '*Communicative language testing: revolution or evolution?*', this volume, p. 143.

Morrow, K. and Johnson, K. 1979, *Communicate*, Cambridge University Press.

Munby, J. 1978, *Communicative Syllabus Design*, Cambridge University Press.

Newmark, L. 1966, 'How not to interfere with language learning', *International Journal of American Linguistics*, 32, 1, II, 77–83, reprinted in Lester (ed.) 1970 and in this volume, p. 160.

Newmark, L., 1971, 'A minimal language teaching program' in Pimsleur and Quinn, 1971.

Newmark L. and Reibel, D. 1968, 'Necessity and sufficiency in language learning', *International Review of Applied Linguistics*, 6, 2, 145–64, reprinted in Lester (ed.) 1970.

Oller, J. 1971, 'Dictation as a device for testing foreign language proficiency', *English Language Teaching Journal*, 25, 3.

Oller, J. 1973, 'Cloze tests of second language proficiency and what they measure', *Language Learning*, 23, 1.

O'Neill, T. and Snow, P. 1977, *Crescent English Course, Book 1*, Oxford University Press. Extract, this volume, p. 212.

Pilliner, A. E. G. 1968, '*Subjective and objective testing*', in Davies (ed.) 1968.

Pimsleur, P. and Quinn, T. (eds) 1971, *The Psychology of Second Language Learning*, Cambridge University Press.

Politzer, R. L. 1961, *Teaching French: an Introduction to Applied Linguistics*, Ginn.

Postal, P. 1970, 'On the surface verb: "remind" ', *Linguistic Inquiry*, 1, 37–120.

Pride, J. and Holmes, J. (eds) 1972, *Sociolinguistics*, Penguin Books.

Quine, W. V. 1968, 'The inscrutability of reference', a part of 'Ontological relativity', *The Journal of Philosophy LXV*, 185–212, reprinted in Steinberg and Jakobovits (eds) 1971.

Quirk, R. 1966, 'Acceptability in language', *Proceedings of the University of Newcastle on Tyne Philosophical Society*, 1, 7, 79–92.

Reed, G. F. 1968, '*Skill*', in Lunzer and Morris 1968.

Richterich, R. 1972, *A Model for the Definition of Language Needs of Adults Learning a Modern Language*, Council of Europe.

Richterich, R. and Marchl, H. 1970, '*The Concept of "Situation" in the Teaching of Modern Languages*', Council of Europe.

Robinson, P. 1973, 'Oral expression tests', *English Language Teaching*, 25, 2–3.

Robinson, W. P. 1972, *Language and Social Behaviour*, Penguin Books.

Roget, P. M. 1852, *Thesaurus of English Words and Phrases*, Longman (more recent editions from various publishers).

Romney, A. K. and D'Andrade, R. G. (eds) 1964, *Transcultural Studies of Cognition*, American Anthropological Association.

Ross, J. R. 1970, '*On declarative sentences*', in Jacobs and Rosenbaum (eds) 1970.

Sapir, E. 1925, 'Sound patterns in language', *Language*, Vol. 1, 37–51.

Sapon, S. 1961, *Spanish A, TEMAC Series for Encyclopaedia Britannica Films*.

Saporta, S. 1964, 'Psycholinguistic research and language learning', *NAFSA Studies and Papers, English Language Series no. 9*.

Saporta, S. 1966, '*Applied linguistics and generative grammar*', in Valdman (ed.) 1966, 81–92.

Savignon, S. 1972a, 'Teaching for communicative competence', *AVLA Journal*, 3, 153–62.

Savignon, S. 1972b, *Communicative Competence: an Experiment in Foreign Language Teaching*, Center for Curriculum Development.

Searle, J. 1965, '*What is a speech act?*', in Black (ed.) 1965.

Searle, J. 1967, 'Human communication theory and the philosophy of language: some remarks', in Dance (ed.) 1967.

Searle, J. 1969, *Speech Acts*, Cambridge University Press.

Sebeck, T. 1959, '*Folksong viewed as code and message*', Anthropos, 54, 141–53.

Selinker, L. 1972, 'Interlanguage', *International Review of Applied Linguistics*, 10, 3.

Sen, A. 1970, *Problems of Overseas Students and Nurses*, National Foundation for Educational Research.

Shuy, R. (ed.) 1965, *Social Dialects and Language Learning*, National Council of Teachers of English.

Sinclair, J. and Coulthard, M. 1975, *Towards an Analysis of Discourse*, Oxford University Press.

Singer, M. 1955, 'The cultural pattern of Indian civilization: a preliminary report of a methodological field study', *Far Eastern Quarterly*, 15, 223–36.

Spolsky, B. 1966, 'A psycholinguistic critique of programmed foreign language instruction', *International Review of Applied Linguistics*, 4, 2.

Spolsky, B. 1975, 'Language testing: art or science?' *Address to the Fourth AILA Congress*, Stuttgart. Summarized in *Valette* 1977.

Stevick, E. Q. 1976, *Memory Meaning and Method* Newbury House.

Strawson P. F. 1950, '*On referring*', Mind LIX, reprinted in Strawson (ed.) 1971.

Strawson, P. F. (ed.) 1971, *Logico-linguistics* papers, Methuen.

Steinberg, D. and Jakobovits, L. (eds) 1971, *Semantics*, Cambridge University Press.

Strevens, P. (ed.) 1978, *In Honour of A. S. Hornby*, Oxford University Press.

Swift, L. B. *et al.* 1962, *Igbo:* Basic Course, Foreign Services Institute.

Thomas, O. 1965, *Transformational Grammar and the Teacher of English*, Holt Rinehart and Winston.

Trim, J. L. M. 1973, 'Draft outline of a European unit/credit system for modern languages', *in Systems Development in Adult Language Learning*, Council of Europe. Extract, this volume, p. 100.

Turner, G. J. 1973, 'Social class and children's language of control at age 5 and age 7' in Bernstein, 1973.

Turner, R. (ed.) 1974, *Ethnomethodology*, Penguin Books.

Valdman, A. (ed.) 1966, *Trends in Language Teaching*, McGraw Hill.

Valette, R. M. 1967, *Modern Language Testing:* a Handbook, Harcourt Brace and World.

Valette, R. M. 1977, *Modern Language Testing*, 2nd edition, Harcourt Brace Jovanovich.

Van Buren, P. 1974, '*Contrastive analysis*', in Allen and Corder (eds) 1974, 279–312.

Van Ek, J. 1975, *The Threshold Level*, Council of Europe. Extracts, this volume, p. 103.

Wallace, A. F. C. 1961a, 'On being just complicated enough', *Proceedings of the National Academy of Sciences*, Vol. 47, 438–64.

Wallace, A. F. C. 1961b, *Culture and Personality*, Random House.

West, M. 1954, 'Vocabulary selection and the minimum adequate vocabulary', *English Language Teaching*, 8, 4.

Whorf, B. L. 1956, *Language, Thought and Reality*, ed. J. B. Carroll, M.I.T. Press.

Widdowson, H. G. 1968, '*The teaching of English through science*', in Dakin, Tiffen and Widdowson 1968.

Widdowson, H. G. 1971, 'The teaching of rhetoric to students of science and technology', in *Science and Technology in a Second Language*, Centre for Information on Language Teaching.

Widdowson, H. G. 1972, 'The teaching of English as communication', *English Language Teaching*, 27, 1, 15–19, and this volume, p. 117.

Widdowson, H. G. 1973a, 'Two types of communication exercise', in *Preprints of AILA/BAAL Seminar, The Communicative Teaching of English*, Lancaster University, mimeo.

Widdowson, H. G. 1973b, '*Directions in the teaching of discourse*', in Corder and Roulet (eds) 1973 and this volume, p. 49.

Widdowson, H. G. 1974, '*The deep structure of discourse and the use of translation*', in Corder and Roulet (eds) 1974 and this volume, p. 61.

Widdowson, H. G. 1978, *Teaching Language as Communication*, Oxford University Press.

Wilkins, D. A. 1972a, *An Investigation into the Linguistic and Situational Common Core in a Unit/Credit System*, Council of Europe.

Wilkins, D. A. 1972b, 'Grammatical, situational and notional syllabuses', *Proceedings of the Third International Congress of Applied Linguistics*, Copenhagen 1972, Julius Groos Verlag, Heidelberg, and this volume, p. 82.

Wilkins, D. A. 1974, '*Notional syllabuses and the concept of a minimum adequate grammar*', in Corder and Roulet (eds) 1974, and this volume, p. 91.

Wilkins, D. A. 1976, Notional Syllabuses, Oxford University Press.

Wolf, E. 1964, *Anthropology*, Prentice Hall.

Woodworth, R. S. 1938, *Experimental Psychology*, Holt.

Wright, A. 1976, *Visual Materials for the Language Teacher*, Longman.

Yates, A. (ed.) 1971, *Students from Overseas*, National Foundation for Educational Research.

Young, M. F. D. (ed.) 1971, *Knowledge and Control*, Collier–Macmillan.

Index